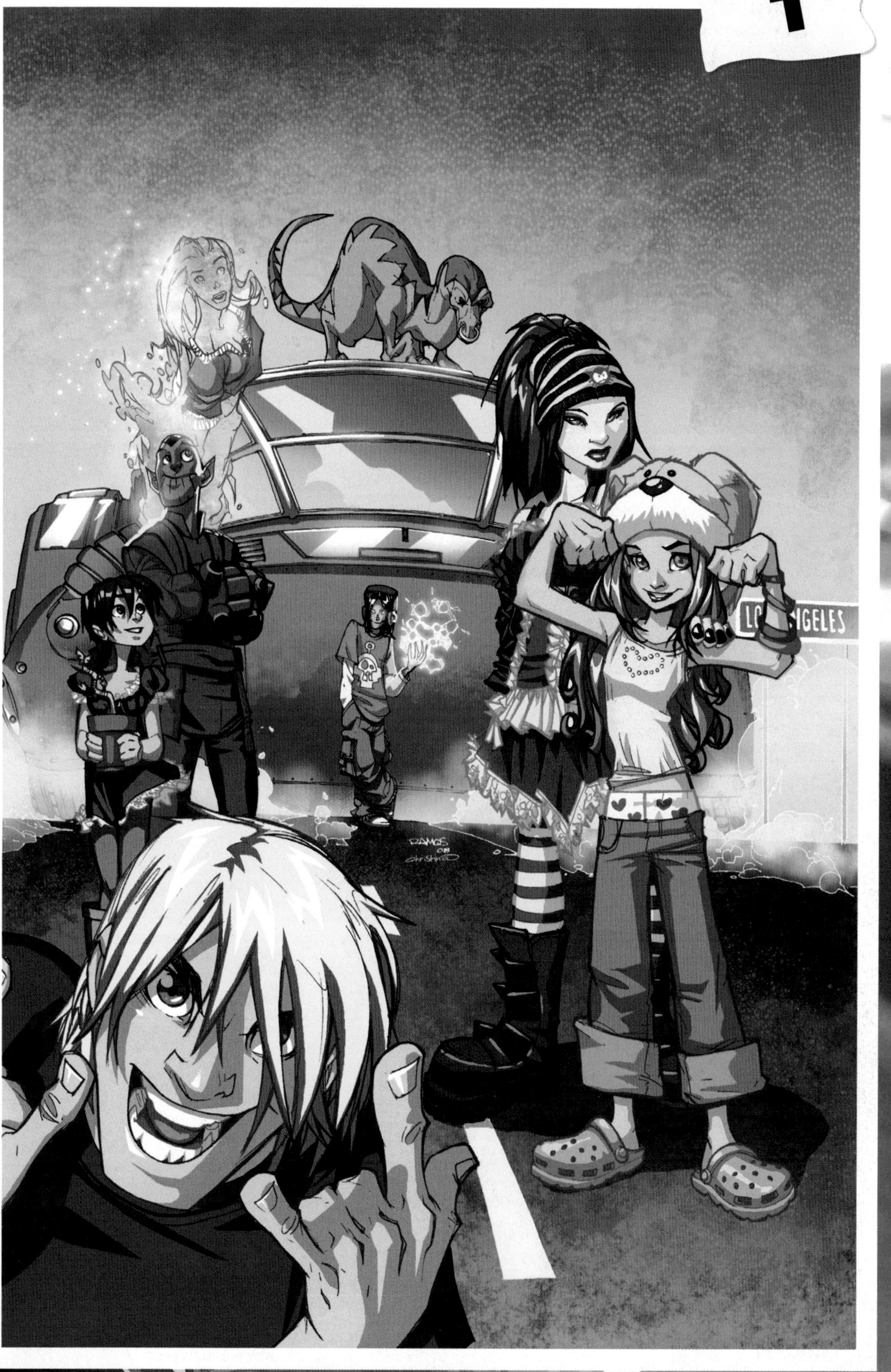

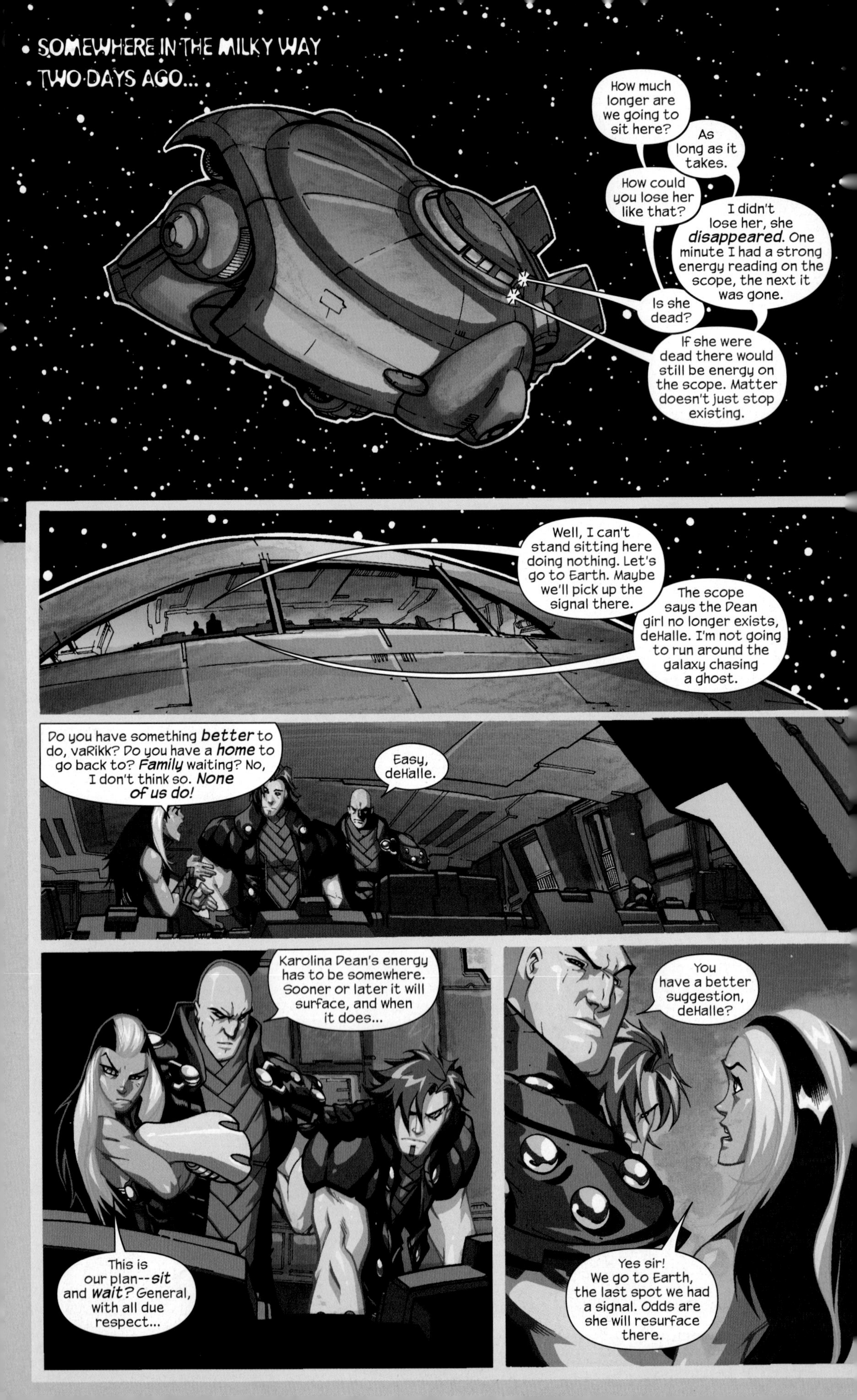
SOMEWHERE IN THE MILKY WAY
TWO DAYS AGO...
How much longer are we going to sit here?
As long as it takes.
How could you lose her like that?
I didn't lose her, she *disappeared*. One minute I had a strong energy reading on the scope, the next it was gone.
Is she dead?
If she were dead there would still be energy on the scope. Matter doesn't just stop existing.
Well, I can't stand sitting here doing nothing. Let's go to Earth. Maybe we'll pick up the signal there.
The scope says the Dean girl no longer exists, deHalle. I'm not going to run around the galaxy chasing a ghost.
Do you have something *better* to do, vaRikk? Do you have a *home* to go back to? *Family* waiting? No, I don't think so. *None of us do!*
Easy, deHalle.
Karolina Dean's energy has to be somewhere. Sooner or later it will surface, and when it does...
This is our plan--*sit* and *wait?* General, with all due respect...
You have a better suggestion, deHalle?
Yes sir! We go to Earth, the last spot we had a signal. Odds are she will resurface there.

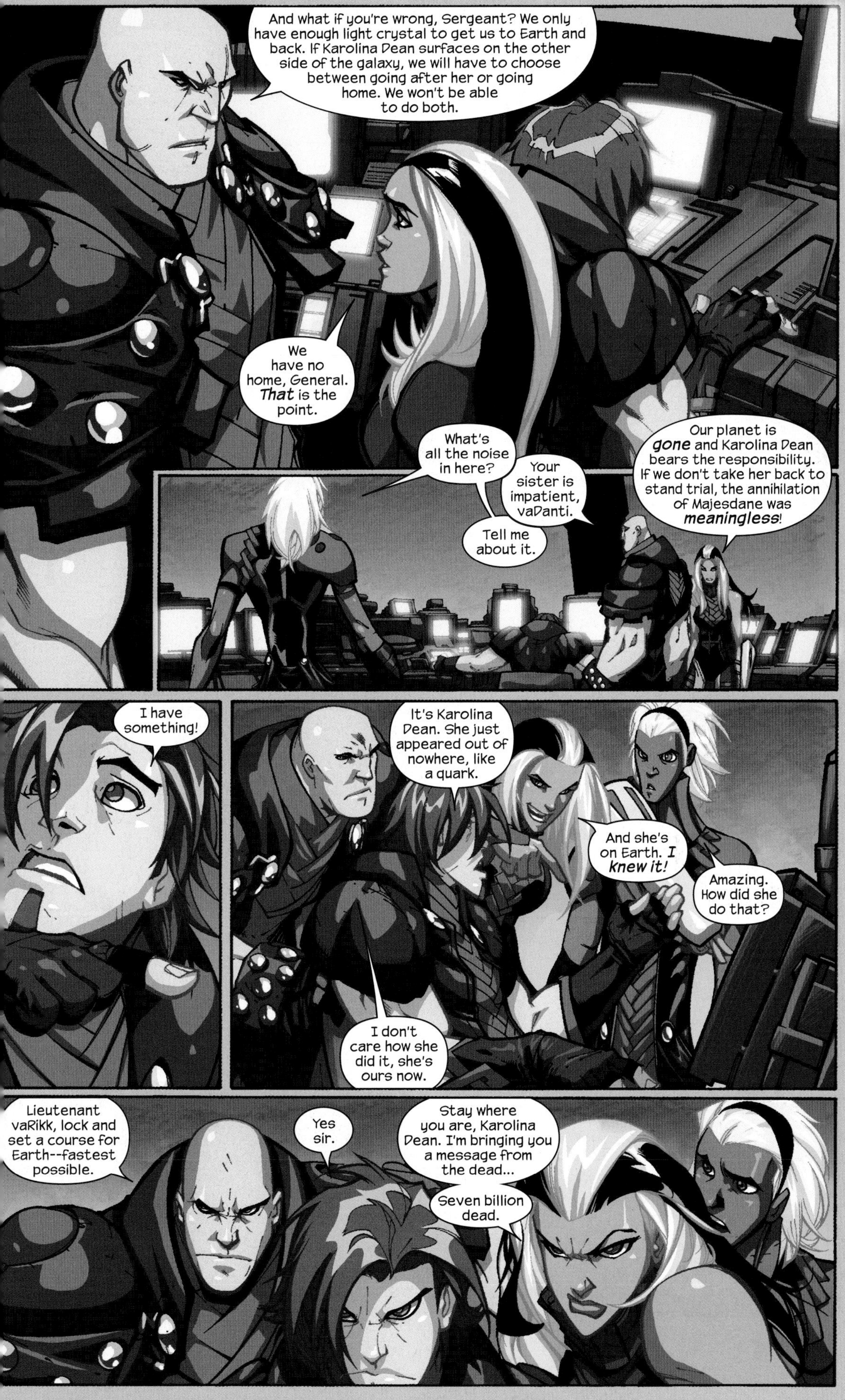
And what if you're wrong, Sergeant? We only have enough light crystal to get us to Earth and back. If Karolina Dean surfaces on the other side of the galaxy, we will have to choose between going after her or going home. We won't be able to do both.
We have no home, General. *That* is the point.
What's all the noise in here?
Your sister is impatient, vaDanti.
Tell me about it.
Our planet is **gone** and Karolina Dean bears the responsibility. If we don't take her back to stand trial, the annihilation of Majesdane was **meaningless**!
I have something!
It's Karolina Dean. She just appeared out of nowhere, like a quark.
And she's on Earth. ***I knew it!***
Amazing. How did she do that?
I don't care how she did it, she's ours now.
Lieutenant vaRikk, lock and set a course for Earth--fastest possible.
Yes sir.
Stay where you are, Karolina Dean. I'm bringing you a message from the dead...
Seven billion dead.

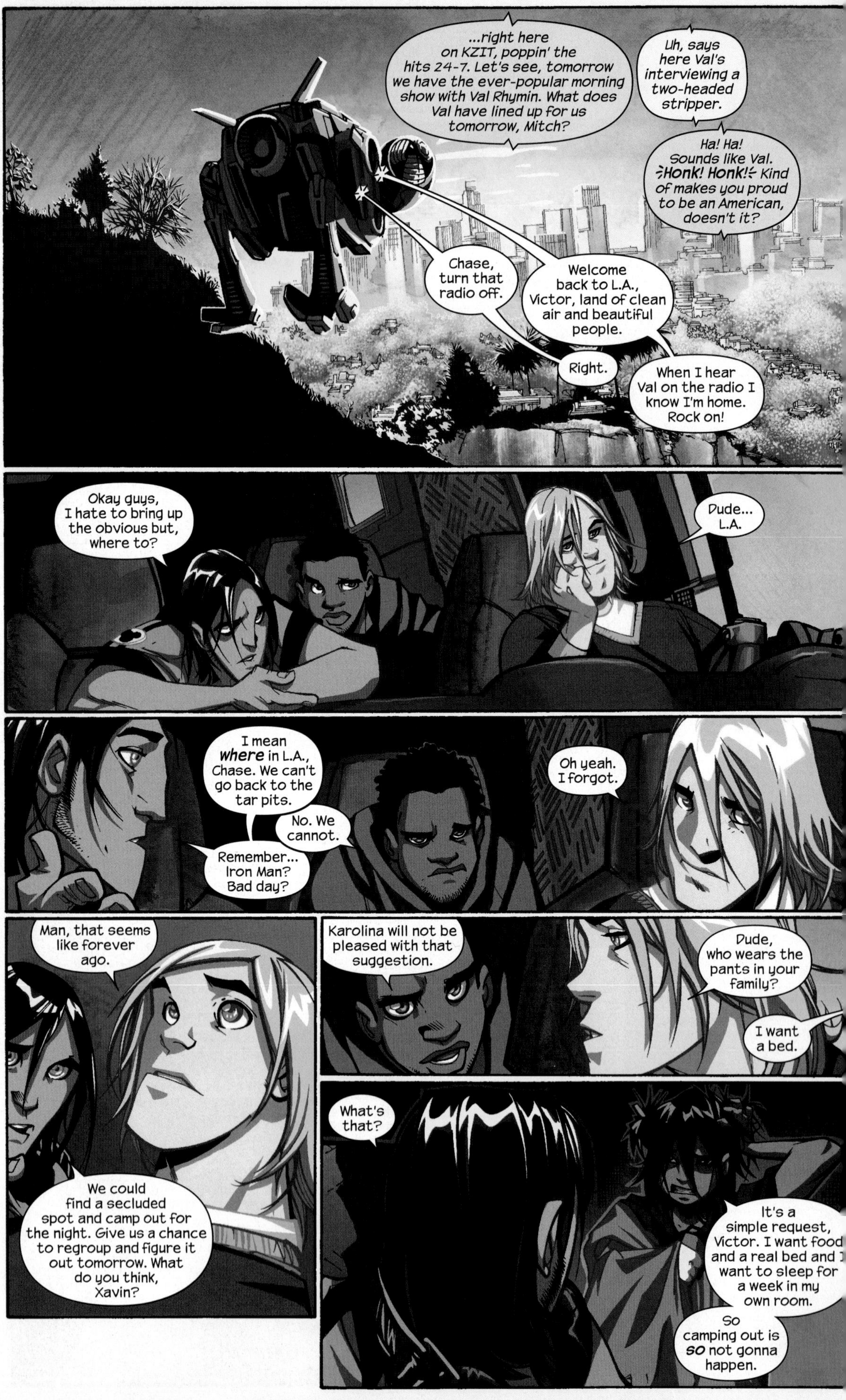
...right here on KZIT, poppin' the hits 24-7. Let's see, tomorrow we have the ever-popular morning show with Val Rhymin. What does Val have lined up for us tomorrow, Mitch?
Uh, says here Val's interviewing a two-headed stripper.
Ha! Ha! Sounds like Val. *Honk! Honk!* Kind of makes you proud to be an American, doesn't it?
Chase, turn that radio off.
Welcome back to L.A., Victor, land of clean air and beautiful people.
Right.
When I hear Val on the radio I know I'm home. Rock on!
Okay guys, I hate to bring up the obvious but, where to?
Dude... L.A.
I mean *where* in L.A., Chase. We can't go back to the tar pits.
Oh yeah. I forgot.
Remember... Iron Man? Bad day?
No. We cannot.
Man, that seems like forever ago.
We could find a secluded spot and camp out for the night. Give us a chance to regroup and figure it out tomorrow. What do you think, Xavin?
Karolina will not be pleased with that suggestion.
Dude, who wears the pants in your family?
I want a bed.
What's that?
It's a simple request, Victor. I want food and a real bed and I want to sleep for a week in my own room.
So camping out is *so* not gonna happen.

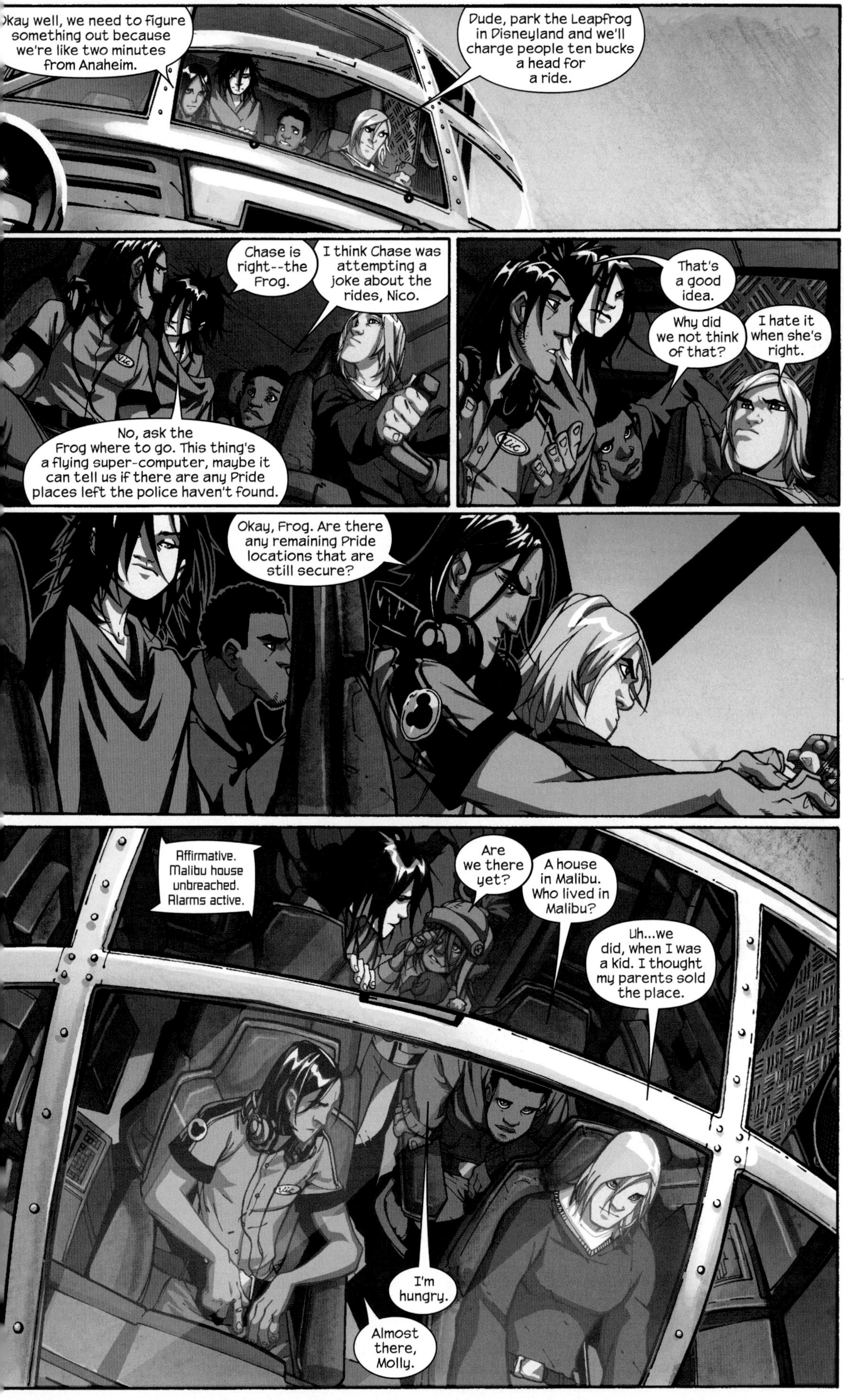
Okay well, we need to figure something out because we're like two minutes from Anaheim.
Dude, park the Leapfrog in Disneyland and we'll charge people ten bucks a head for a ride.
Chase is right--the Frog.
I think Chase was attempting a joke about the rides, Nico.
No, ask the Frog where to go. This thing's a flying super-computer, maybe it can tell us if there are any Pride places left the police haven't found.
That's a good idea.
Why did we not think of that?
I hate it when she's right.
Okay, Frog. Are there any remaining Pride locations that are still secure?
Affirmative. Malibu house unbreached. Alarms active.
Are we there yet?
A house in Malibu. Who lived in Malibu?
Uh...we did, when I was a kid. I thought my parents sold the place.
I'm hungry.
Almost there, Molly.

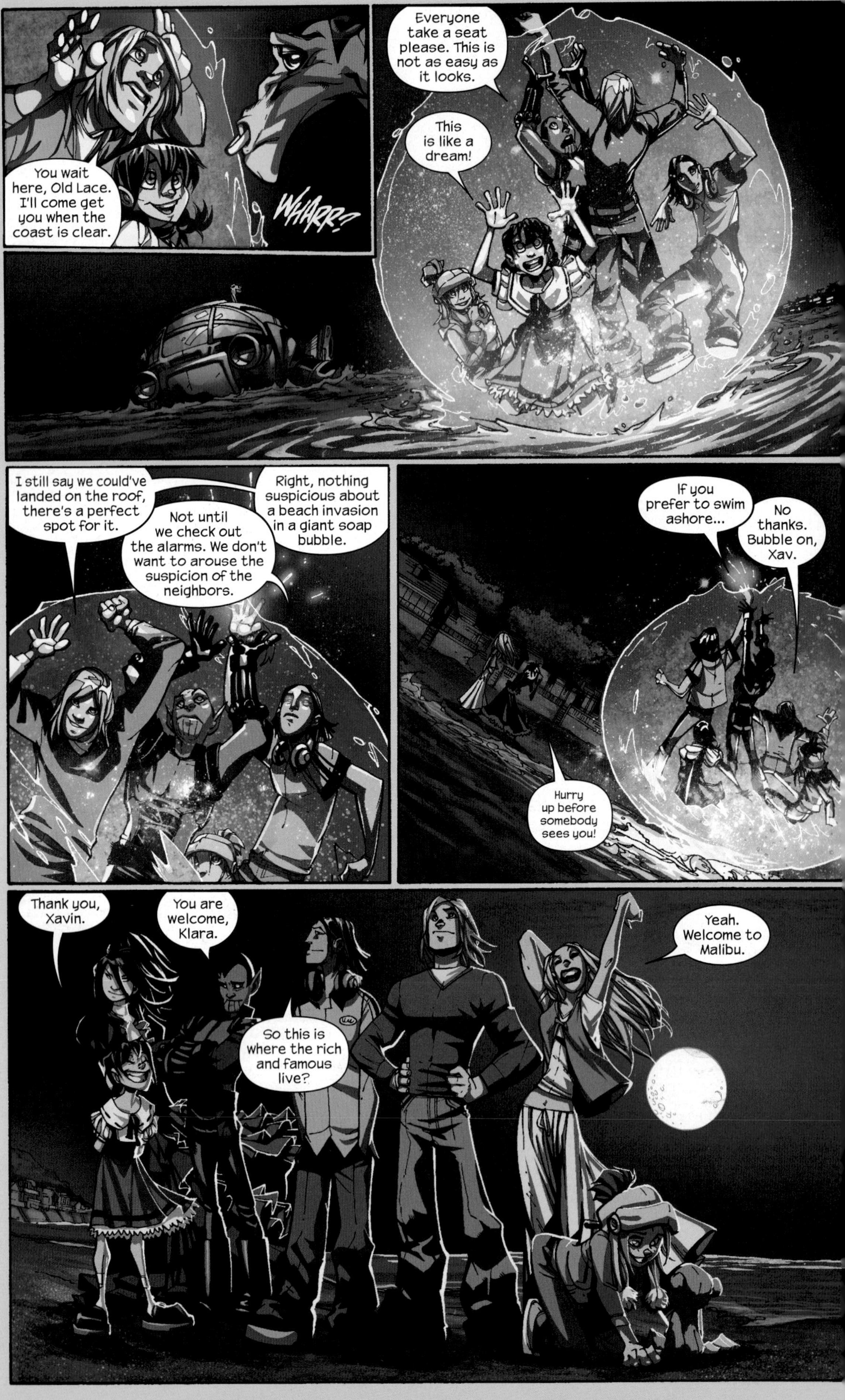

You wait here, Old Lace. I'll come get you when the coast is clear.
WHARR?
Everyone take a seat please. This is not as easy as it looks.
This is like a dream!
I still say we could've landed on the roof, there's a perfect spot for it.
Right, nothing suspicious about a beach invasion in a giant soap bubble.
Not until we check out the alarms. We don't want to arouse the suspicion of the neighbors.
If you prefer to swim ashore...
No thanks. Bubble on, Xav.
Hurry up before somebody sees you!
Thank you, Xavin.
You are welcome, Klara.
So this is where the rich and famous live?
Yeah. Welcome to Malibu.

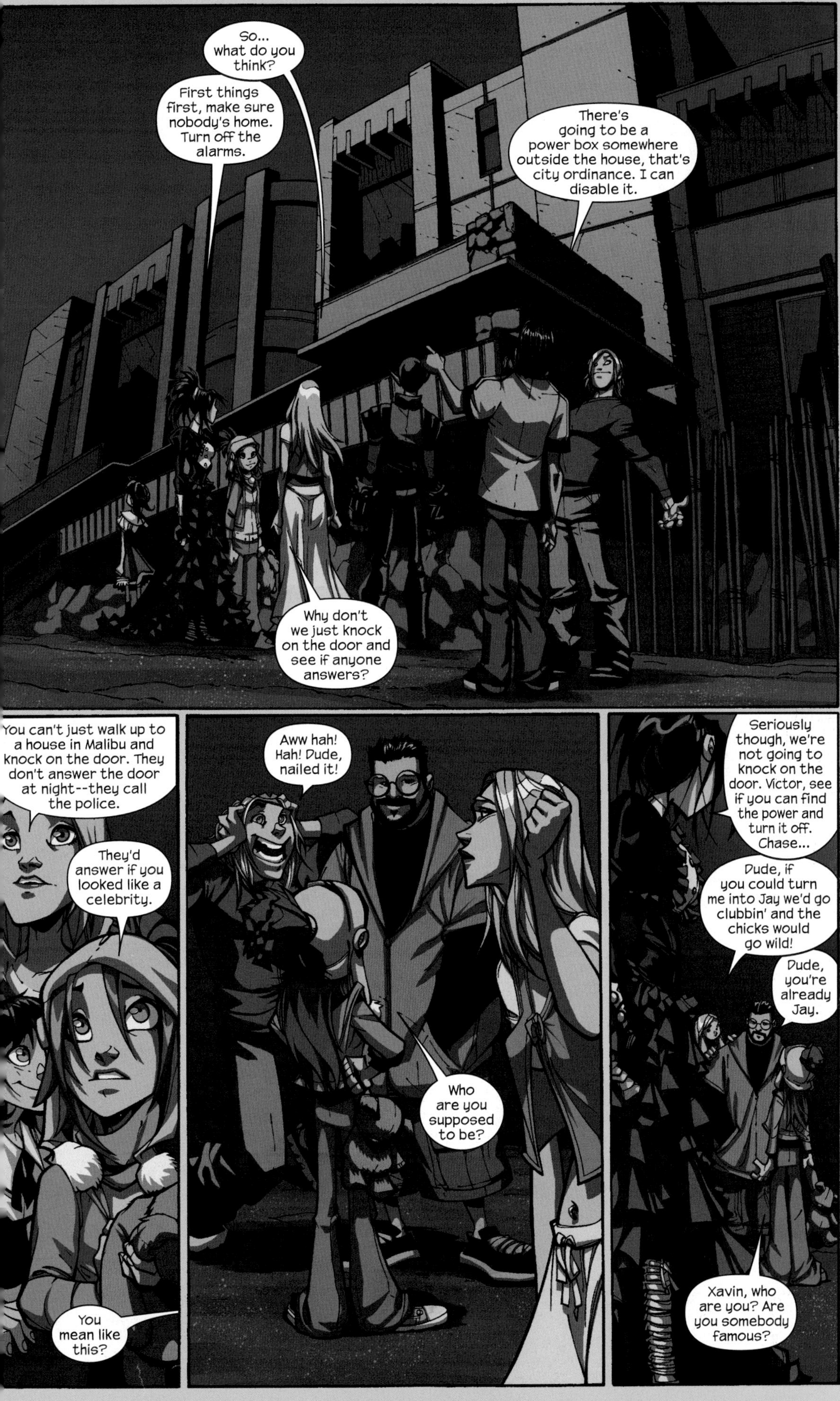
So... what do you think?
First things first, make sure nobody's home. Turn off the alarms.
There's going to be a power box somewhere outside the house, that's city ordinance. I can disable it.
Why don't we just knock on the door and see if anyone answers?
You can't just walk up to a house in Malibu and knock on the door. They don't answer the door at night--they call the police.
They'd answer if you looked like a celebrity.
You mean like this?
Aww hah! Hah! Dude, nailed it!
Who are you supposed to be?
Seriously though, we're not going to knock on the door. Victor, see if you can find the power and turn it off. Chase...
Dude, if you could turn me into Jay we'd go clubbin' and the chicks would go wild!
Dude, you're already Jay.
Xavin, who are you? Are you somebody famous?

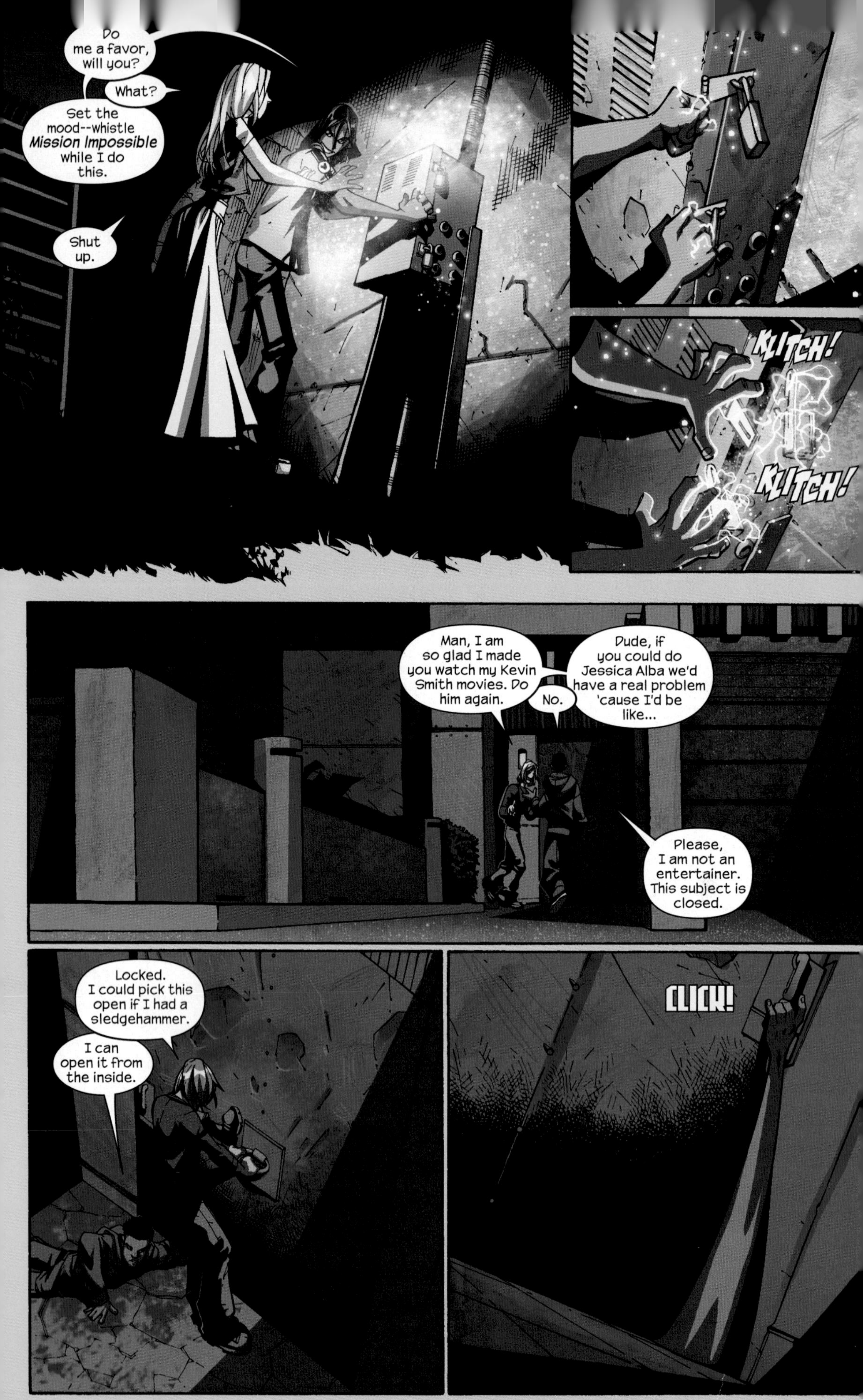

Do me a favor, will you?
What?
Set the mood--whistle *Mission Impossible* while I do this.
Shut up.
KLITCH!
KLITCH!
Man, I am so glad I made you watch my Kevin Smith movies. Do him again.
Dude, if you could do Jessica Alba we'd have a real problem 'cause I'd be like...
No.
Please, I am not an entertainer. This subject is closed.
Locked. I could pick this open if I had a sledgehammer.
I can open it from the inside.
CLICK!

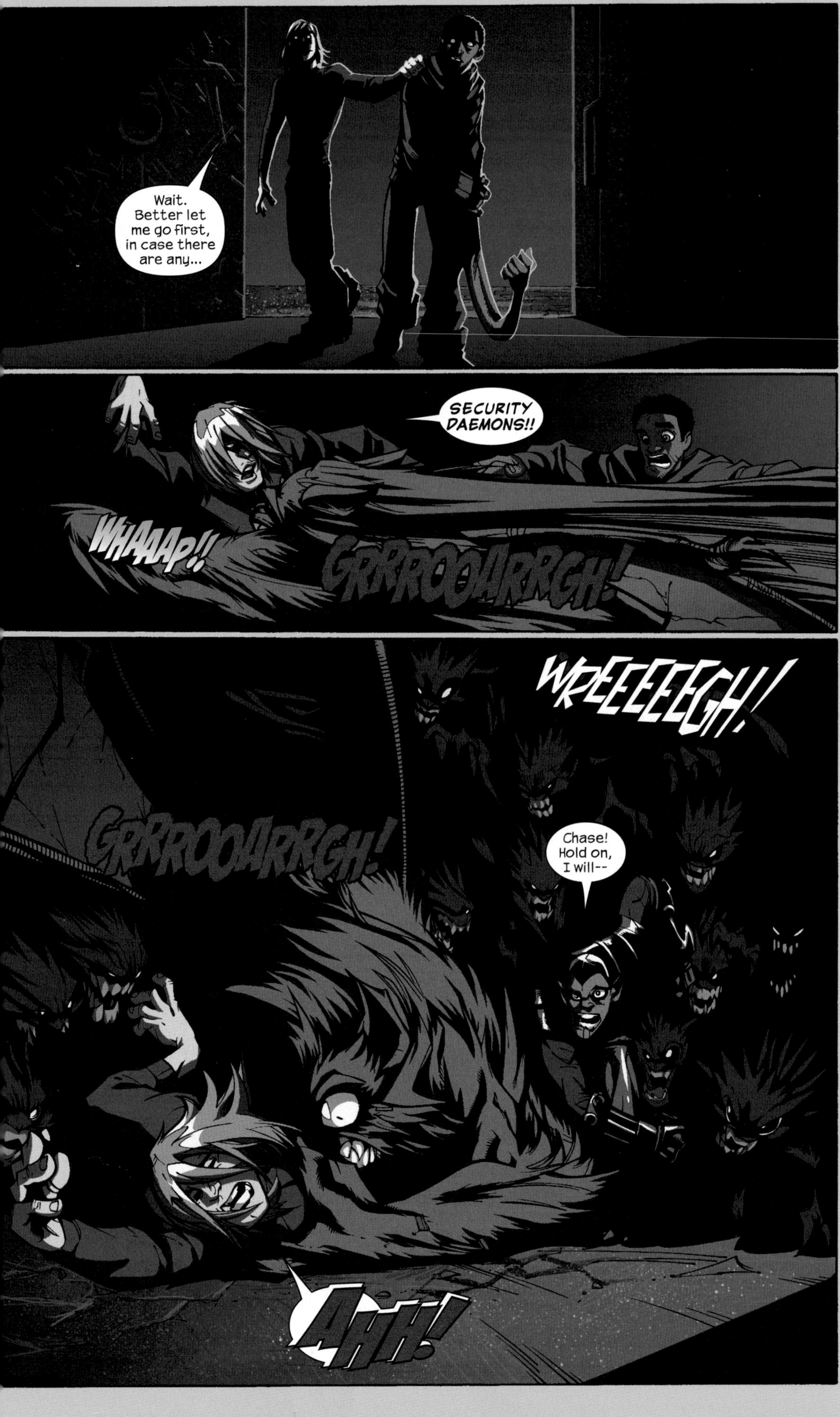
Wait. Better let me go first, in case there are any...
SECURITY DAEMONS!!
WHAAAP!!
GRRROOARRRGH!
WREEEEEGH!
GRRROOARRRGH!
Chase! Hold on, I will--
AHH!

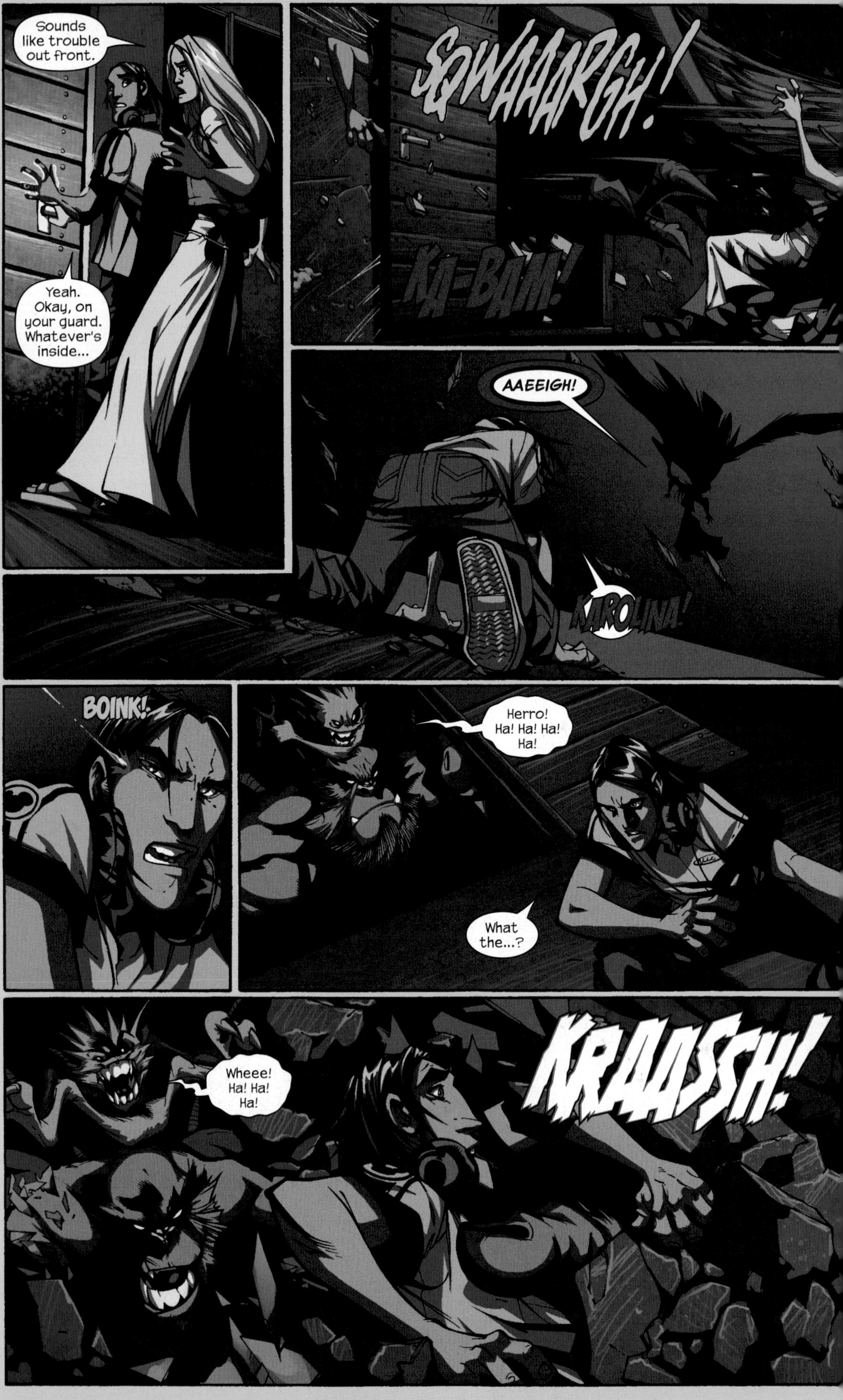
Sounds like trouble out front.
Yeah. Okay, on your guard. Whatever's inside...
SQWAAARGH!
KA-BAM!
AAEEIGH!
KAROLINA!
BOINK!
Herro! Ha! Ha! Ha! Ha!
What the...?
Wheee! Ha! Ha! Ha!
KRAASSH!

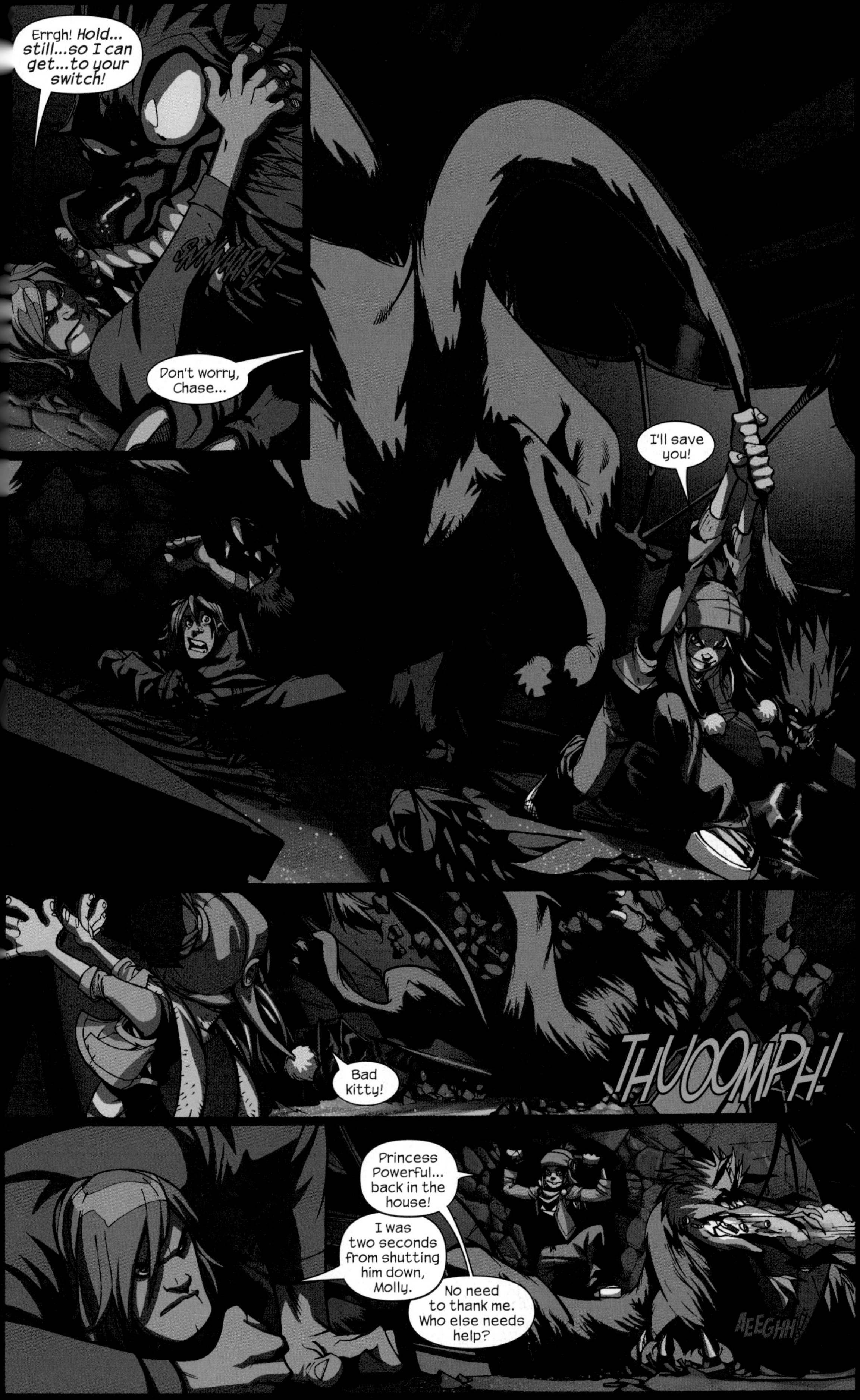
Errgh! Hold... still...so I can get...to your switch!
Don't worry, Chase...
I'll save you!
Bad kitty!
THUOOMPH!
Princess Powerful... back in the house!
I was two seconds from shutting him down, Molly.
No need to thank me. Who else needs help?
AEEGHH!

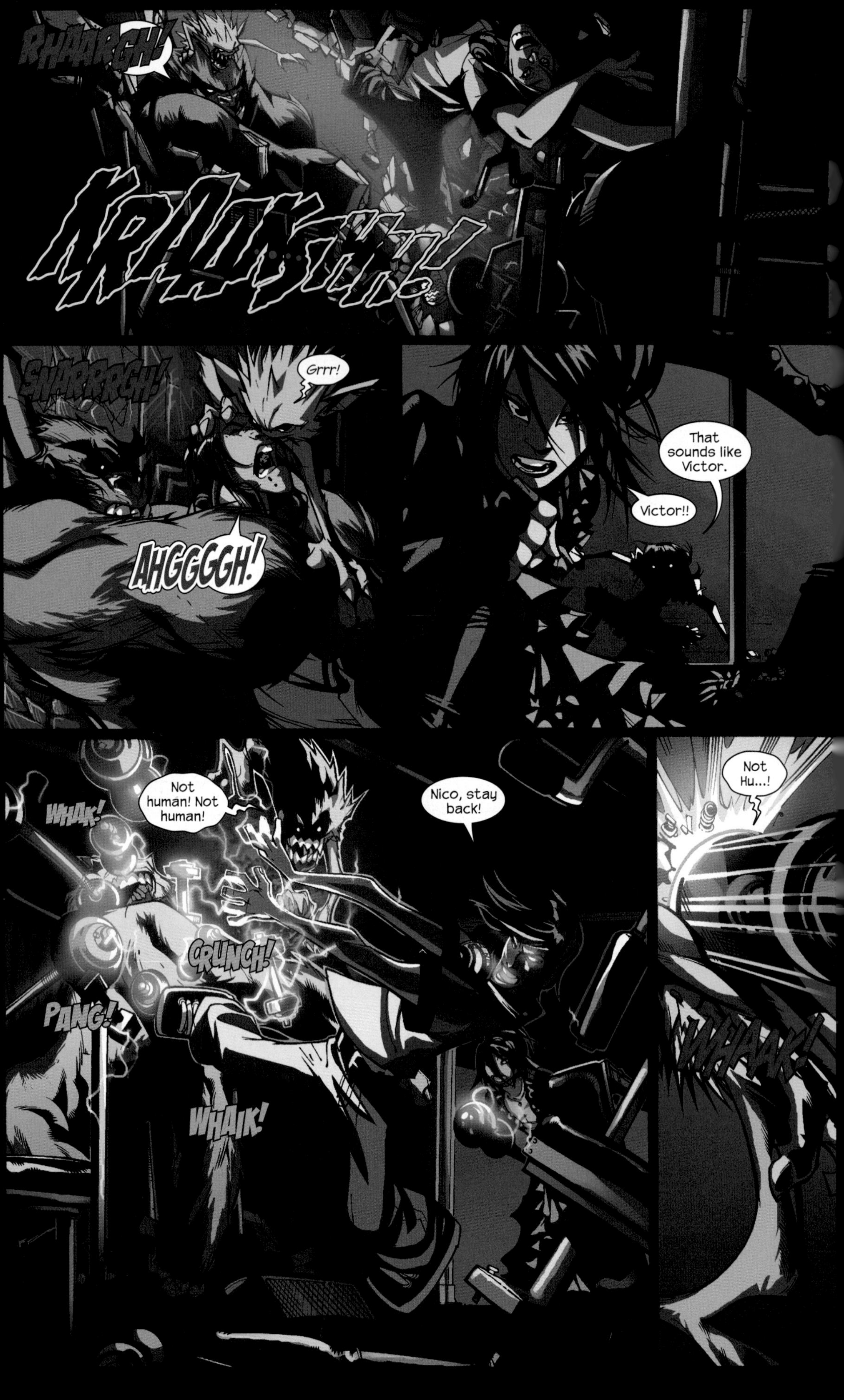
RHAARGH!
KRAASHHH!!
SNARRRGH!
Grrr!
AHGGGGH!
That sounds like Victor.
Victor!!
WHAK!
Not human! Not human!
Nico, stay back!
CRUNCH!
PANG!
WHAIK!
Not Hu...!
WHAAK!

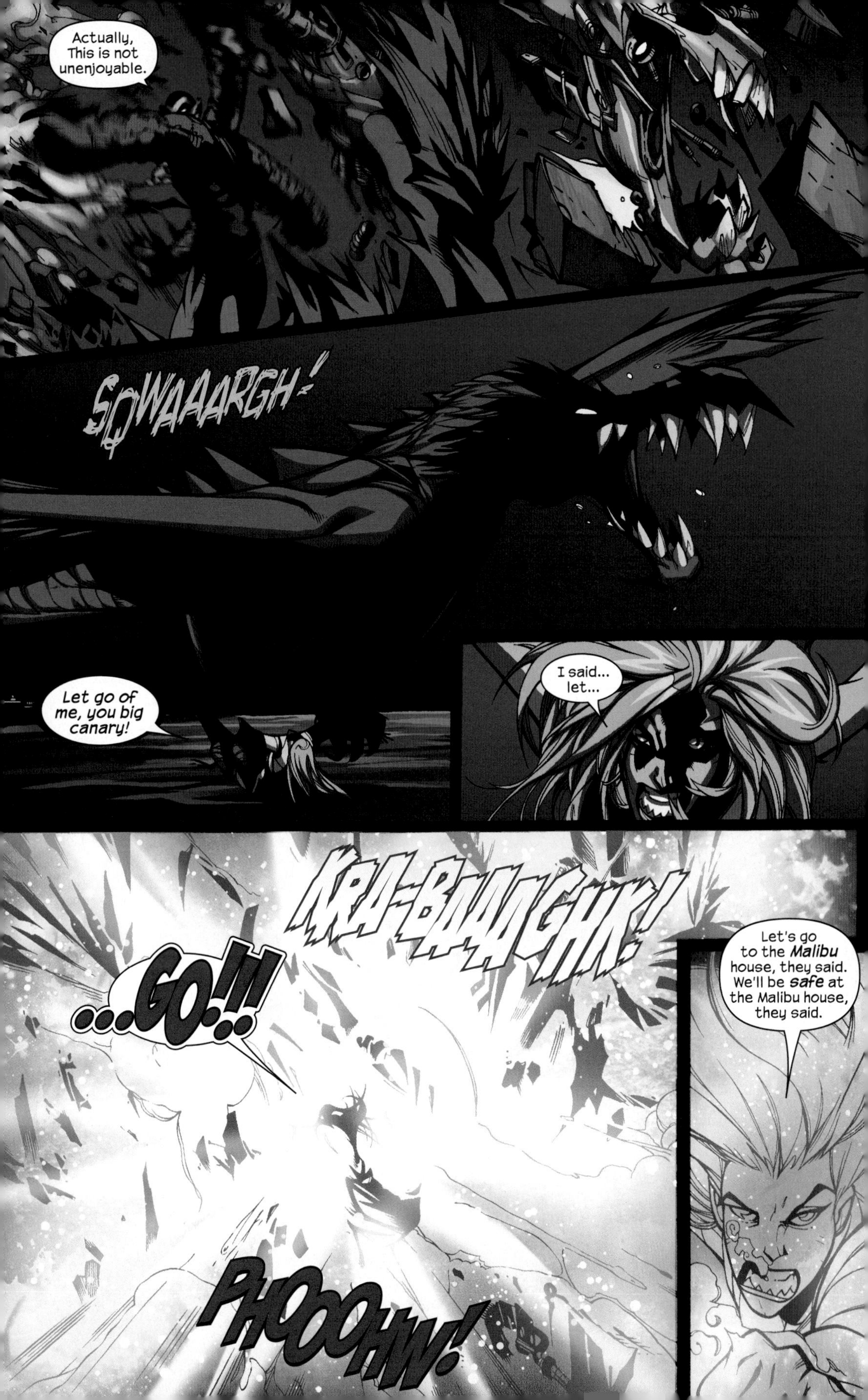

Actually, This is not unenjoyable.
SQWAAARGH!
Let go of me, you big canary!
I said... let...
...GO!!!
KRA-BAAAGHK!
PHOOOHW!
Let's go to the *Malibu* house, they said. We'll be *safe* at the Malibu house, they said.

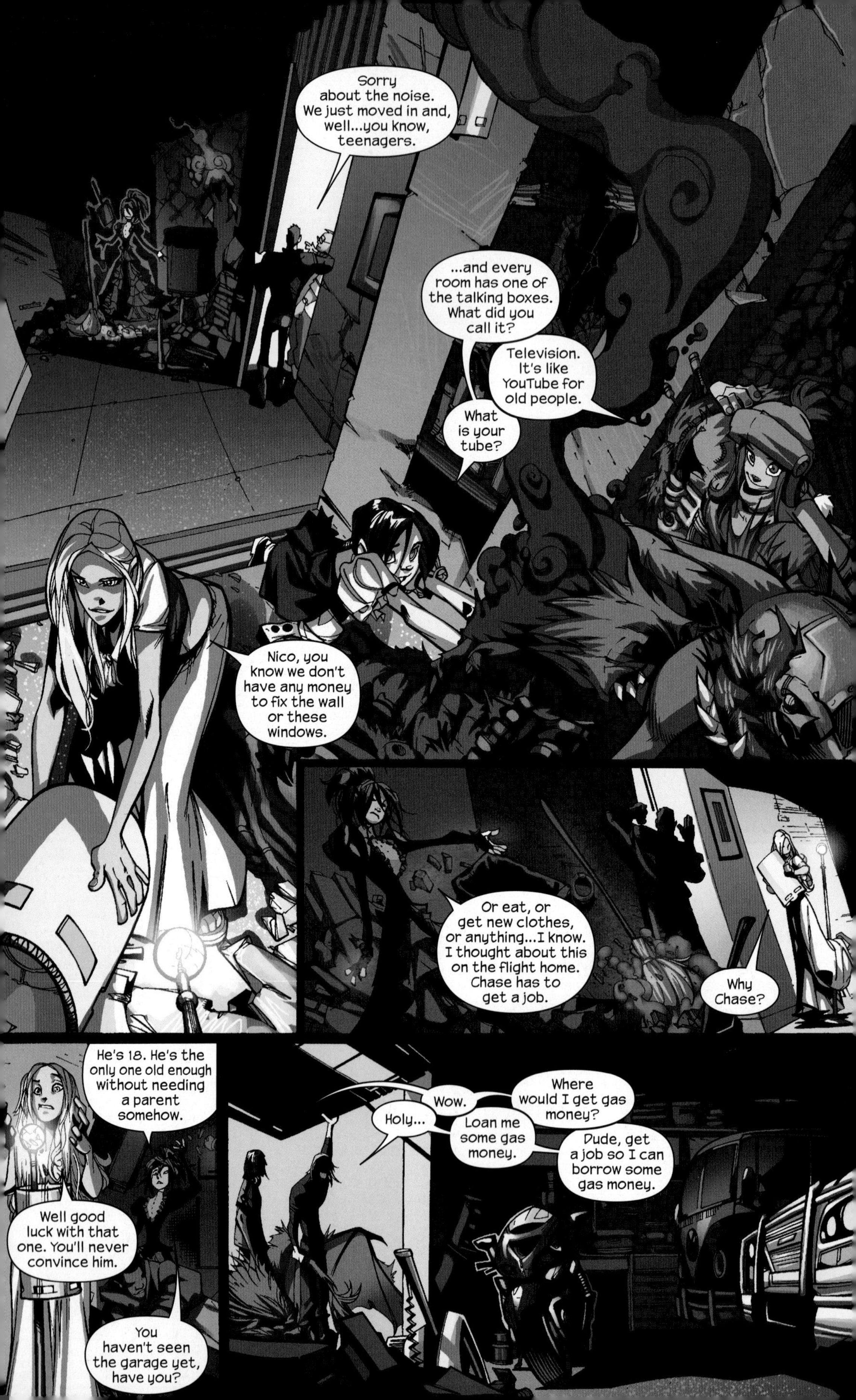
Sorry about the noise. We just moved in and, well...you know, teenagers.
...and every room has one of the talking boxes. What did you call it?
Television. It's like YouTube for old people.
What is your tube?
Nico, you know we don't have any money to fix the wall or these windows.
Or eat, or get new clothes, or anything...I know. I thought about this on the flight home. Chase has to get a job.
Why Chase?
He's 18. He's the only one old enough without needing a parent somehow.
Well good luck with that one. You'll never convince him.
You haven't seen the garage yet, have you?
Wow.
Holy...
Where would I get gas money?
Loan me some gas money.
Dude, get a job so I can borrow some gas money.

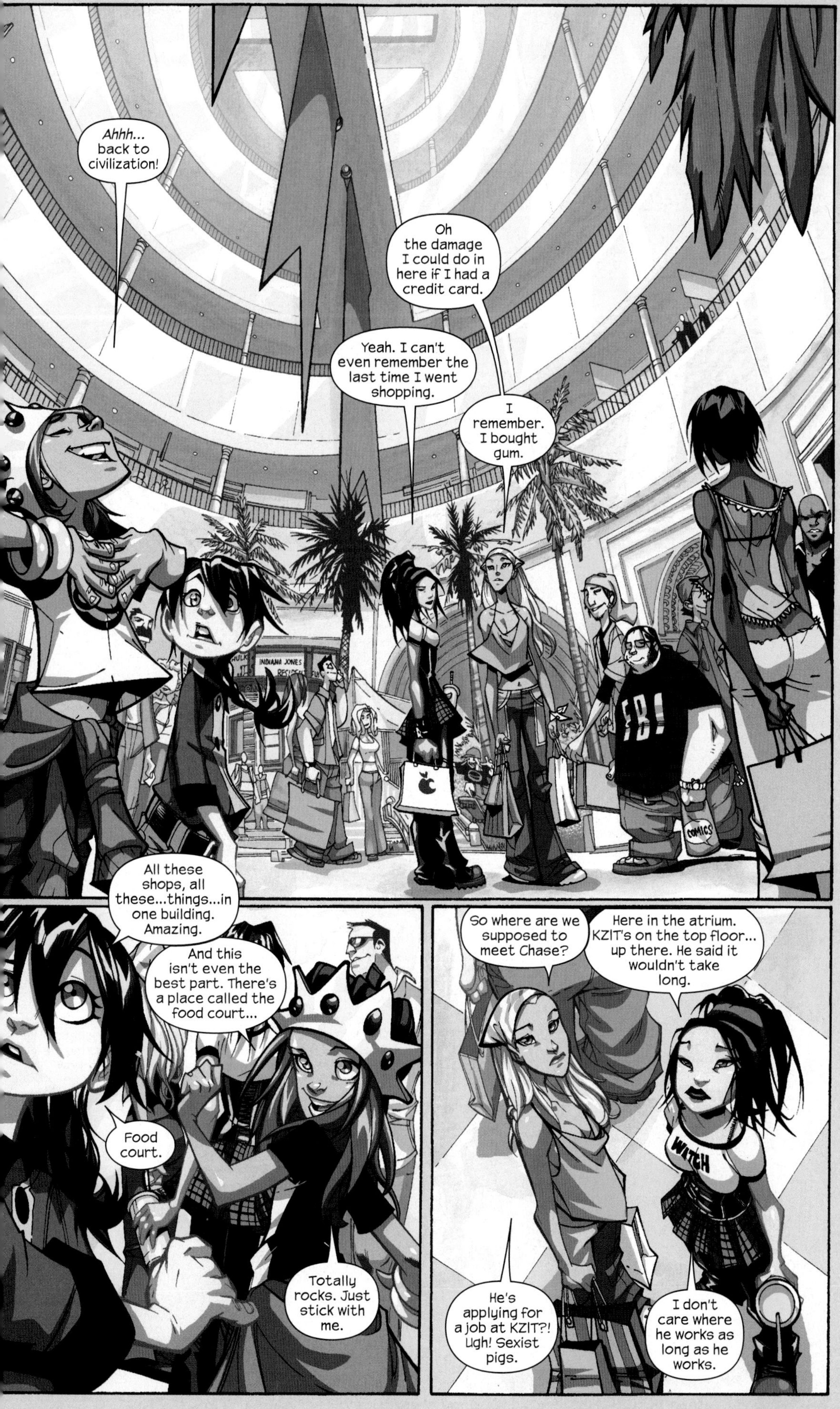
Ahhh... back to civilization!
Oh the damage I could do in here if I had a credit card.
Yeah. I can't even remember the last time I went shopping.
I remember. I bought gum.
INDIANA JONES
FBI
COMICS
All these shops, all these...things...in one building. Amazing.
And this isn't even the best part. There's a place called the food court...
Food court.
Totally rocks. Just stick with me.
So where are we supposed to meet Chase?
Here in the atrium. KZIT's on the top floor... up there. He said it wouldn't take long.
WITCH
He's applying for a job at KZIT?! Ugh! Sexist pigs.
I don't care where he works as long as he works.

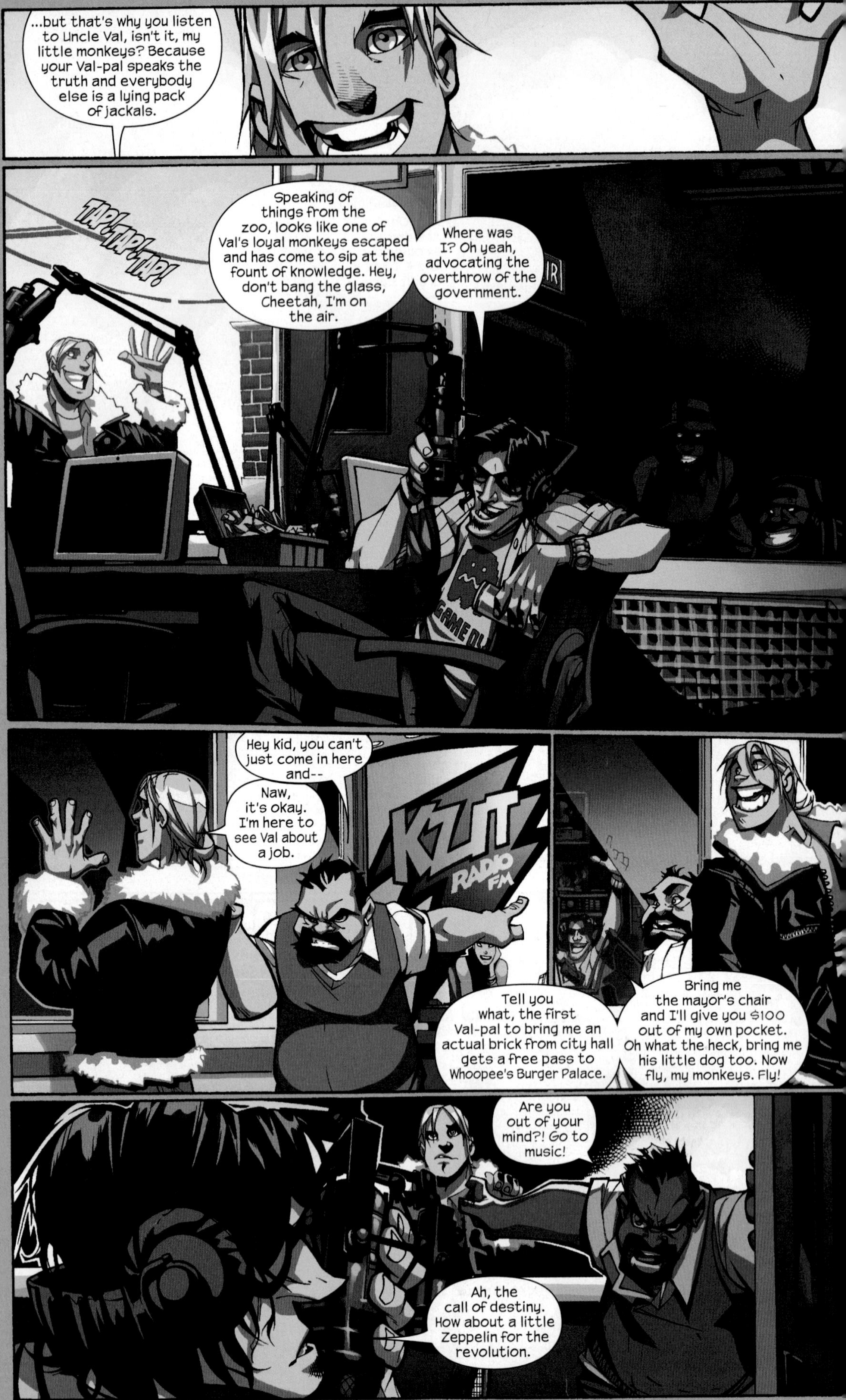
...but that's why you listen to Uncle Val, isn't it, my little monkeys? Because your Val-pal speaks the truth and everybody else is a lying pack of jackals.
TAP! TAP! TAP!
Speaking of things from the zoo, looks like one of Val's loyal monkeys escaped and has come to sip at the fount of knowledge. Hey, don't bang the glass, Cheetah, I'm on the air.
Where was I? Oh yeah, advocating the overthrow of the government.
Hey kid, you can't just come in here and--
Naw, it's okay. I'm here to see Val about a job.
KZIT RADIO FM
Tell you what, the first Val-pal to bring me an actual brick from city hall gets a free pass to Whoopee's Burger Palace.
Bring me the mayor's chair and I'll give you $100 out of my own pocket. Oh what the heck, bring me his little dog too. Now fly, my monkeys. Fly!
Are you out of your mind?! Go to music!
Ah, the call of destiny. How about a little Zeppelin for the revolution.

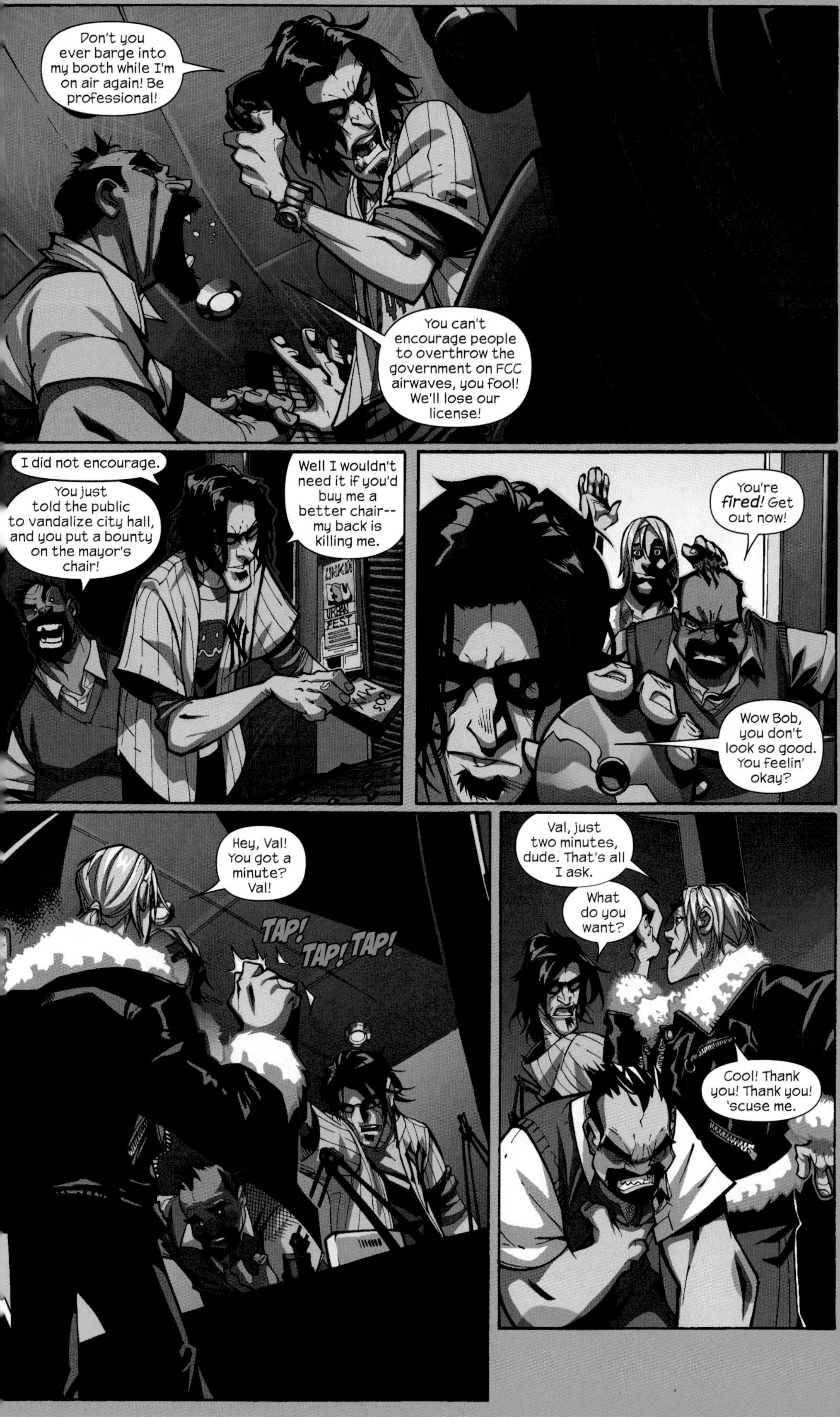

Don't you ever barge into my booth while I'm on air again! Be professional!
You can't encourage people to overthrow the government on FCC airwaves, you fool! We'll lose our license!
I did not encourage.
You just told the public to vandalize city hall, and you put a bounty on the mayor's chair!
Well I wouldn't need it if you'd buy me a better chair-- my back is killing me.
URBAN FEST
You're *fired!* Get out now!
Wow Bob, you don't look so good. You feelin' okay?
Hey, Val! You got a minute? Val!
TAP! TAP! TAP!
Val, just two minutes, dude. That's all I ask.
What do you want?
Cool! Thank you! Thank you! 'scuse me.

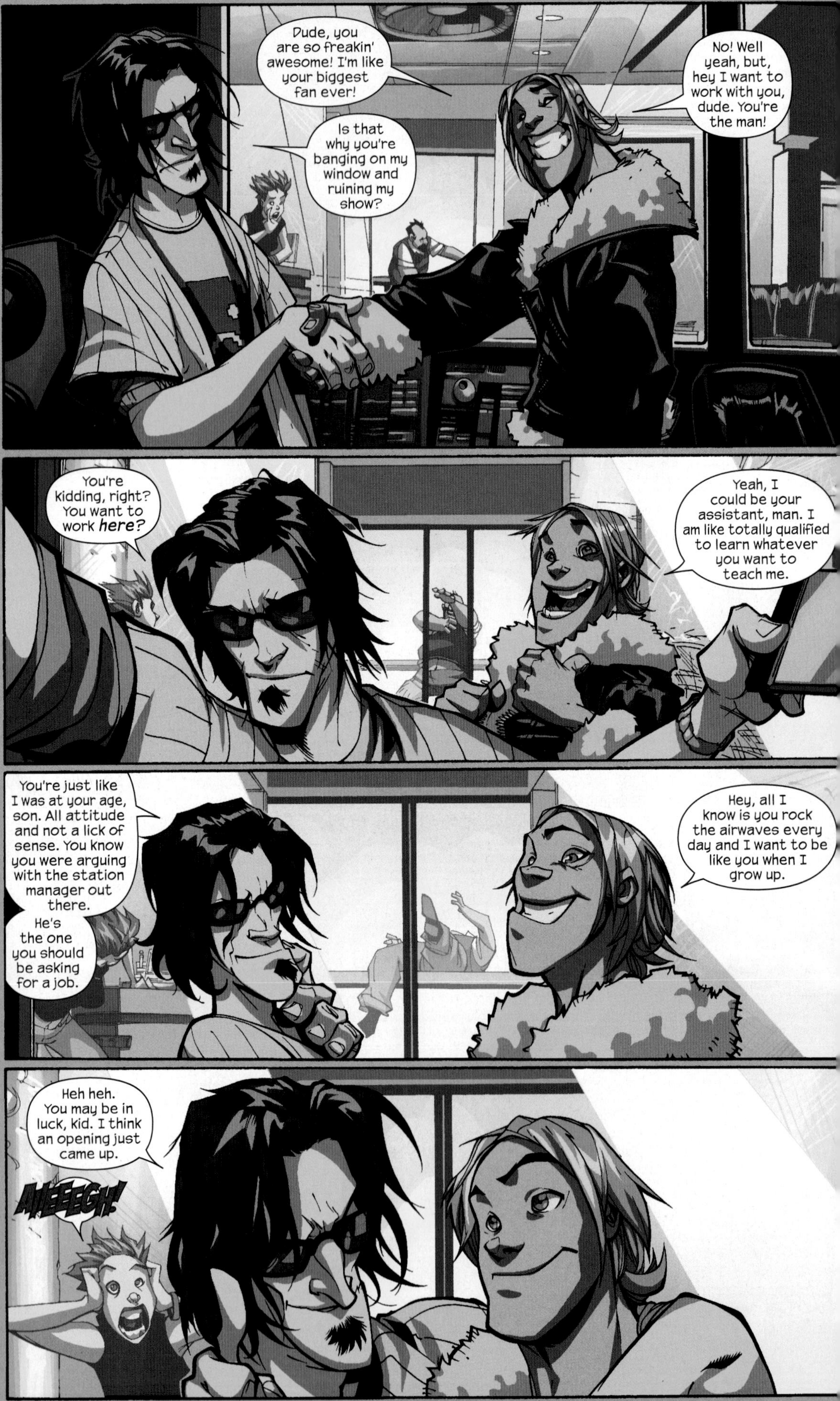
Dude, you are so freakin' awesome! I'm like your biggest fan ever!
Is that why you're banging on my window and ruining my show?
No! Well yeah, but, hey I want to work with you, dude. You're the man!
You're kidding, right? You want to work *here*?
Yeah, I could be your assistant, man. I am like totally qualified to learn whatever you want to teach me.
You're just like I was at your age, son. All attitude and not a lick of sense. You know you were arguing with the station manager out there.
He's the one you should be asking for a job.
Hey, all I know is you rock the airwaves every day and I want to be like you when I grow up.
Heh heh. You may be in luck, kid. I think an opening just came up.
AIEEEEGH!

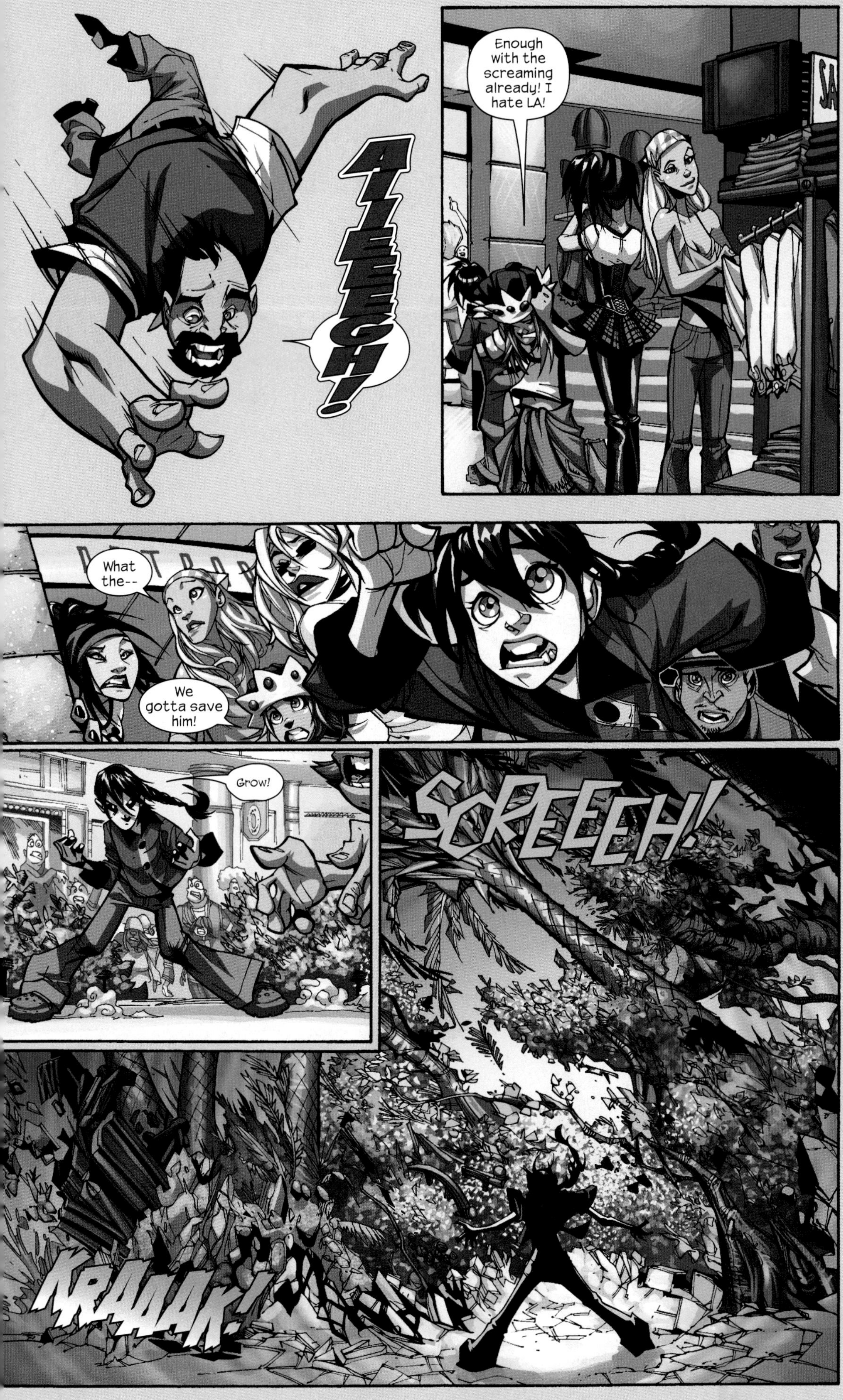
AIIEEEGH!
Enough with the screaming already! I hate LA!
What the--
We gotta save him!
Grow!
SCREEEEH!
KRAAAK!

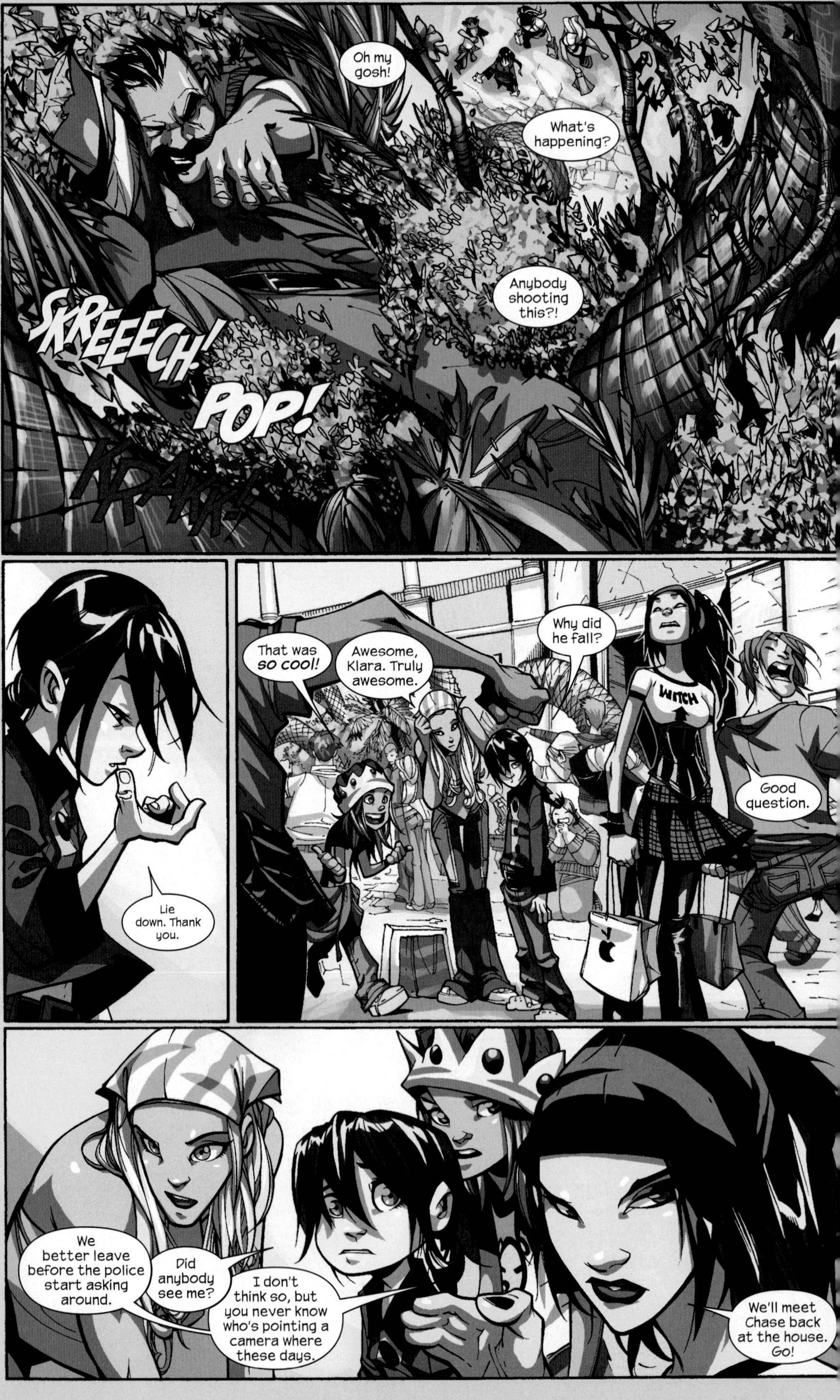
Oh my gosh!
What's happening?
Anybody shooting this?!
SKREEECH!
POP!
KRAWW!
Lie down. Thank you.
That was SO COOL!
Awesome, Klara. Truly awesome.
Why did he fall?
Good question.
We better leave before the police start asking around.
Did anybody see me?
I don't think so, but you never know who's pointing a camera where these days.
We'll meet Chase back at the house. Go!

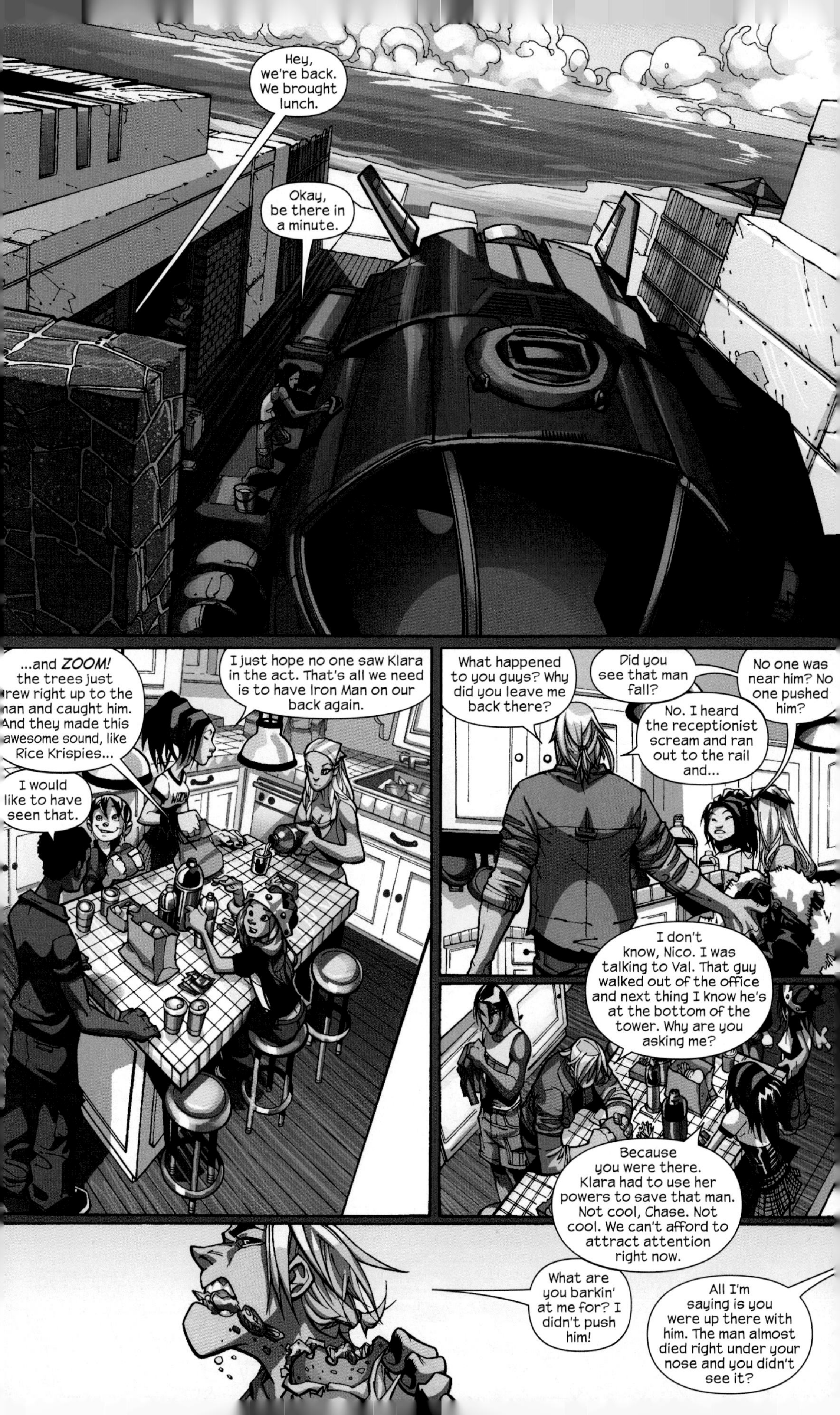
Hey, we're back. We brought lunch.
Okay, be there in a minute.
...and ZOOM! the trees just grew right up to the man and caught him. And they made this awesome sound, like Rice Krispies...
I just hope no one saw Klara in the act. That's all we need is to have Iron Man on our back again.
I would like to have seen that.
What happened to you guys? Why did you leave me back there?
Did you see that man fall?
No one was near him? No one pushed him?
No. I heard the receptionist scream and ran out to the rail and...
I don't know, Nico. I was talking to Val. That guy walked out of the office and next thing I know he's at the bottom of the tower. Why are you asking me?
Because you were there. Klara had to use her powers to save that man. Not cool, Chase. Not cool. We can't afford to attract attention right now.
What are you barkin' at me for? I didn't push him!
All I'm saying is you were up there with him. The man almost died right under your nose and you didn't see it?

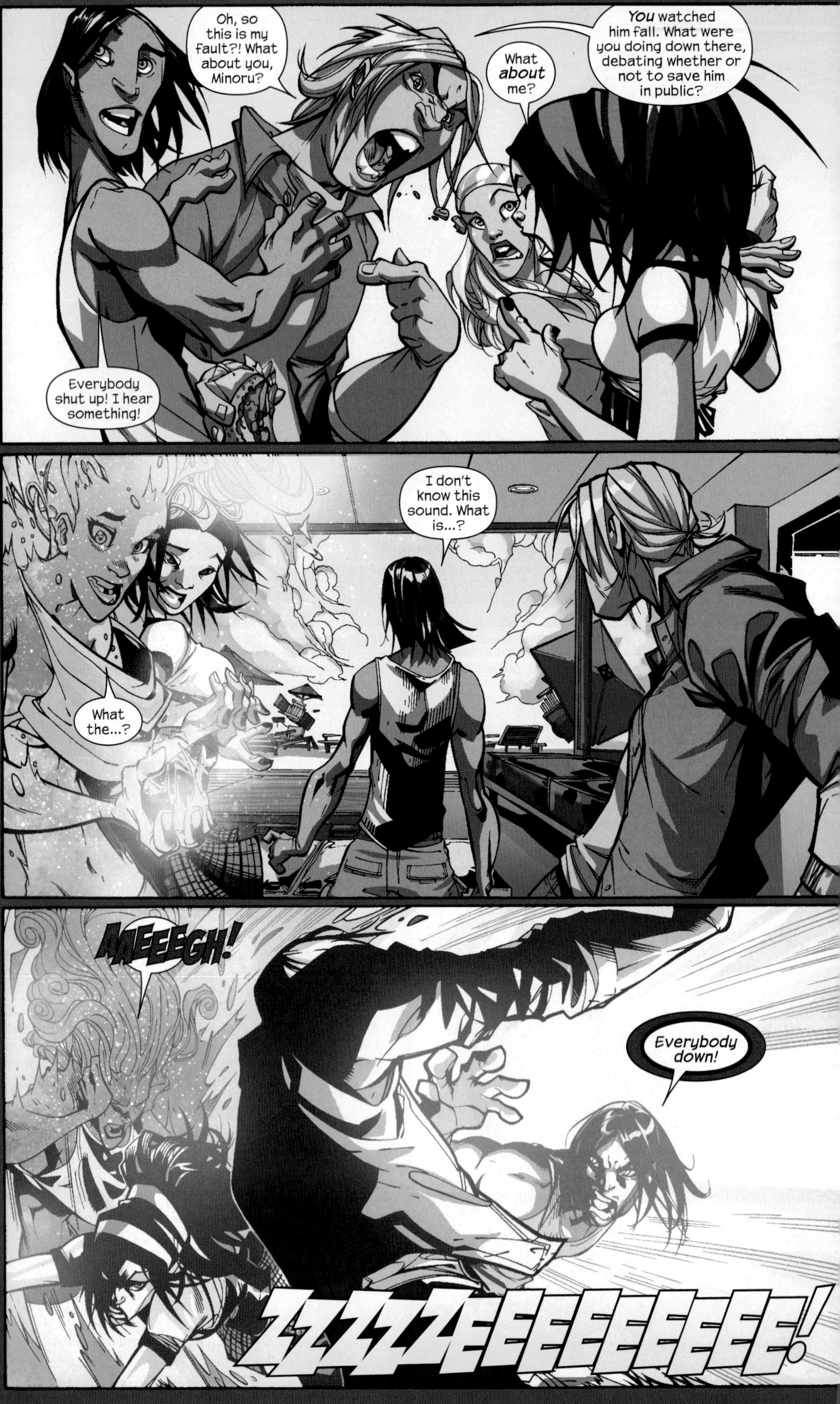
Oh, so this is my fault?! What about you, Minoru?
What about me?
You watched him fall. What were you doing down there, debating whether or not to save him in public?
Everybody shut up! I hear something!
I don't know this sound. What is...?
What the...?
MEEEGH!
Everybody down!
ZZZZEEEEEEEEEEE!

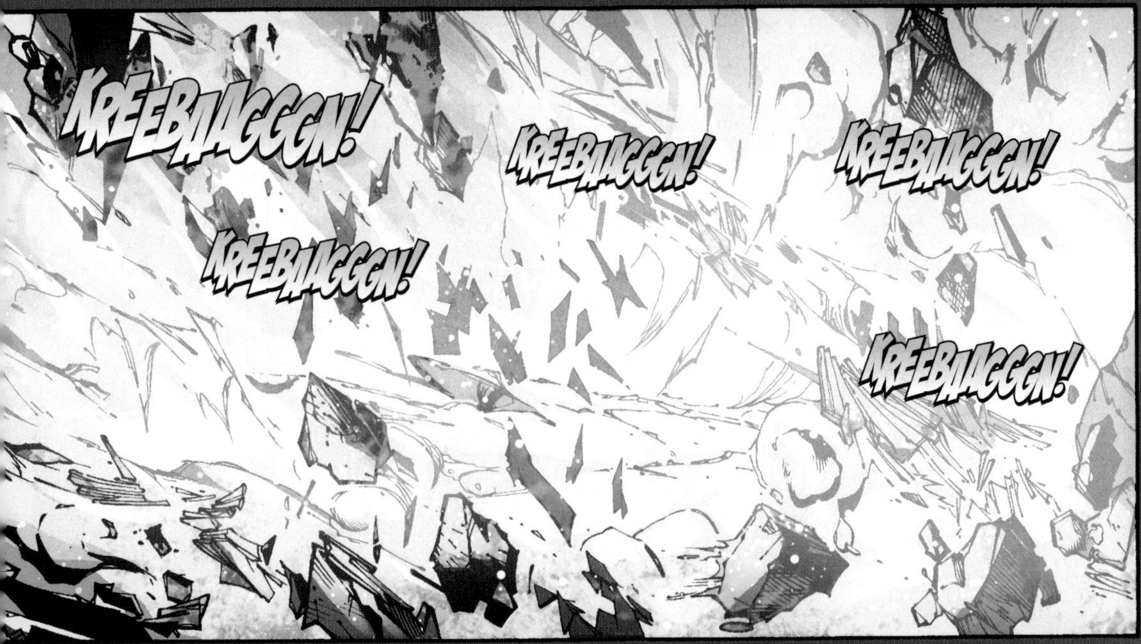
KREEBAAGGGN!
KREEBAAGGGN!
KREEBAAGGGN!
KREEBAAGGGN!
KREEBAAGGGN!

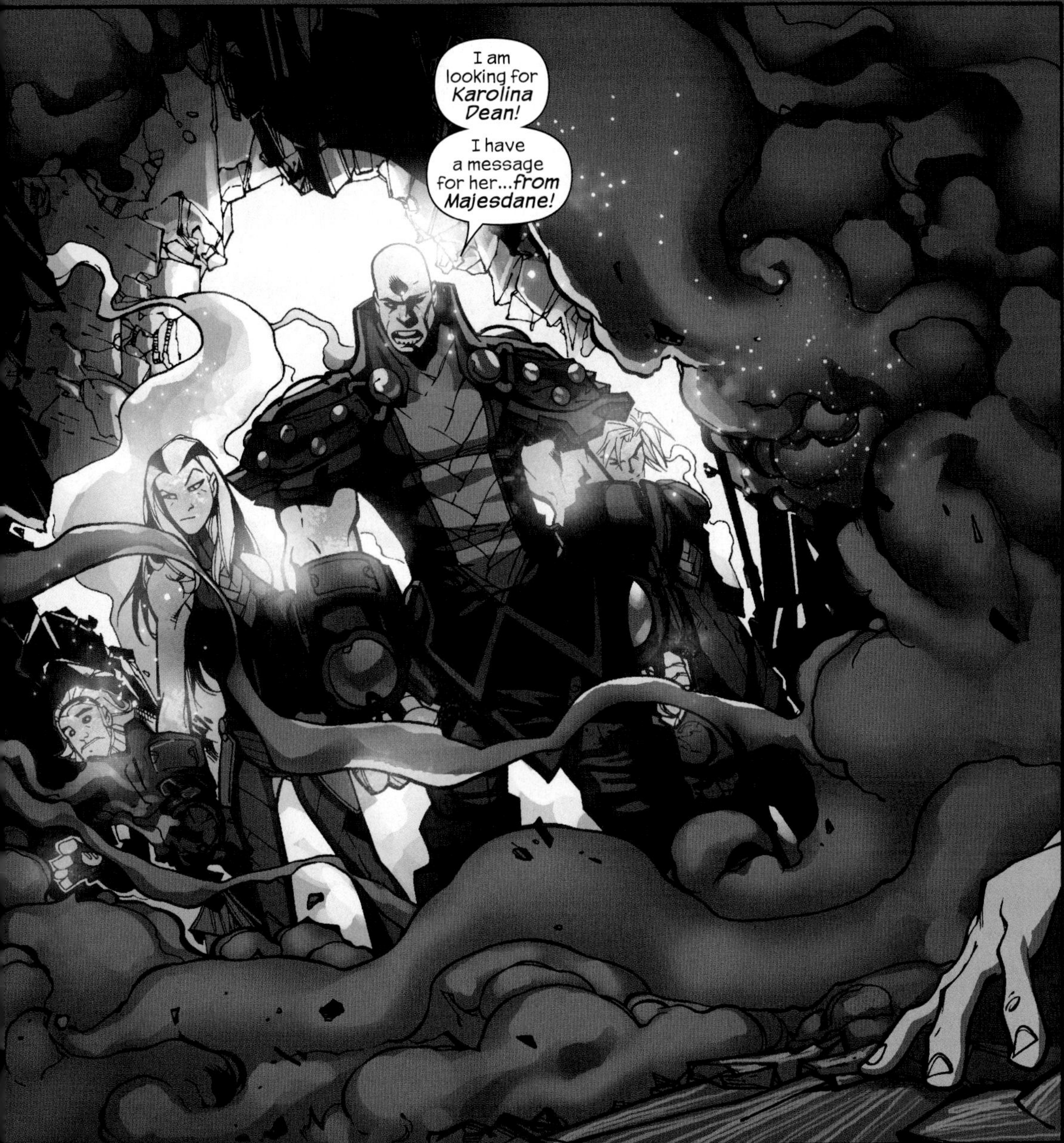
I am looking for *Karolina Dean!*
I have a message for her...*from Majesdane!*

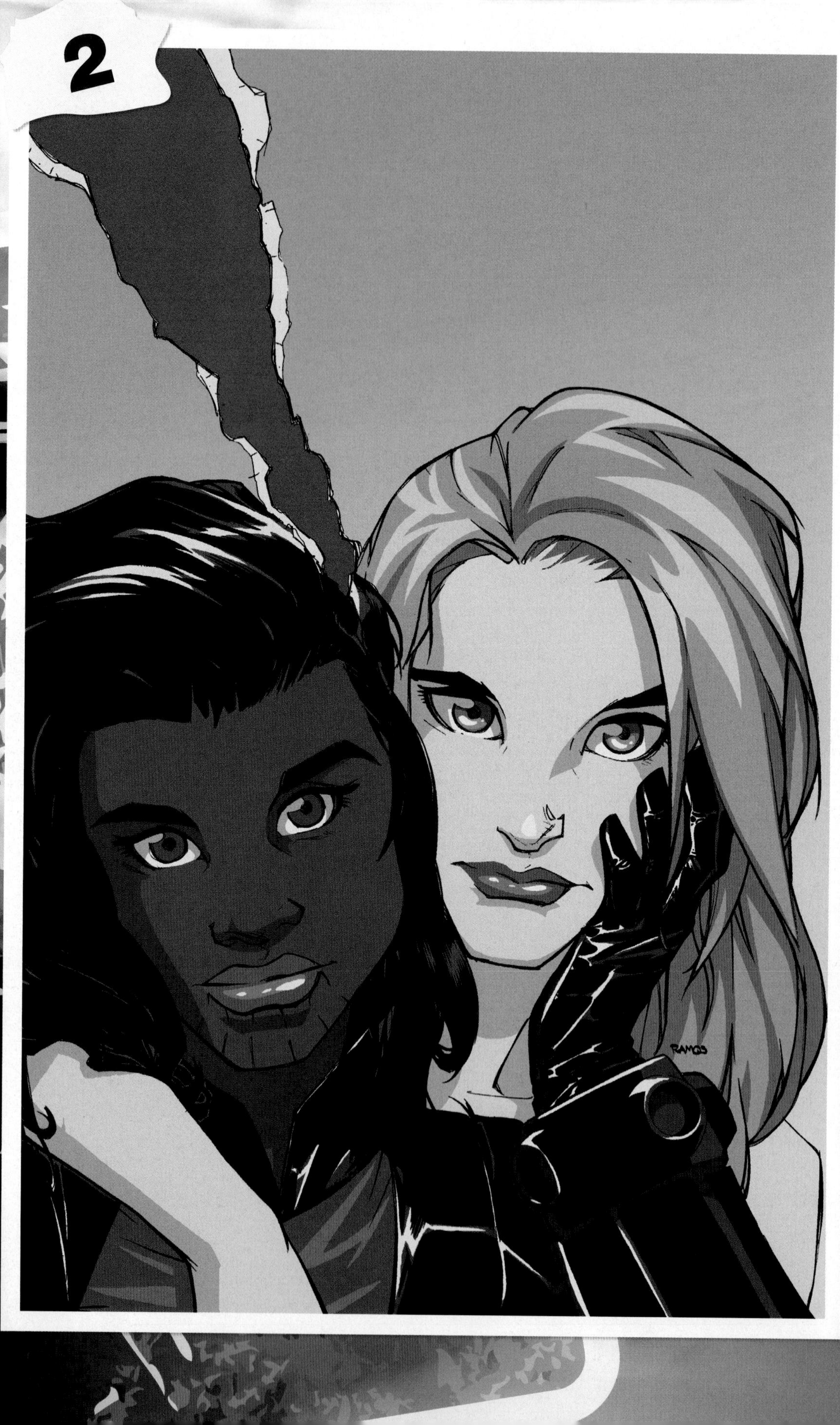
2
RAMOS

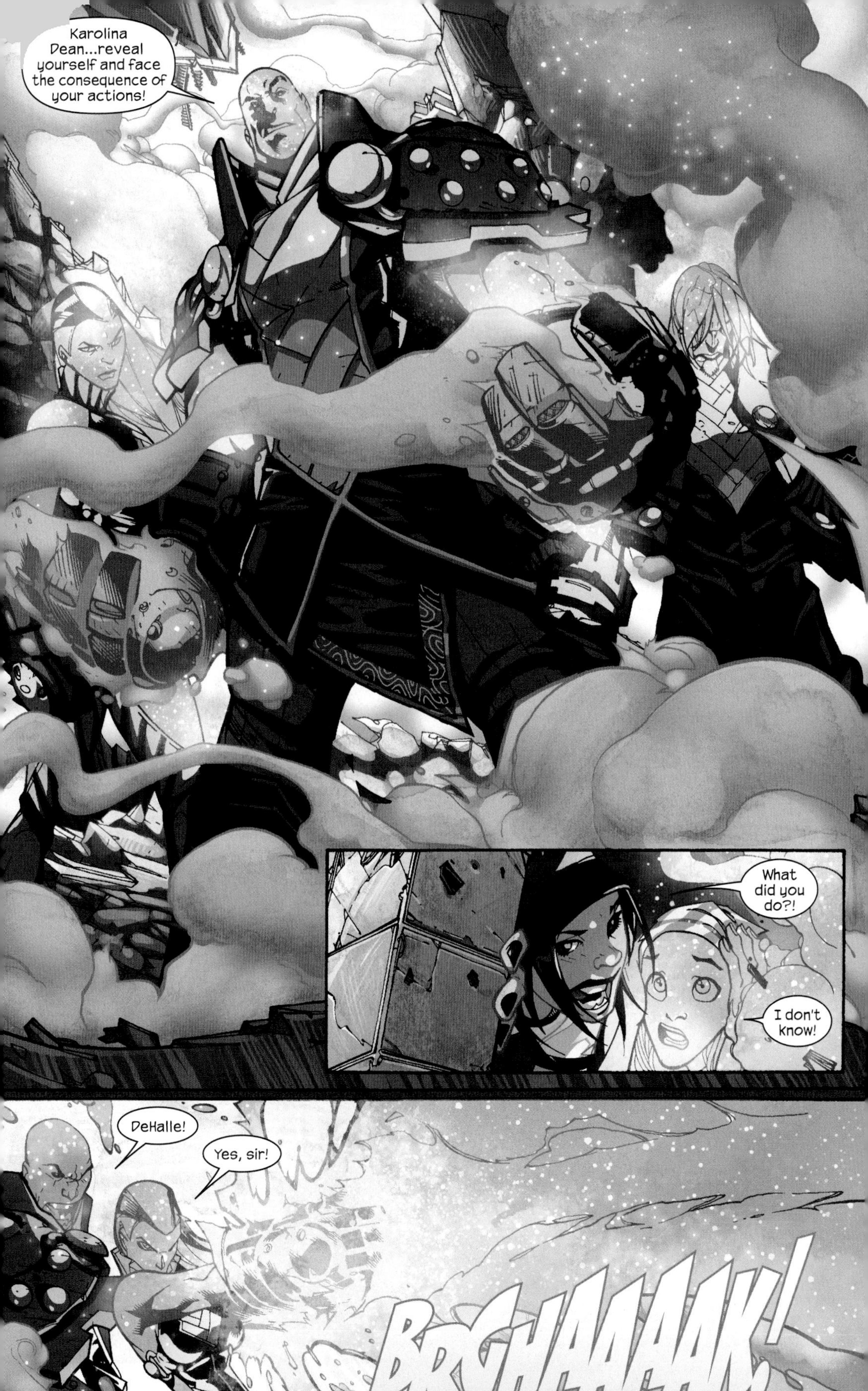
Karolina Dean...reveal yourself and face the consequence of your actions!
What did you do?!
I don't know!
DeHalle!
Yes, sir!
BRGHAAAAK!

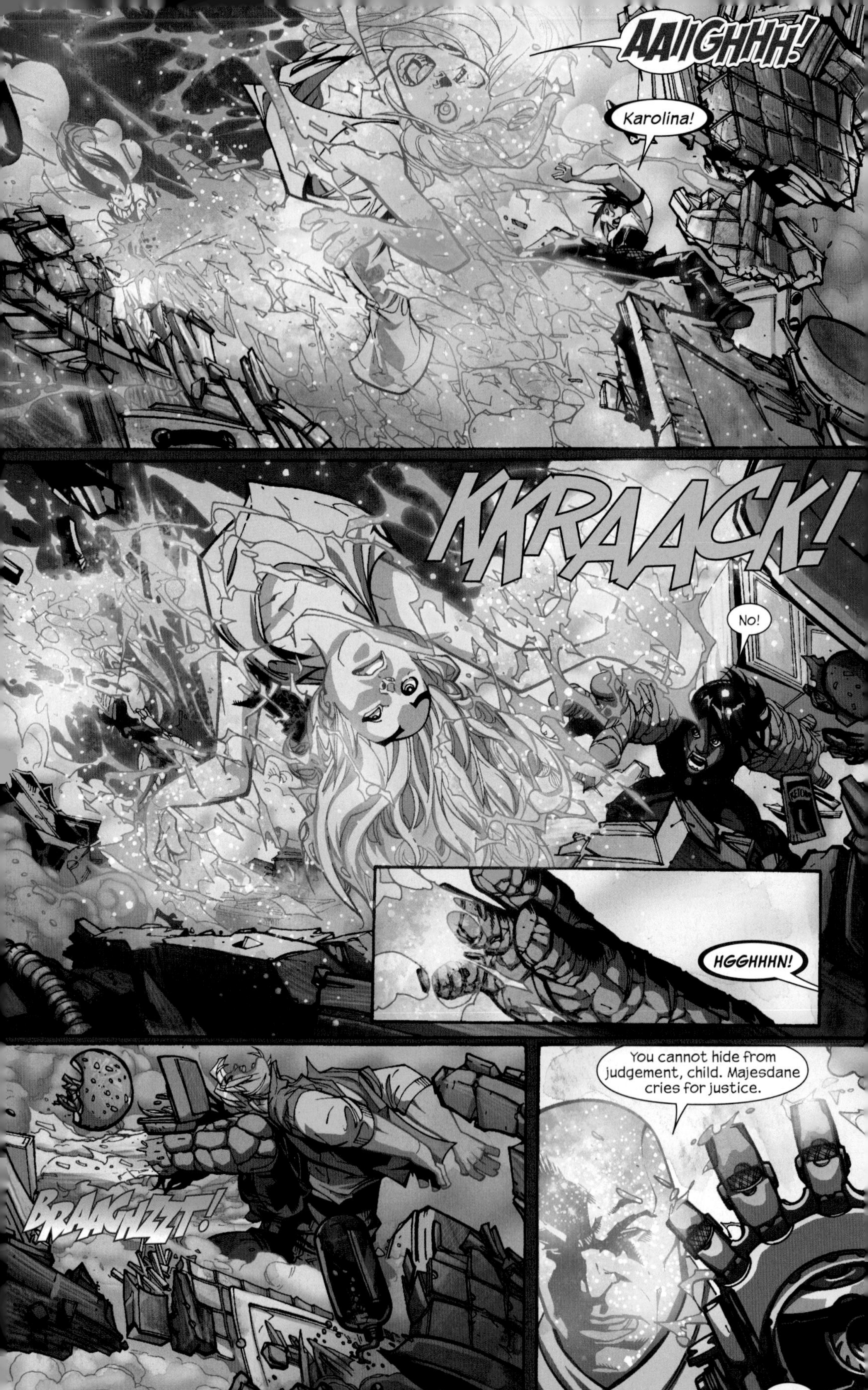
AAIIGHHH!
Karolina!
KKRAACK!
No!
HGGHHHN!
BRAAGHZZT!
You cannot hide from judgement, child. Majesdane cries for justice.
Nico!
CHK-CHINK!

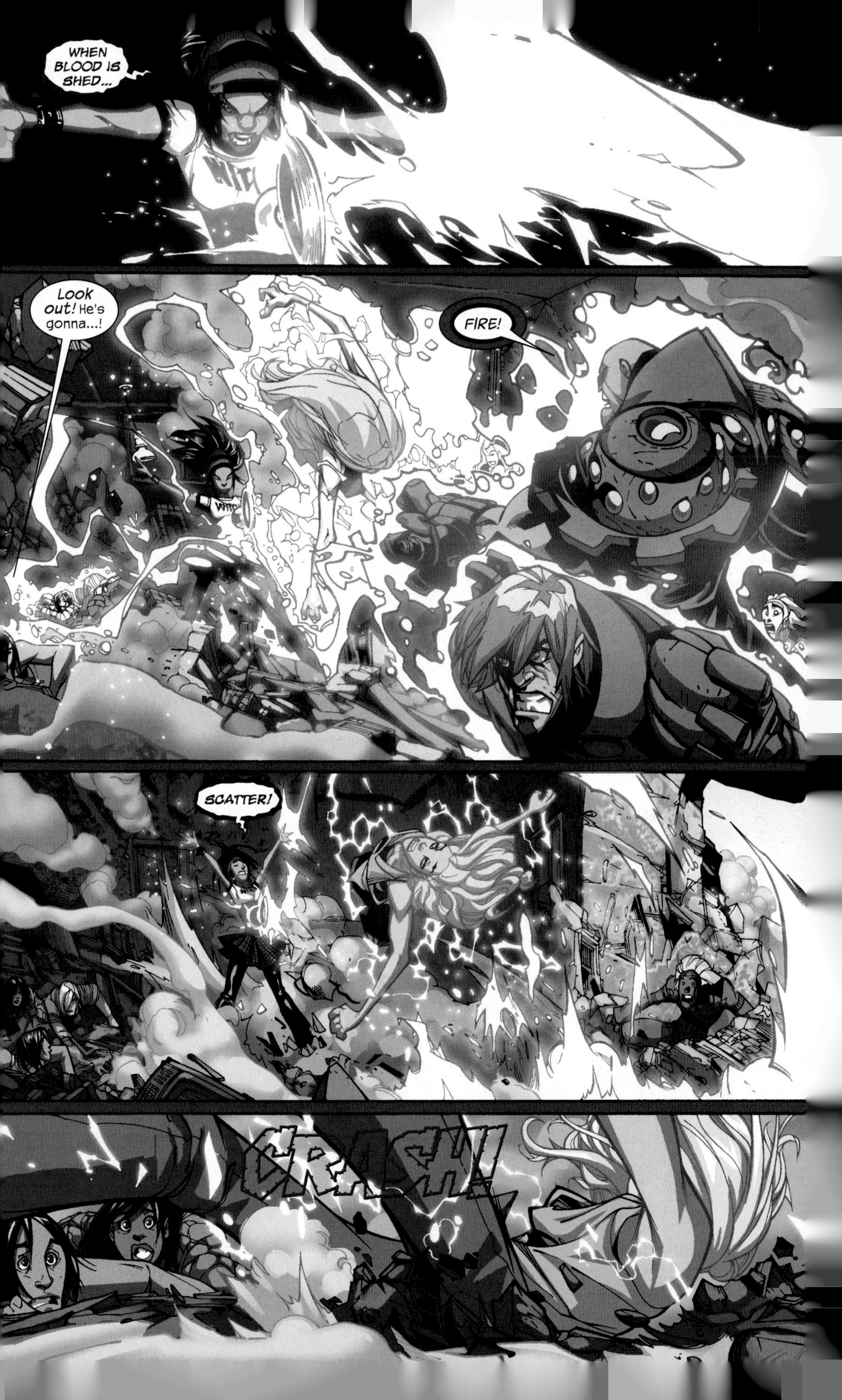

WHEN BLOOD IS SHED...
Look out! He's gonna...!
FIRE!
SCATTER!
CRASH!

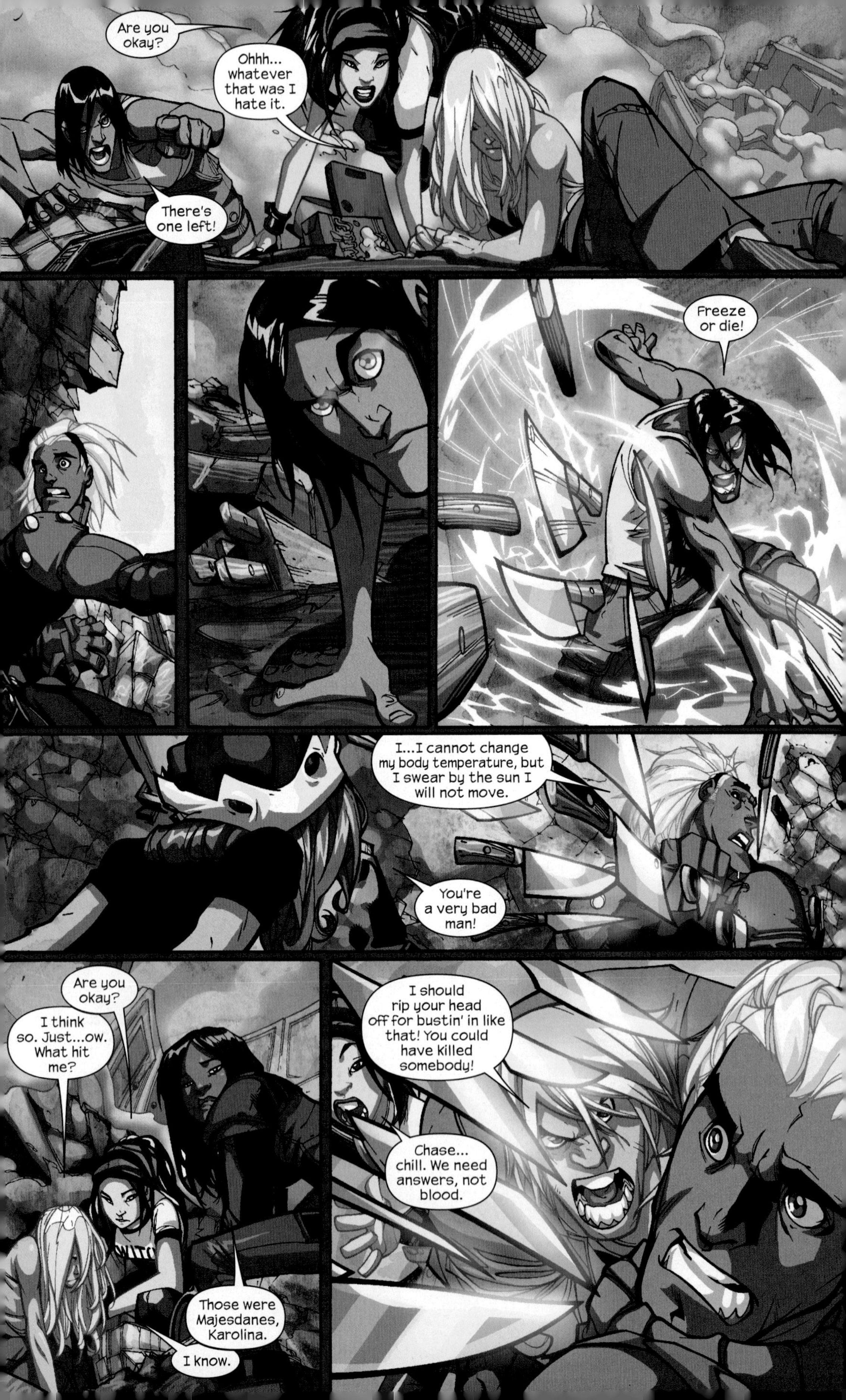
Are you okay?
Ohhh... whatever that was I hate it.
There's one left!
Freeze or die!
I...I cannot change my body temperature, but I swear by the sun I will not move.
You're a very bad man!
Are you okay?
I think so. Just...ow. What hit me?
Those were Majesdanes, Karolina.
I know.
I should rip your head off for bustin' in like that! You could have killed somebody!
Chase... chill. We need answers, not blood.

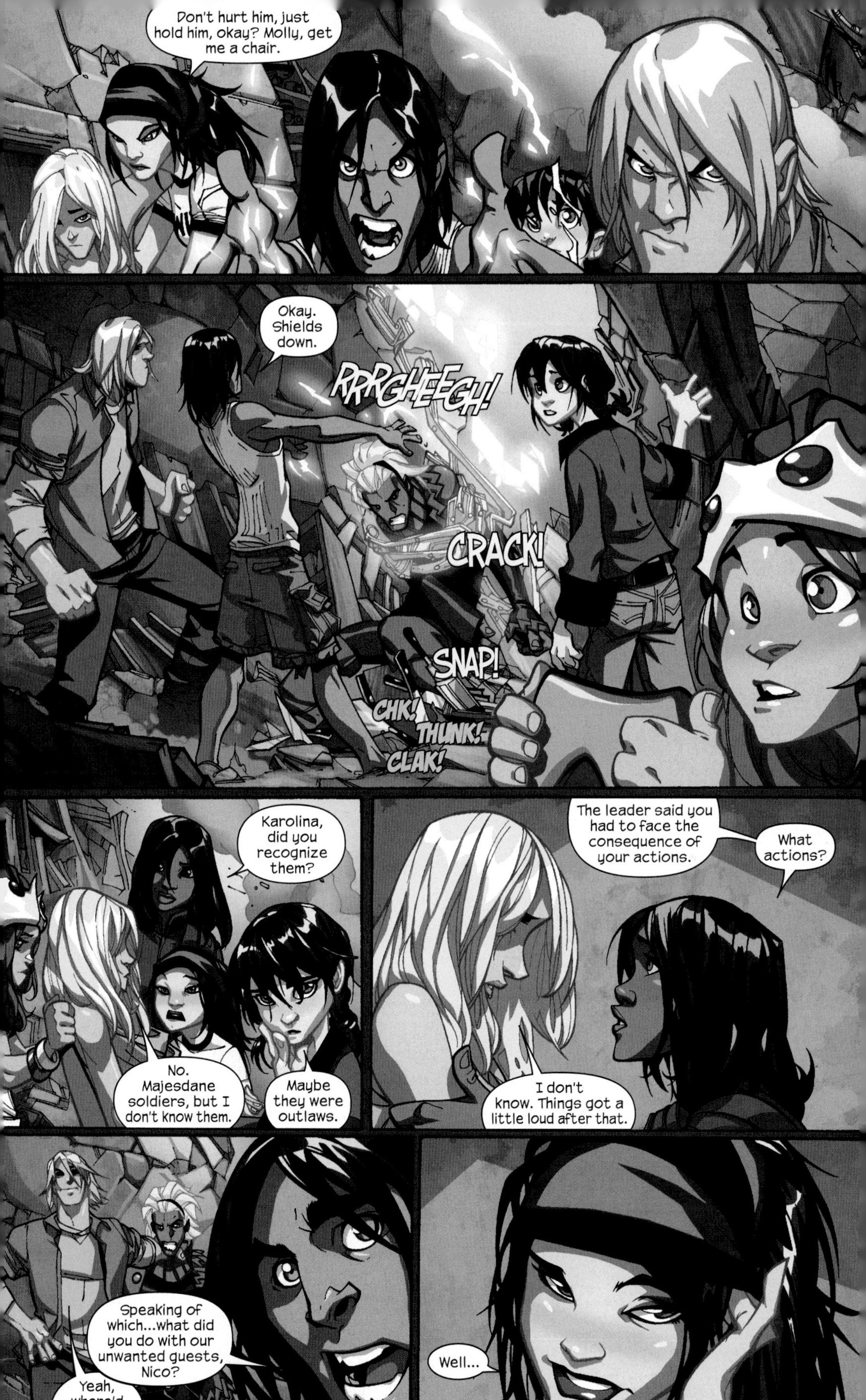
Don't hurt him, just hold him, okay? Molly, get me a chair.
Okay. Shields down.
RRRGHEEGH!
CRACK!
SNAP!
CHK!
THUNK!
CLAK!
Karolina, did you recognize them?
No. Majesdane soldiers, but I don't know them.
Maybe they were outlaws.
The leader said you had to face the consequence of your actions.
What actions?
I don't know. Things got a little loud after that.
Speaking of which...what did you do with our unwanted guests, Nico?
Yeah, where'd everybody go?
Well...

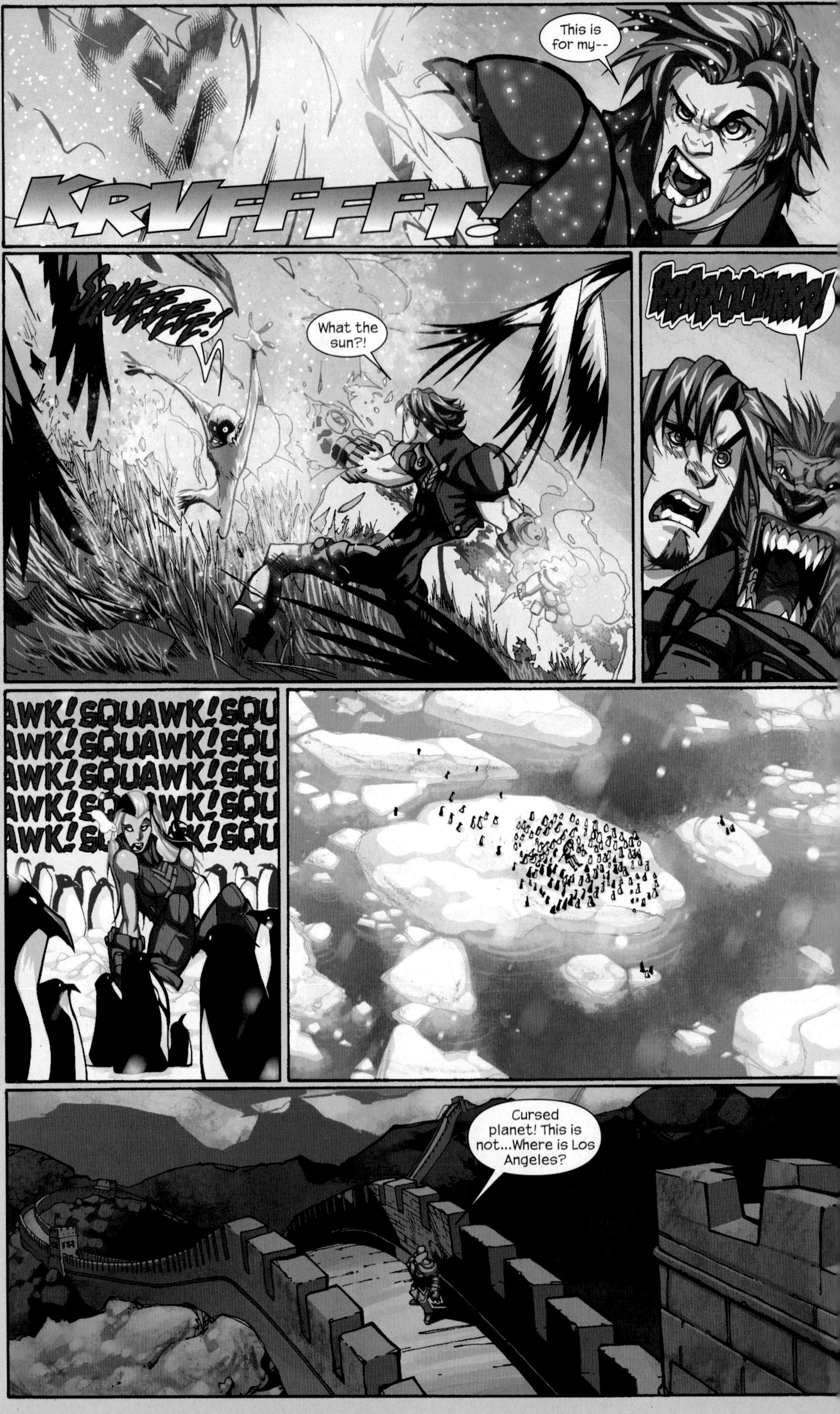
This is for my--
KRVFFFFT!
SQUEEEEE!
What the sun?!
SQUAWK! SQUAWK! SQU
AWK! SQUAWK! SQU
AWK! SQUAWK! SQU
AWK! SQUAWK! SQU
AWK! SQUAWK! SQU
Cursed planet! This is not...Where is Los Angeles?

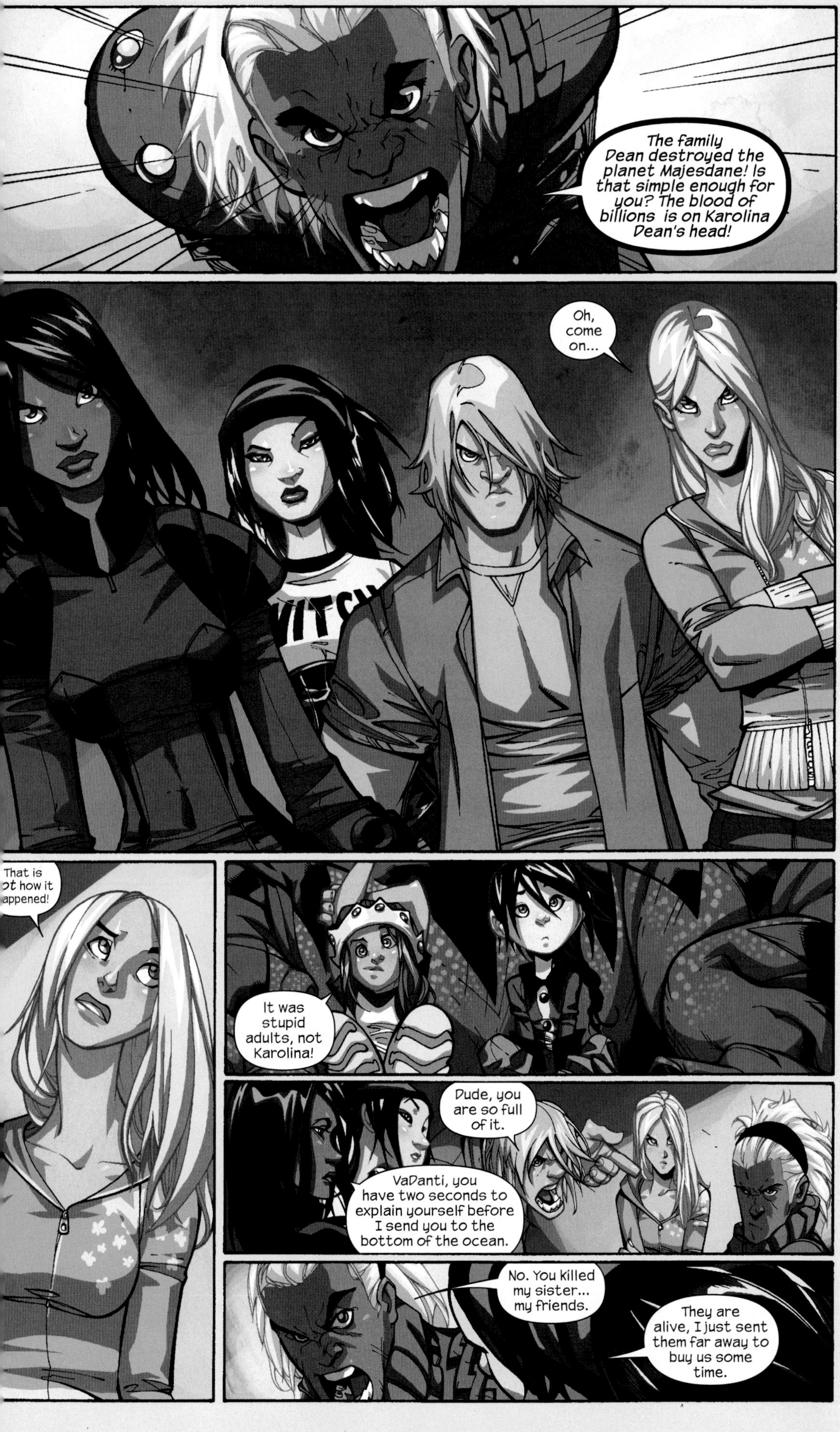

The family Dean destroyed the planet Majesdane! Is that simple enough for you? The blood of billions is on Karolina Dean's head!
Oh, come on...
That is ot how it appened!
It was stupid adults, not Karolina!
Dude, you are so full of it.
VaDanti, you have two seconds to explain yourself before I send you to the bottom of the ocean.
No. You killed my sister... my friends.
They are alive, I just sent them far away to buy us some time.

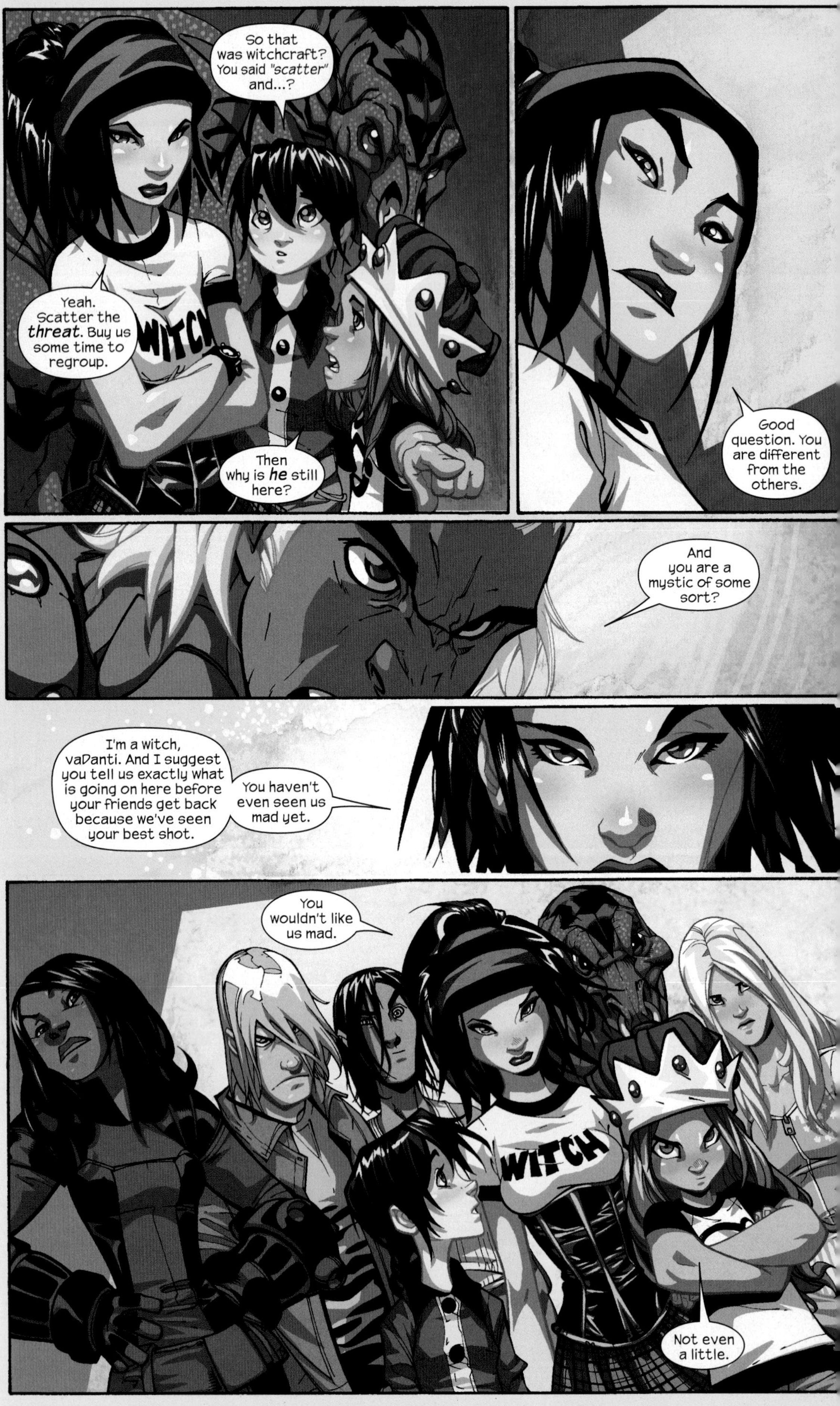

So that was witchcraft? You said "scatter" and...?
Yeah. Scatter the threat. Buy us some time to regroup.
Then why is he still here?
Good question. You are different from the others.
And you are a mystic of some sort?
I'm a witch, vaDanti. And I suggest you tell us exactly what is going on here before your friends get back because we've seen your best shot.
You haven't even seen us mad yet.
You wouldn't like us mad.
Not even a little.

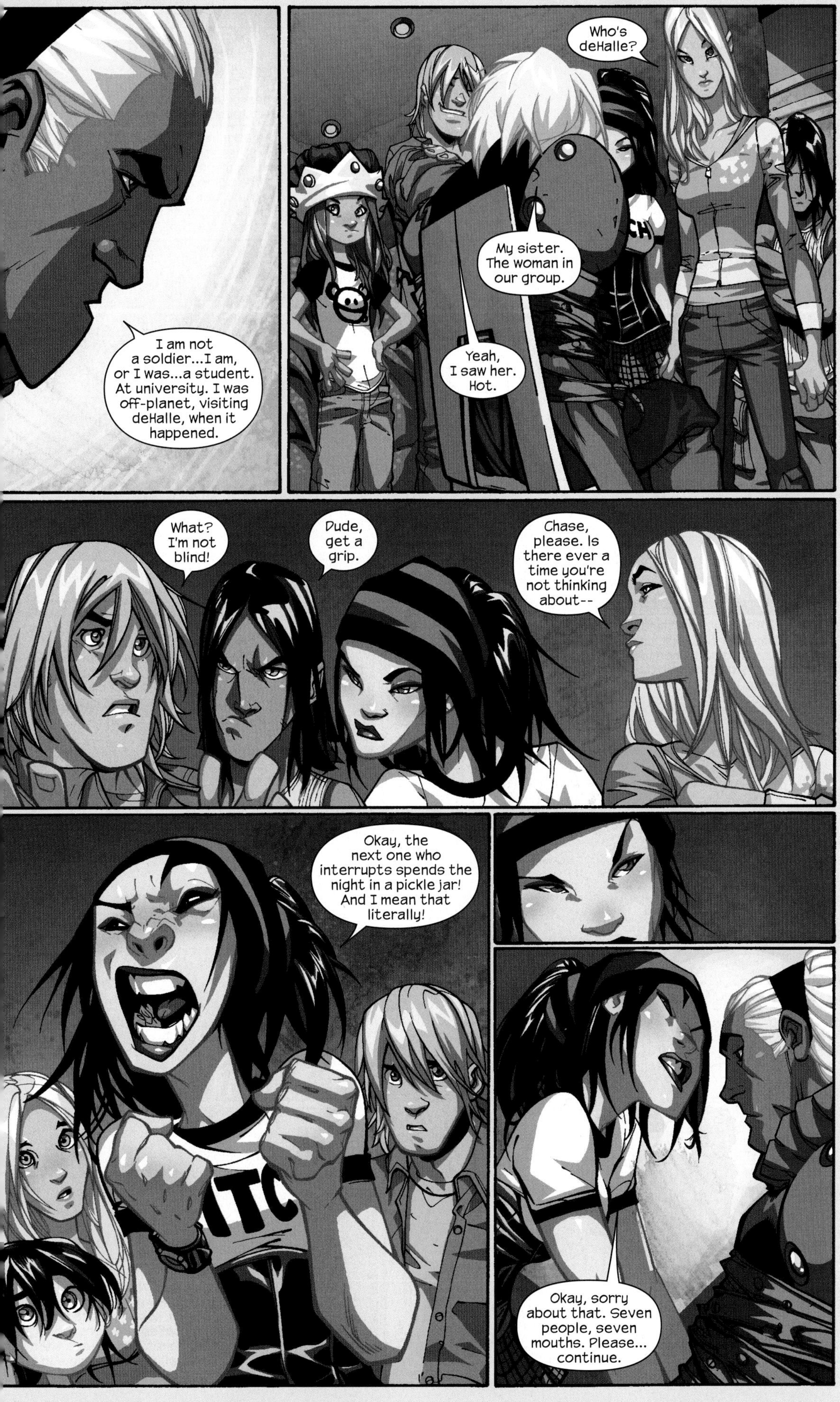
I am not a soldier...I am, or I was...a student. At university. I was off-planet, visiting deHalle, when it happened.
Who's deHalle?
My sister. The woman in our group.
Yeah, I saw her. Hot.
What? I'm not blind!
Dude, get a grip.
Chase, please. Is there ever a time you're not thinking about--
Okay, the next one who interrupts spends the night in a pickle jar! And I mean that literally!
Okay, sorry about that. Seven people, seven mouths. Please... continue.

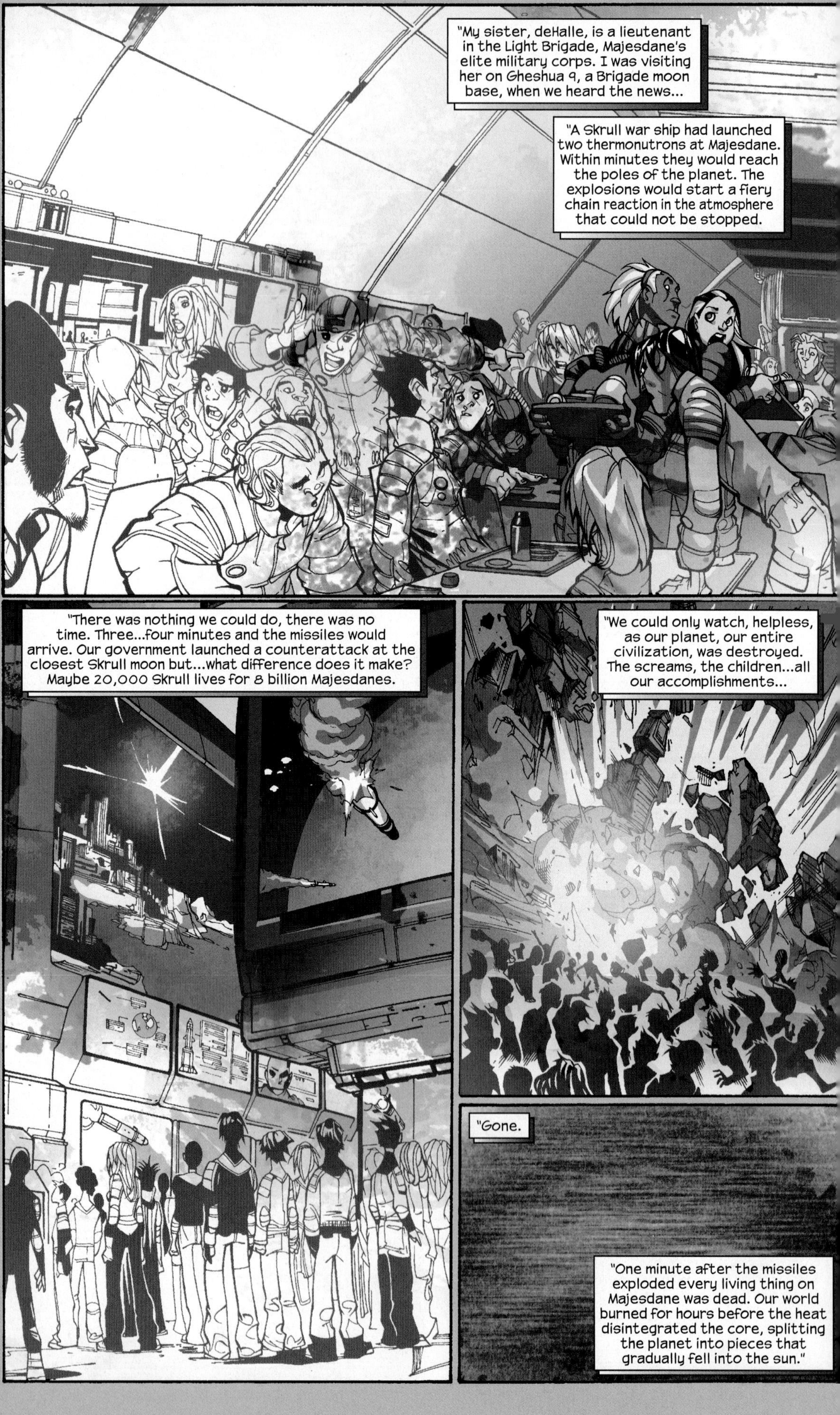
"My sister, deHalle, is a lieutenant in the Light Brigade, Majesdane's elite military corps. I was visiting her on Gheshua 9, a Brigade moon base, when we heard the news...
"A Skrull war ship had launched two thermonutrons at Majesdane. Within minutes they would reach the poles of the planet. The explosions would start a fiery chain reaction in the atmosphere that could not be stopped.
"There was nothing we could do, there was no time. Three...four minutes and the missiles would arrive. Our government launched a counterattack at the closest Skrull moon but...what difference does it make? Maybe 20,000 Skrull lives for 8 billion Majesdanes.
"We could only watch, helpless, as our planet, our entire civilization, was destroyed. The screams, the children...all our accomplishments...
"Gone.
"One minute after the missiles exploded every living thing on Majesdane was dead. Our world burned for hours before the heat disintegrated the core, splitting the planet into pieces that gradually fell into the sun."

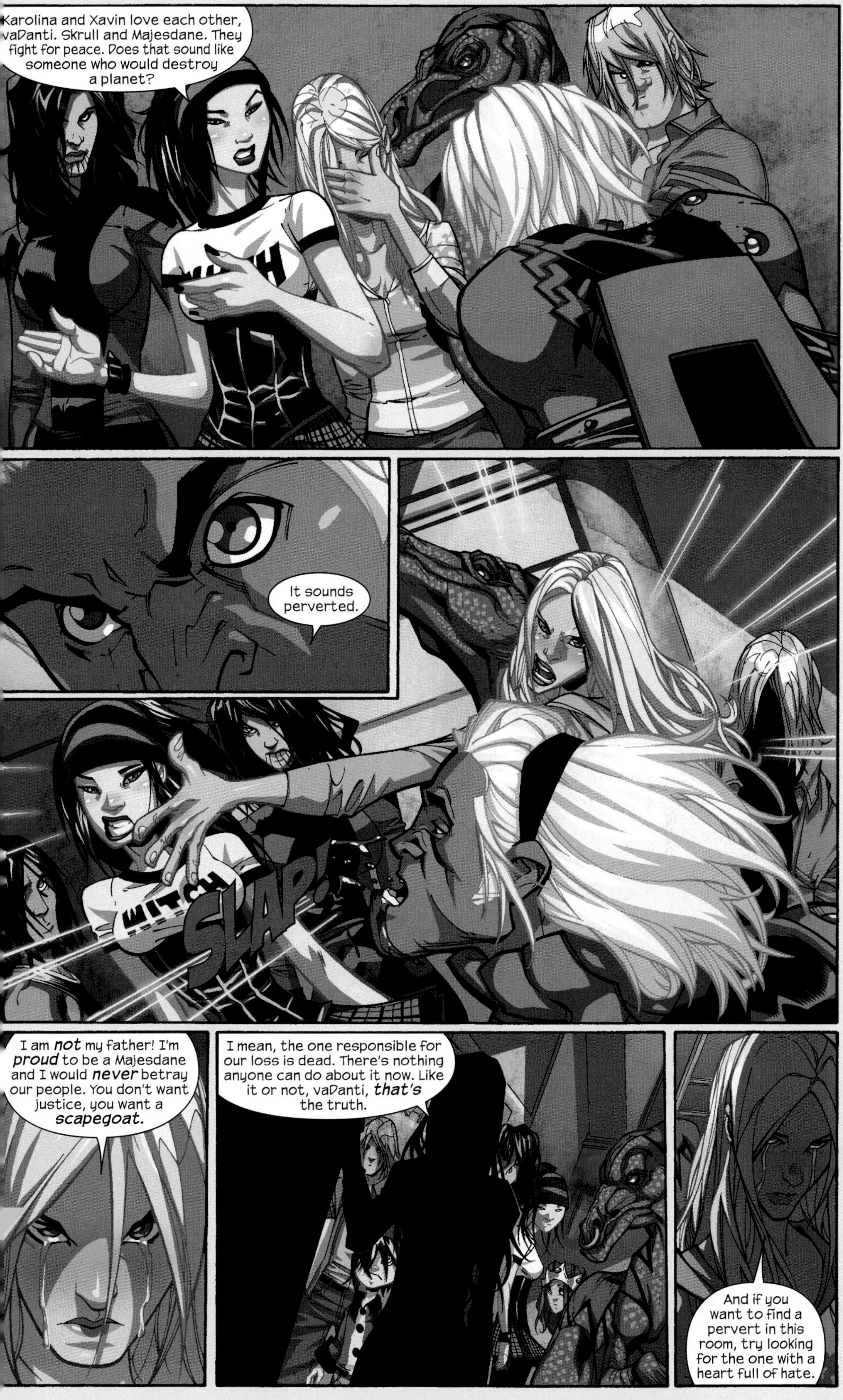

Karolina and Xavin love each other, vaDanti. Skrull and Majesdane. They fight for peace. Does that sound like someone who would destroy a planet?
It sounds perverted.
SLAP!
I am not my father! I'm proud to be a Majesdane and I would never betray our people. You don't want justice, you want a scapegoat.
I mean, the one responsible for our loss is dead. There's nothing anyone can do about it now. Like it or not, vaDanti, that's the truth.
And if you want to find a pervert in this room, try looking for the one with a heart full of hate.

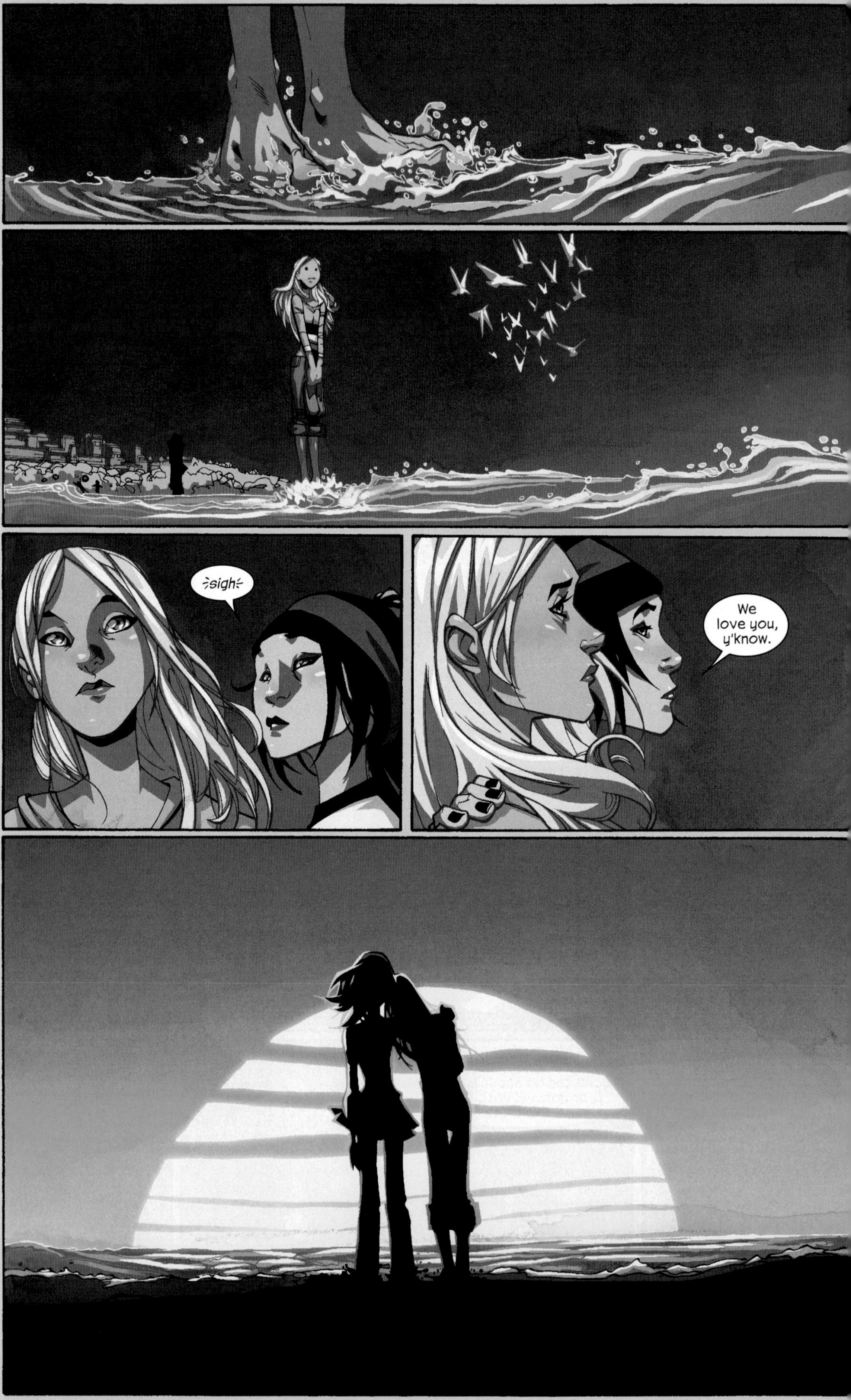

sigh
We love you, y'know.

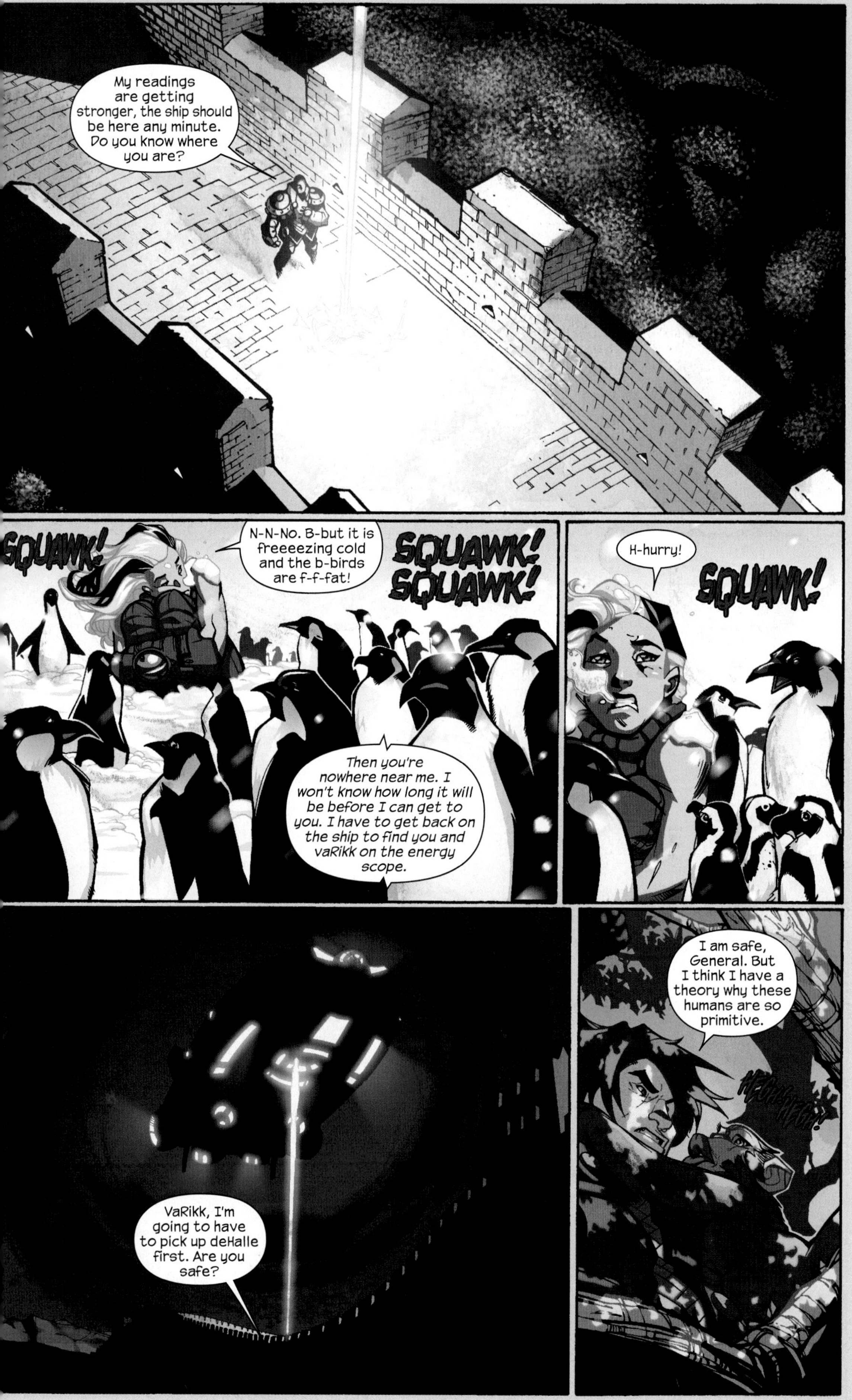
My readings are getting stronger, the ship should be here any minute. Do you know where you are?
SQUAWK!
N-N-No. B-but it is freeeezing cold and the b-birds are f-f-fat!
SQUAWK! SQUAWK!
Then you're nowhere near me. I won't know how long it will be before I can get to you. I have to get back on the ship to find you and vaRikk on the energy scope.
H-hurry!
SQUAWK!
VaRikk, I'm going to have to pick up deHalle first. Are you safe?
I am safe, General. But I think I have a theory why these humans are so primitive.

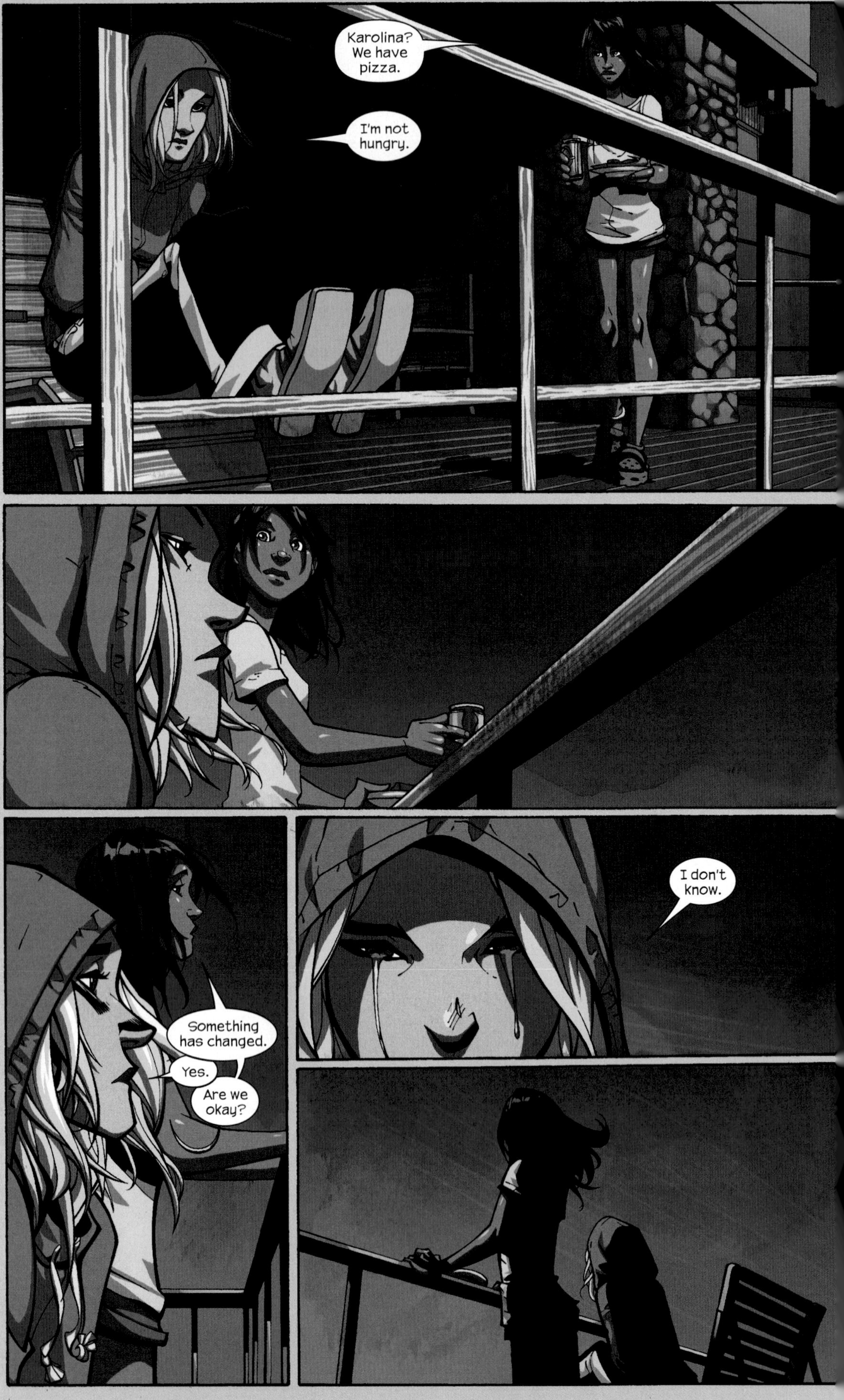
Karolina? We have pizza.
I'm not hungry.
Something has changed.
Yes.
Are we okay?
I don't know.

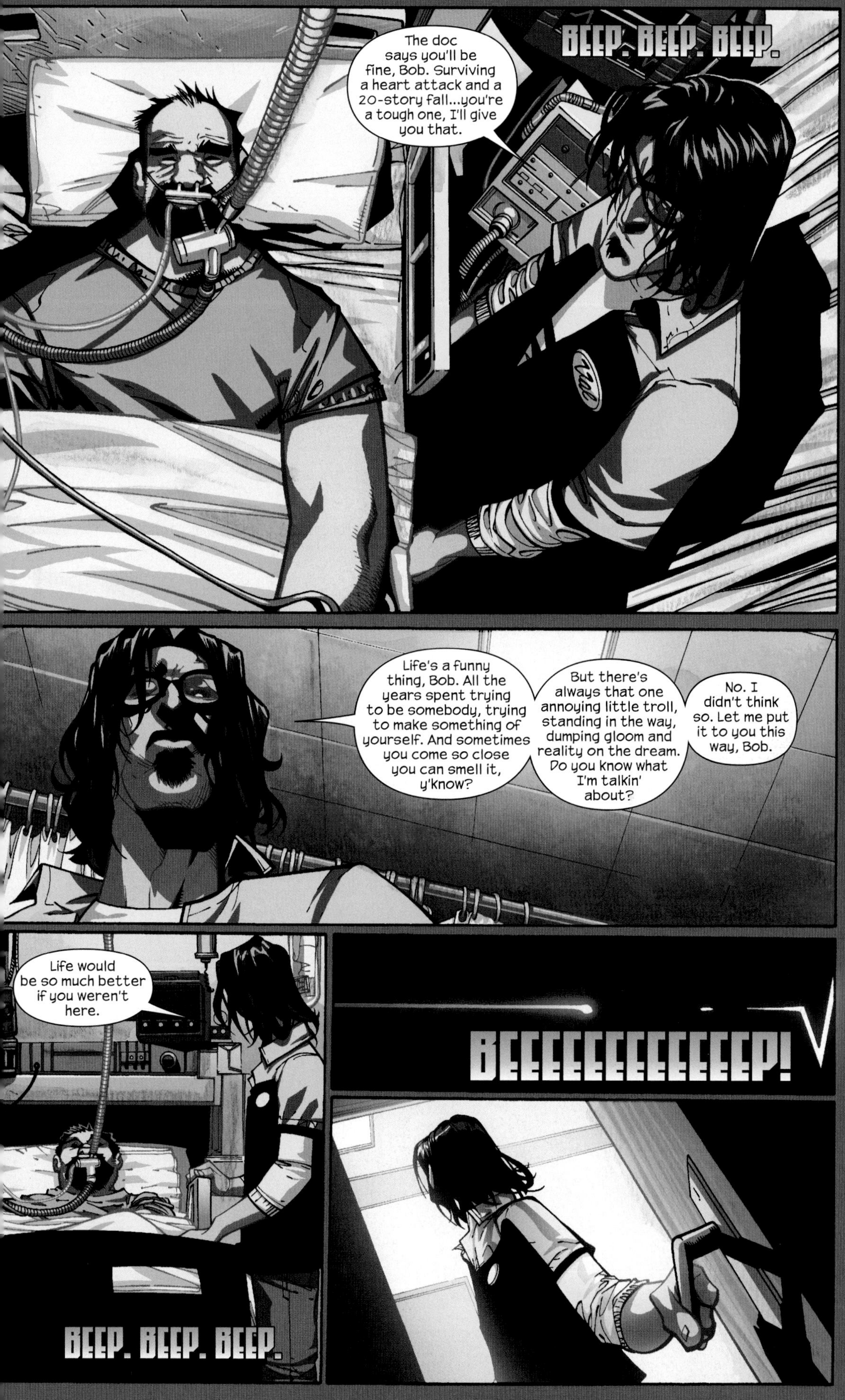
BEEP. BEEP. BEEP.
The doc says you'll be fine, Bob. Surviving a heart attack and a 20-story fall...you're a tough one, I'll give you that.
Life's a funny thing, Bob. All the years spent trying to be somebody, trying to make something of yourself. And sometimes you come so close you can smell it, y'know?
But there's always that one annoying little troll, standing in the way, dumping gloom and reality on the dream. Do you know what I'm talkin' about?
No. I didn't think so. Let me put it to you this way, Bob.
Life would be so much better if you weren't here.
BEEP. BEEP. BEEP.
BEEEEEEEEEEEEP!

3

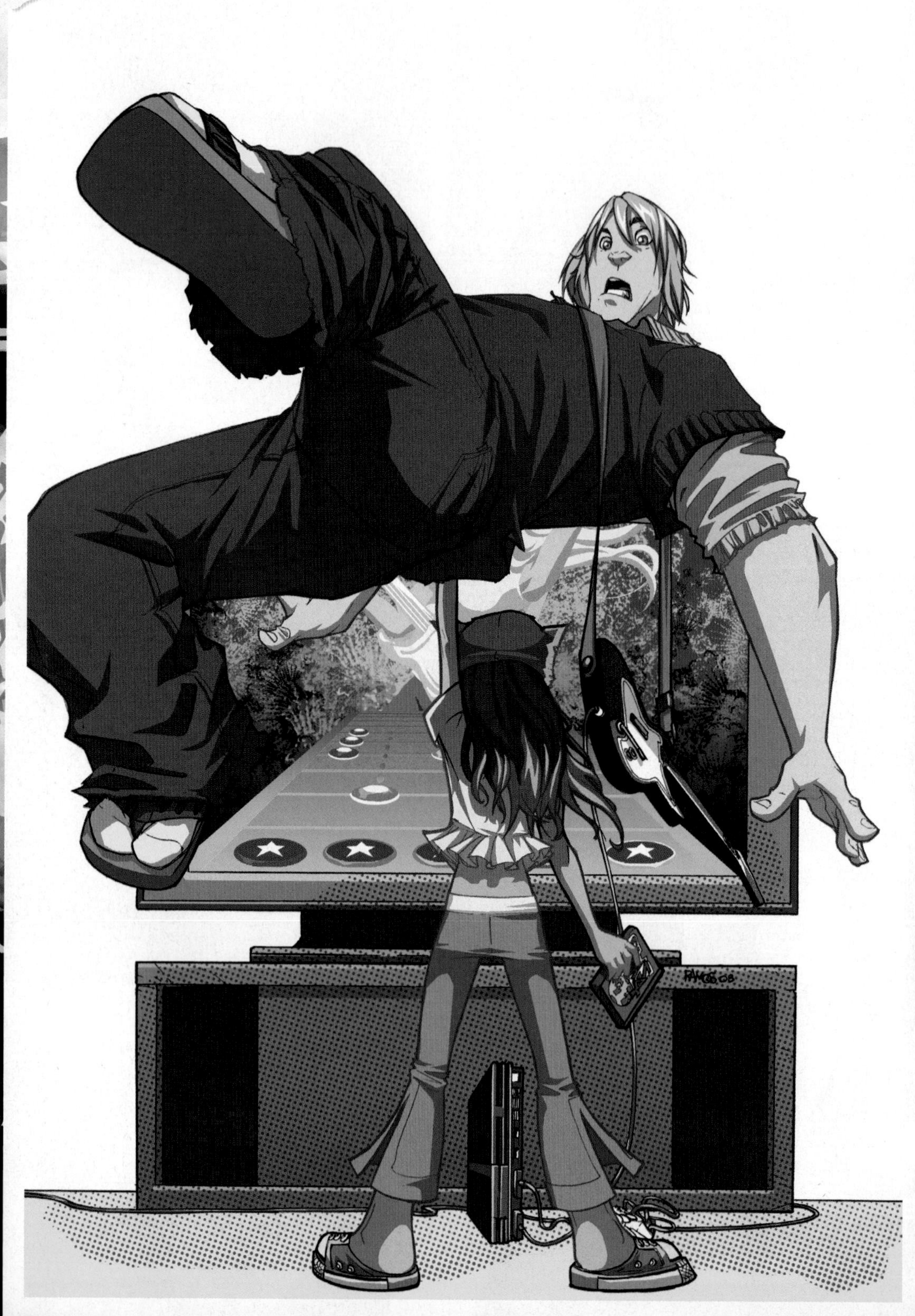

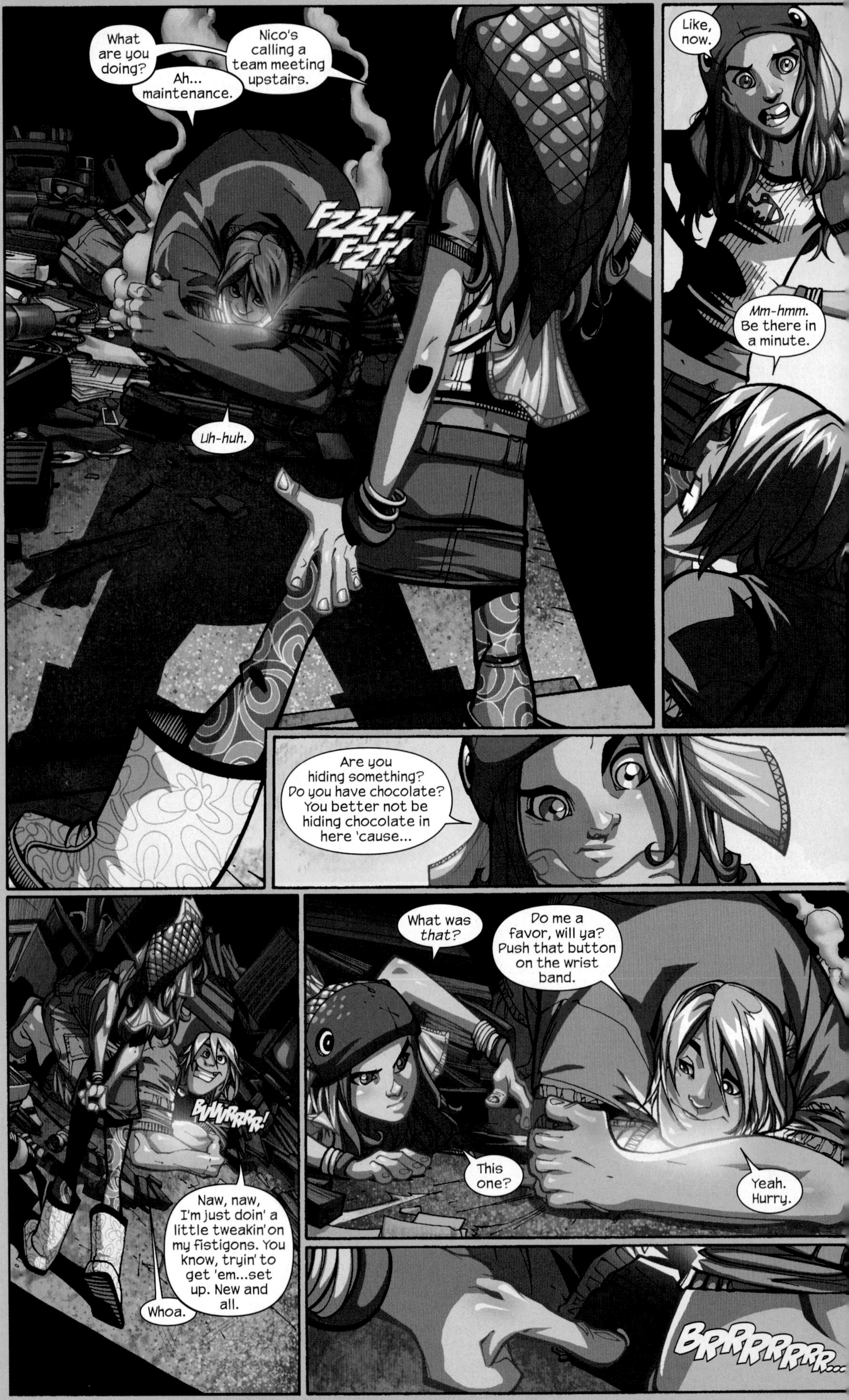
What are you doing?
Nico's calling a team meeting upstairs.
Ah... maintenance.
FZZT! FZT!
Uh-huh.
Like, now.
Mm-hmm. Be there in a minute.
Are you hiding something? Do you have chocolate? You better not be hiding chocolate in here 'cause...
BUUURRRR!
Naw, naw, I'm just doin' a little tweakin' on my fistigons. You know, tryin' to get 'em...set up. New and all.
Whoa.
What was that?
Do me a favor, will ya? Push that button on the wrist band.
This one?
Yeah. Hurry.
BRRRRRRR...

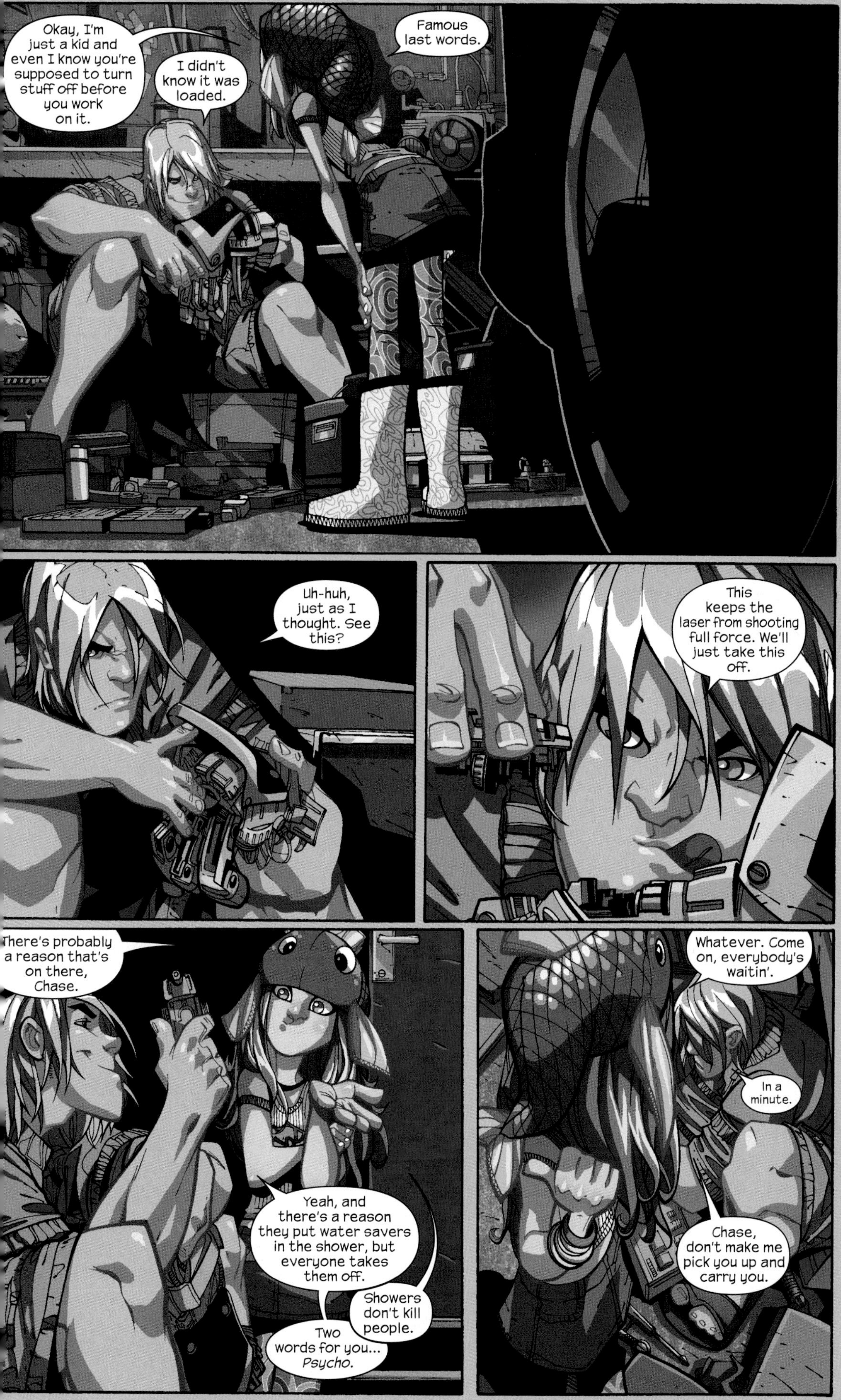
Okay, I'm just a kid and even I know you're supposed to turn stuff off before you work on it.
I didn't know it was loaded.
Famous last words.
Uh-huh, just as I thought. See this?
This keeps the laser from shooting full force. We'll just take this off.
There's probably a reason that's on there, Chase.
Yeah, and there's a reason they put water savers in the shower, but everyone takes them off.
Showers don't kill people.
Two words for you... *Psycho.*
Whatever. Come on, everybody's waitin'.
In a minute.
Chase, don't make me pick you up and carry you.

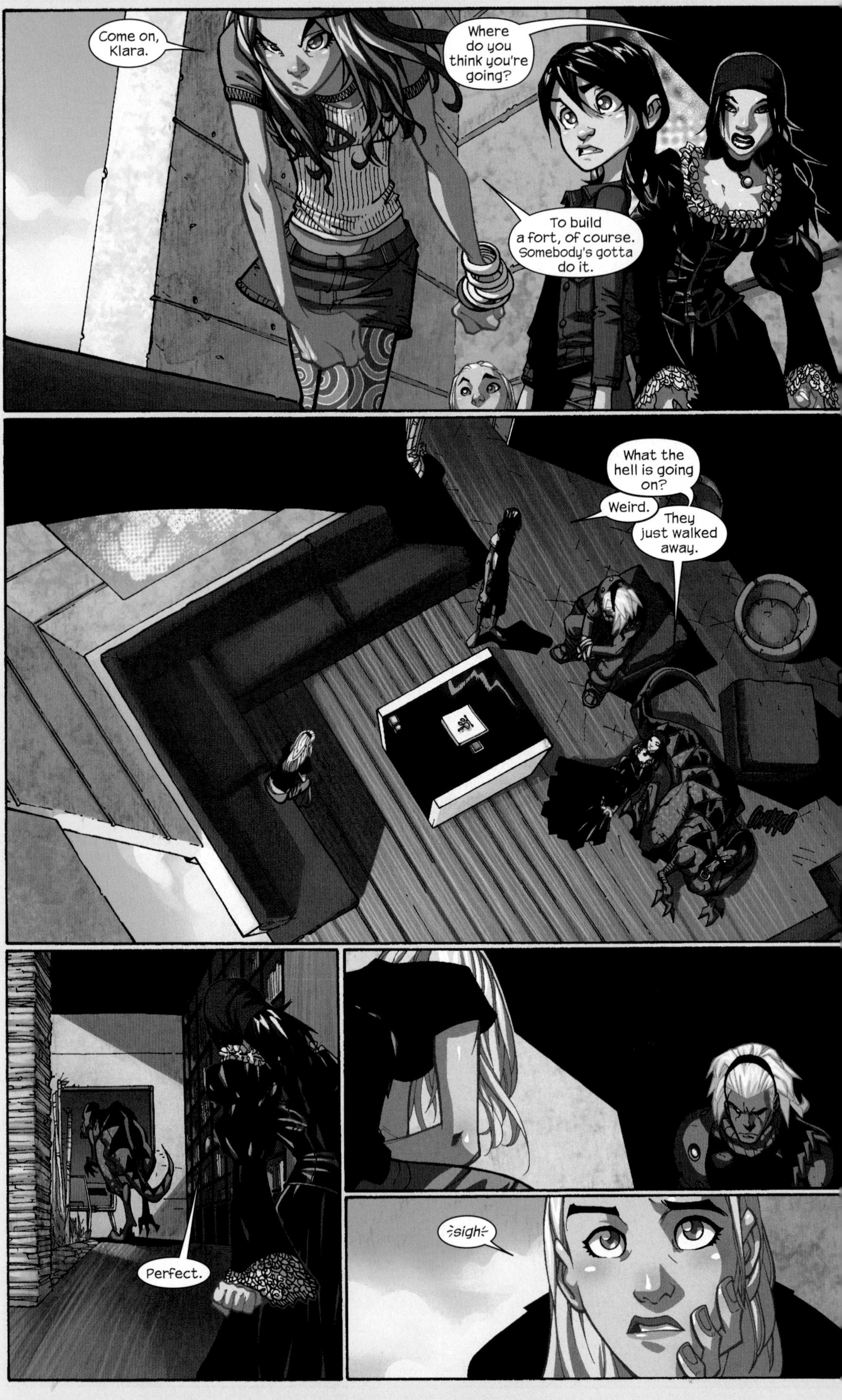
Come on, Klara.
Where do you think you're going?
To build a fort, of course. Somebody's gotta do it.
What the hell is going on?
Weird.
They just walked away.
Perfect.
-sigh-

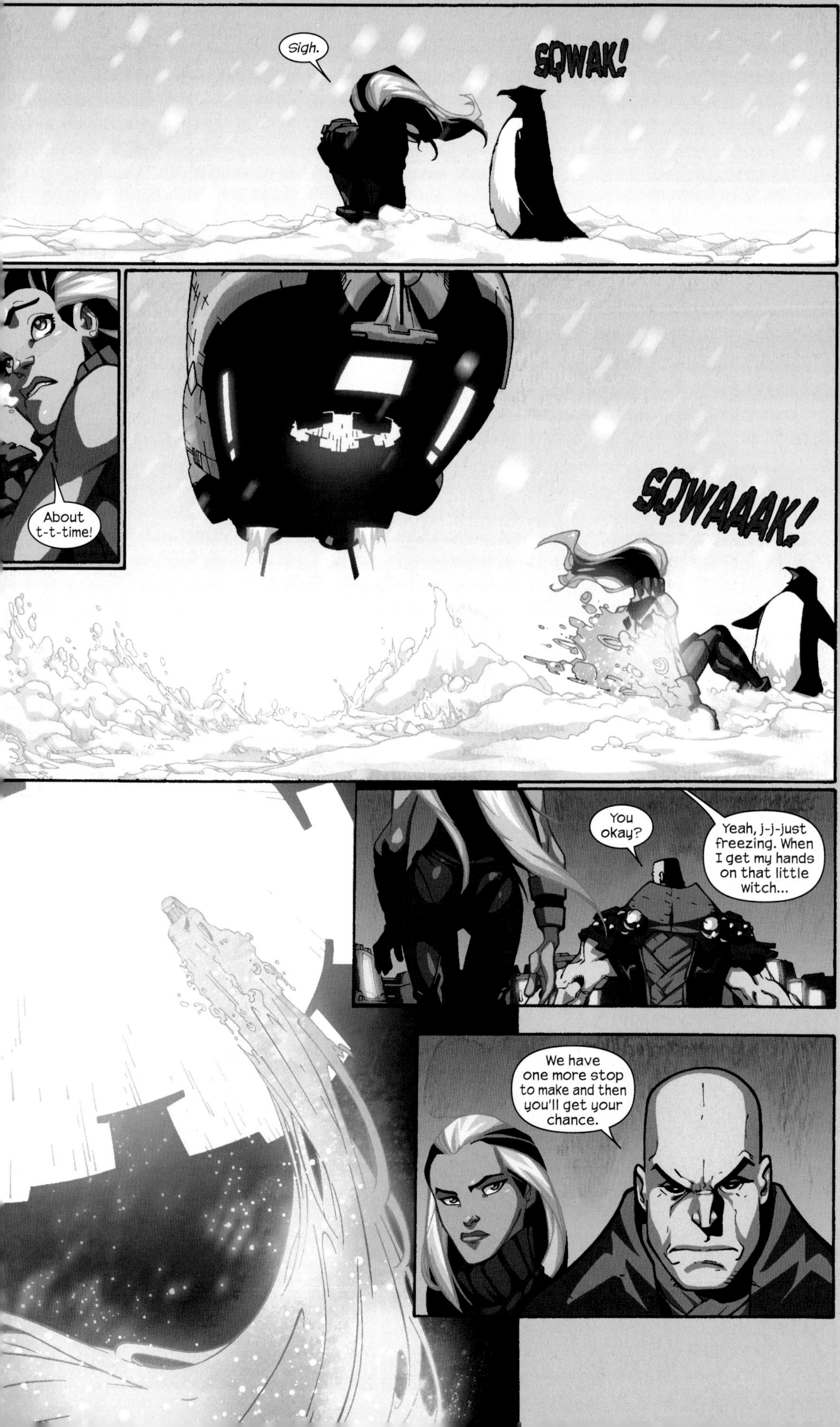

Sigh.
SQWAK!
About t-t-time!
SQWAAAK!
You okay?
Yeah, j-j-just freezing. When I get my hands on that little witch...
We have one more stop to make and then you'll get your chance.

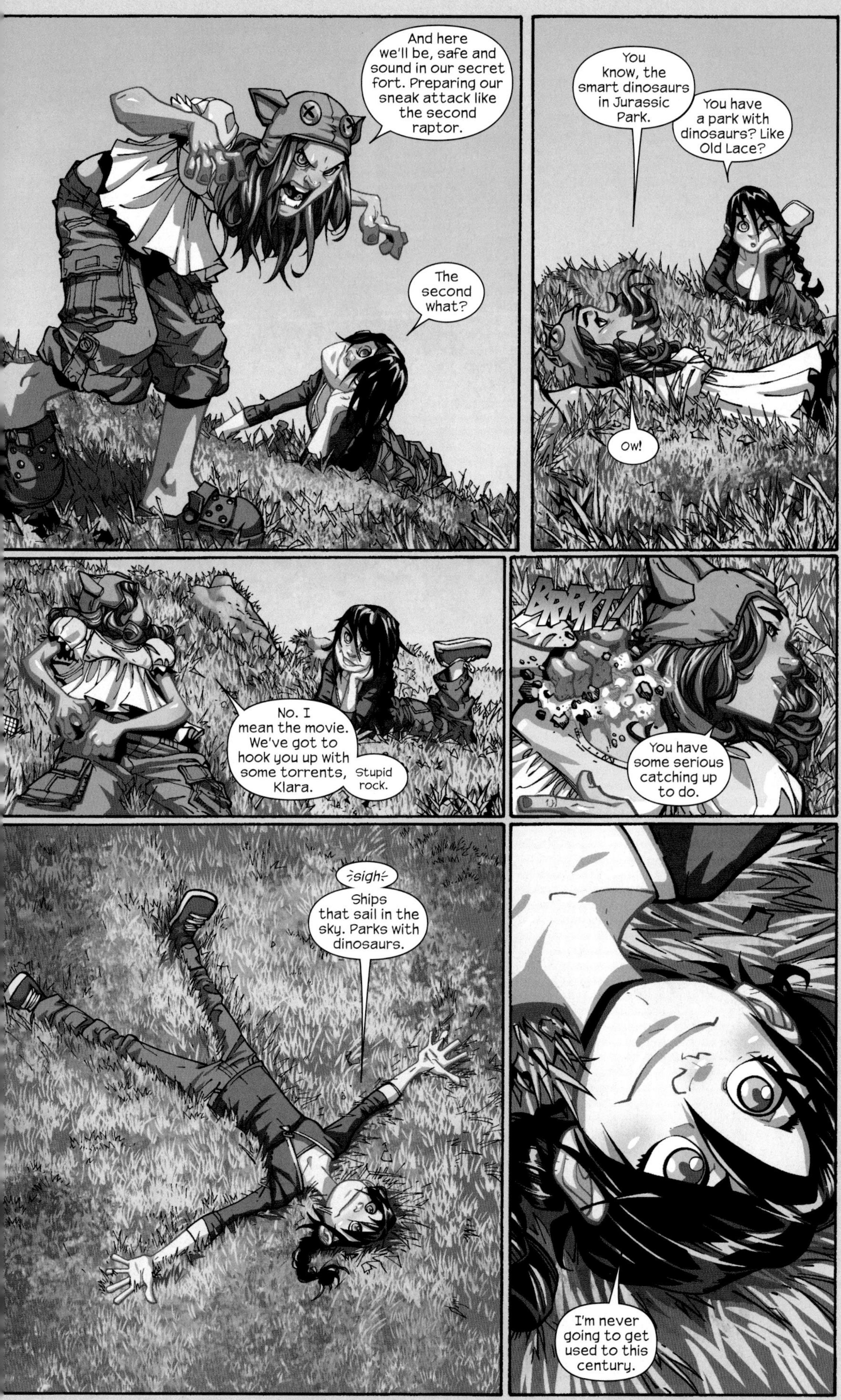
And here we'll be, safe and sound in our secret fort. Preparing our sneak attack like the second raptor.
The second what?
You know, the smart dinosaurs in Jurassic Park.
You have a park with dinosaurs? Like Old Lace?
Ow!
No. I mean the movie. We've got to hook you up with some torrents, Klara.
Stupid rock.
BRRKT!
You have some serious catching up to do.
sigh
Ships that sail in the sky. Parks with dinosaurs.
I'm never going to get used to this century.

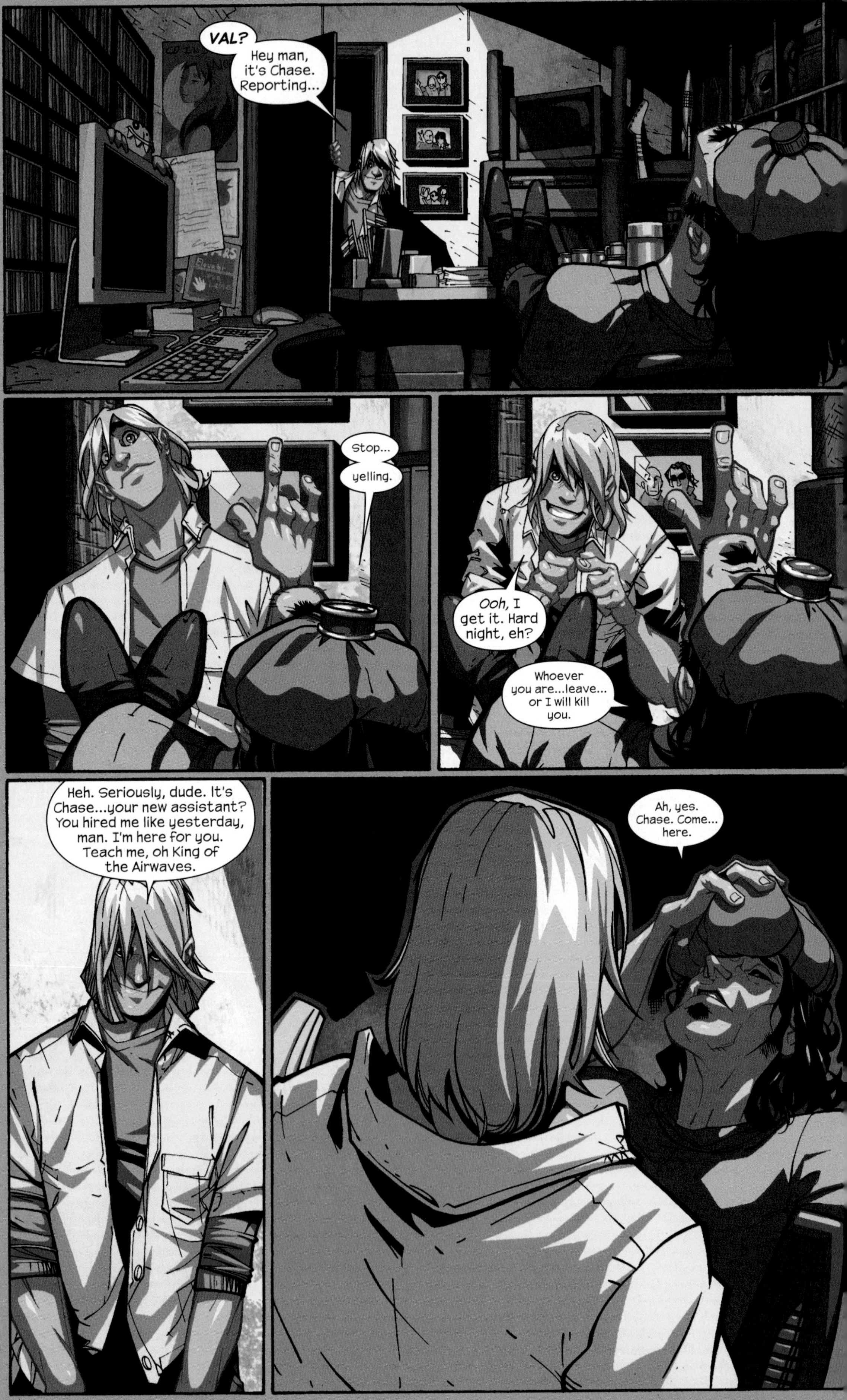
VAL?
Hey man, it's Chase. Reporting...
Stop...
yelling.
Ooh, I get it. Hard night, eh?
Whoever you are...leave... or I will kill you.
Heh. Seriously, dude. It's Chase...your new assistant? You hired me like yesterday, man. I'm here for you. Teach me, oh King of the Airwaves.
Ah, yes. Chase. Come... here.

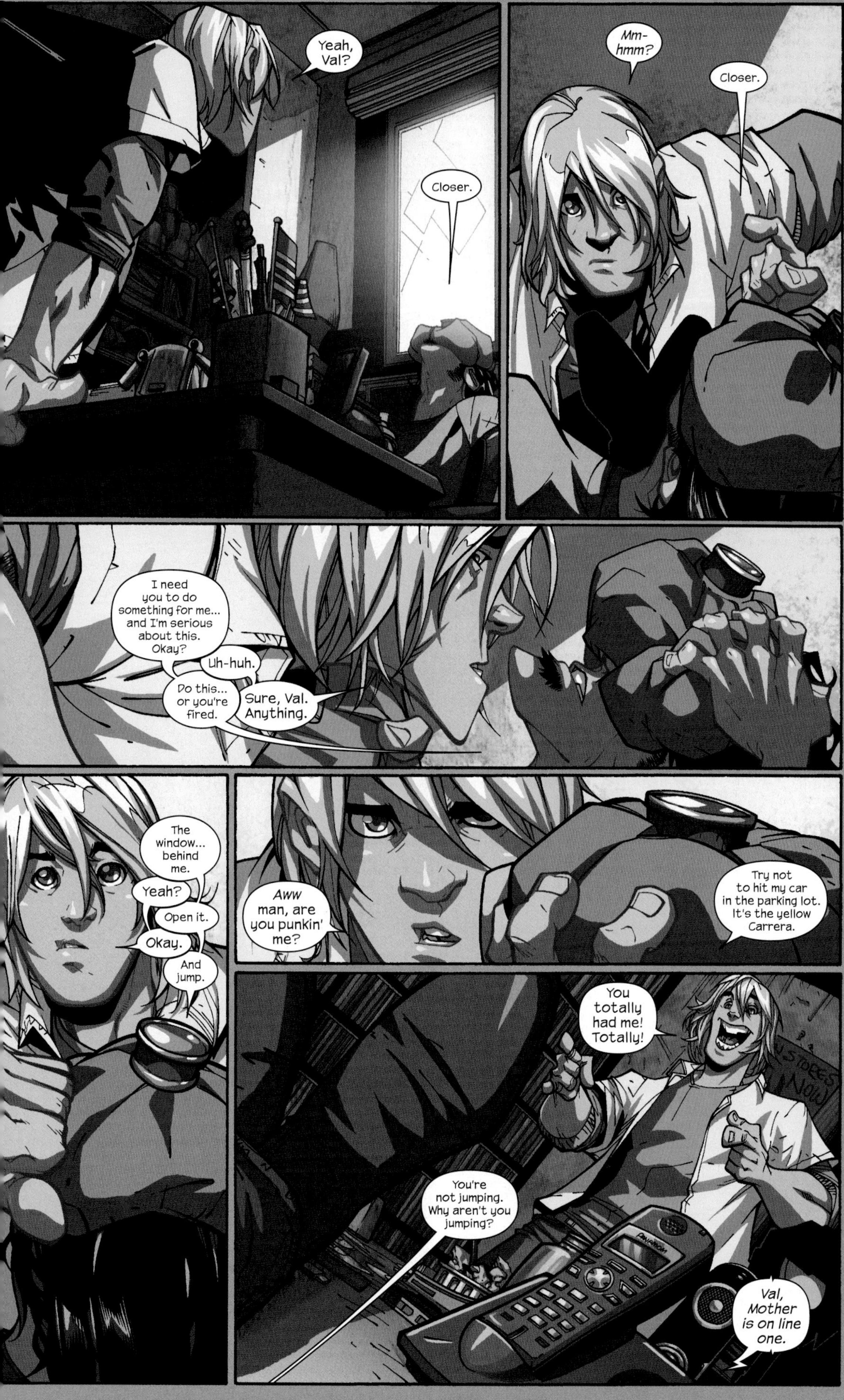
Yeah, Val?
Closer.
Mm-hmm?
Closer.
I need you to do something for me... and I'm serious about this. Okay?
Uh-huh.
Do this... or you're fired.
Sure, Val. Anything.
The window... behind me.
Yeah?
Open it.
Okay.
And jump.
Aww man, are you punkin' me?
Try not to hit my car in the parking lot. It's the yellow Carrera.
You totally had me! Totally!
You're not jumping. Why aren't you jumping?
Val, Mother is on line one.

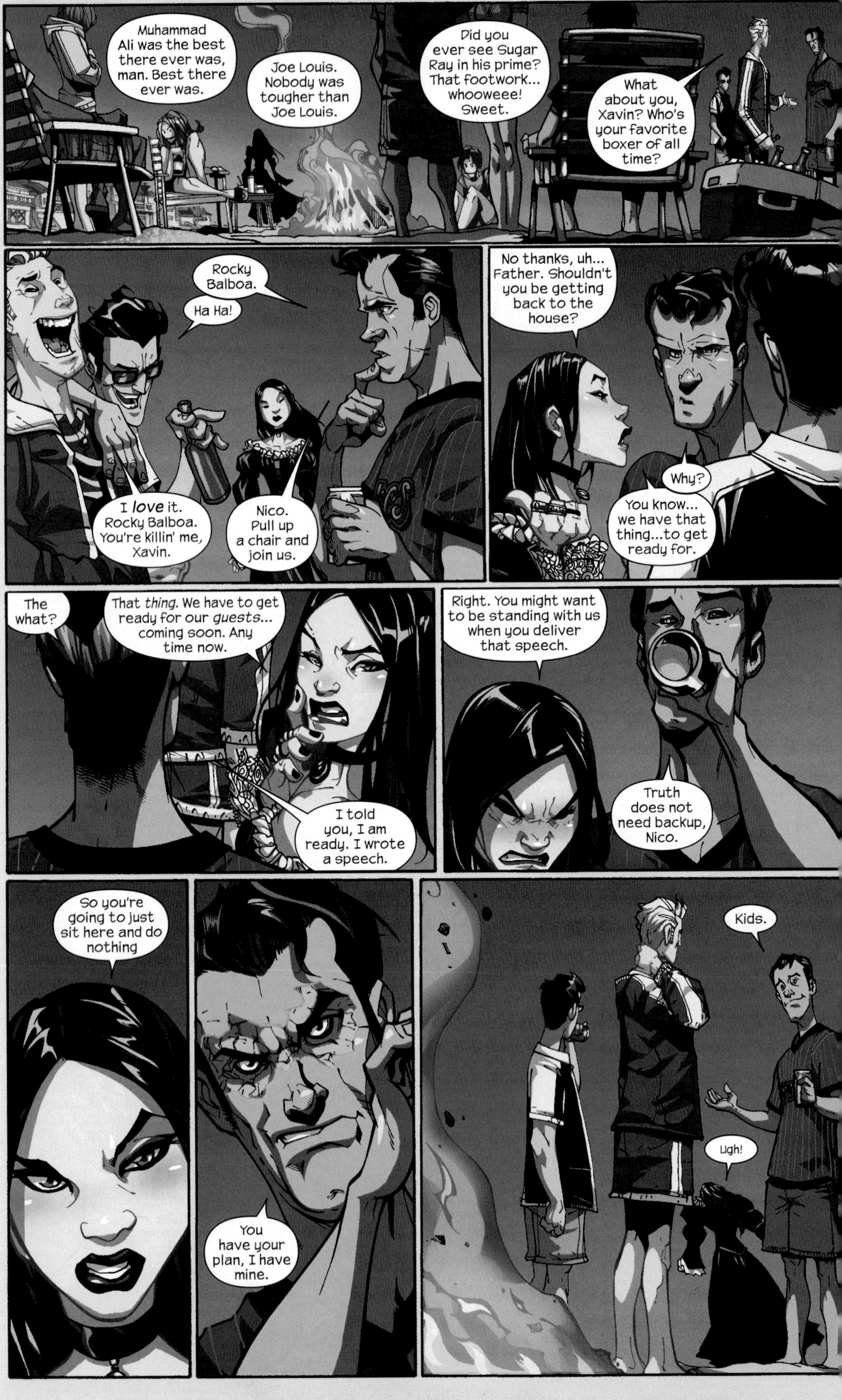
Muhammad Ali was the best there ever was, man. Best there ever was.
Joe Louis. Nobody was tougher than Joe Louis.
Did you ever see Sugar Ray in his prime? That footwork... whooweee! Sweet.
What about you, Xavin? Who's your favorite boxer of all time?
Rocky Balboa.
Ha Ha!
I love it. Rocky Balboa. You're killin' me, Xavin.
Nico. Pull up a chair and join us.
No thanks, uh... Father. Shouldn't you be getting back to the house?
Why?
You know... we have that thing...to get ready for.
The what?
That thing. We have to get ready for our guests... coming soon. Any time now.
I told you, I am ready. I wrote a speech.
Right. You might want to be standing with us when you deliver that speech.
Truth does not need backup, Nico.
So you're going to just sit here and do nothing
You have your plan, I have mine.
Kids.
Ugh!

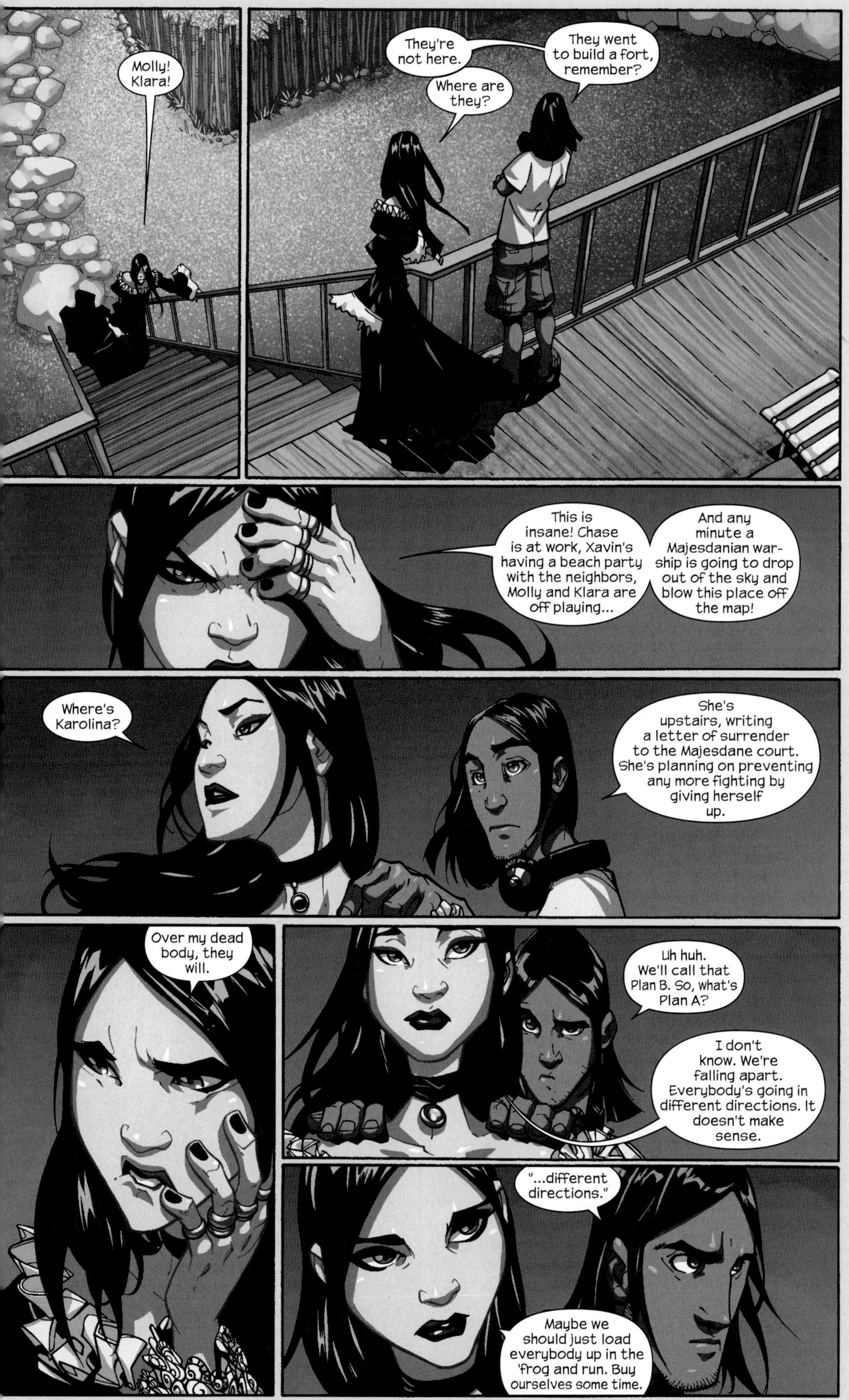
Molly! Klara!
They're not here.
Where are they?
They went to build a fort, remember?
This is insane! Chase is at work, Xavin's having a beach party with the neighbors, Molly and Klara are off playing...
And any minute a Majesdanian war-ship is going to drop out of the sky and blow this place off the map!
Where's Karolina?
She's upstairs, writing a letter of surrender to the Majesdane court. She's planning on preventing any more fighting by giving herself up.
Over my dead body, they will.
Uh huh. We'll call that Plan B. So, what's Plan A?
I don't know. We're falling apart. Everybody's going in different directions. It doesn't make sense.
"...different directions."
Maybe we should just load everybody up in the 'frog and run. Buy ourselves some time.

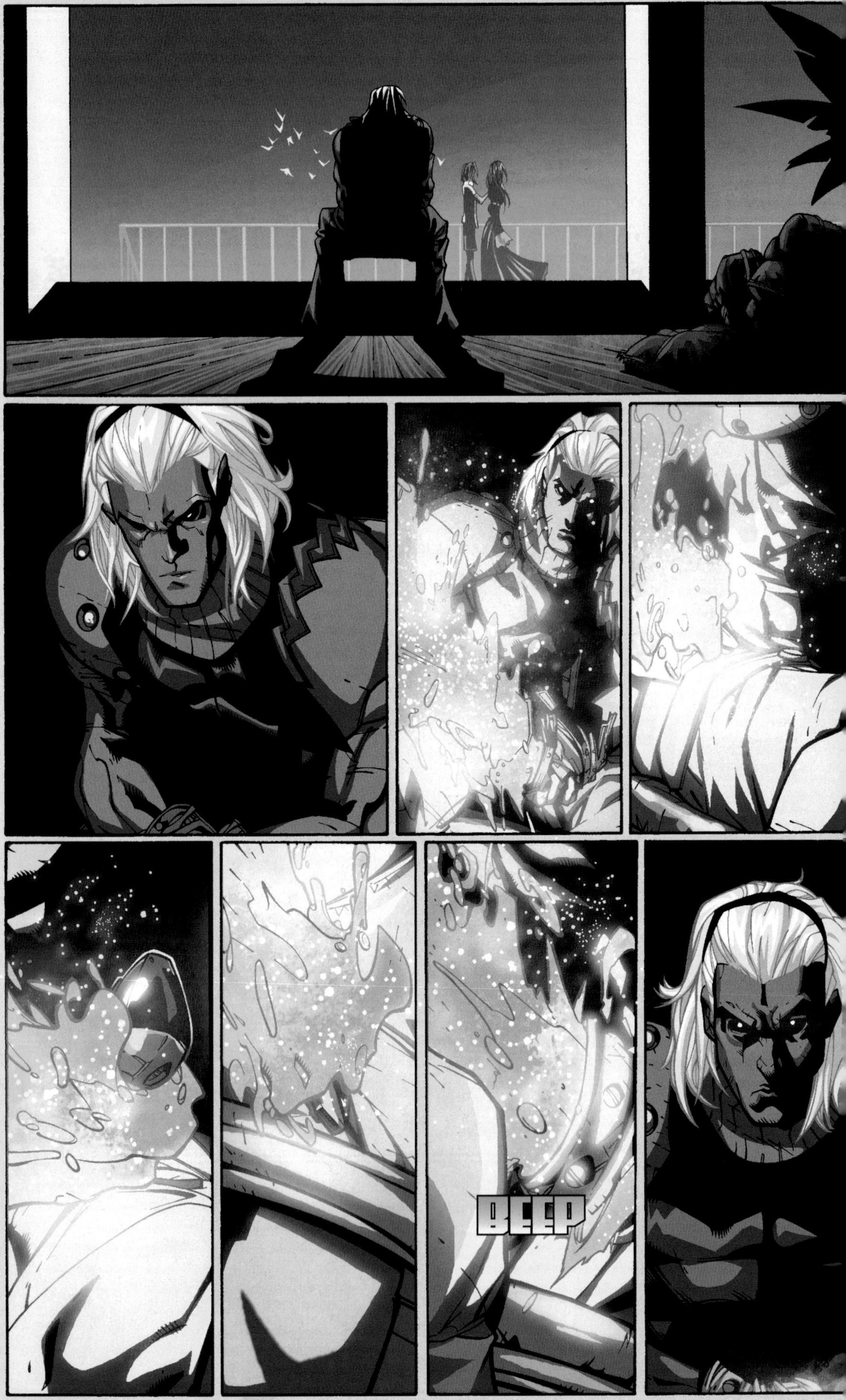
BEEP

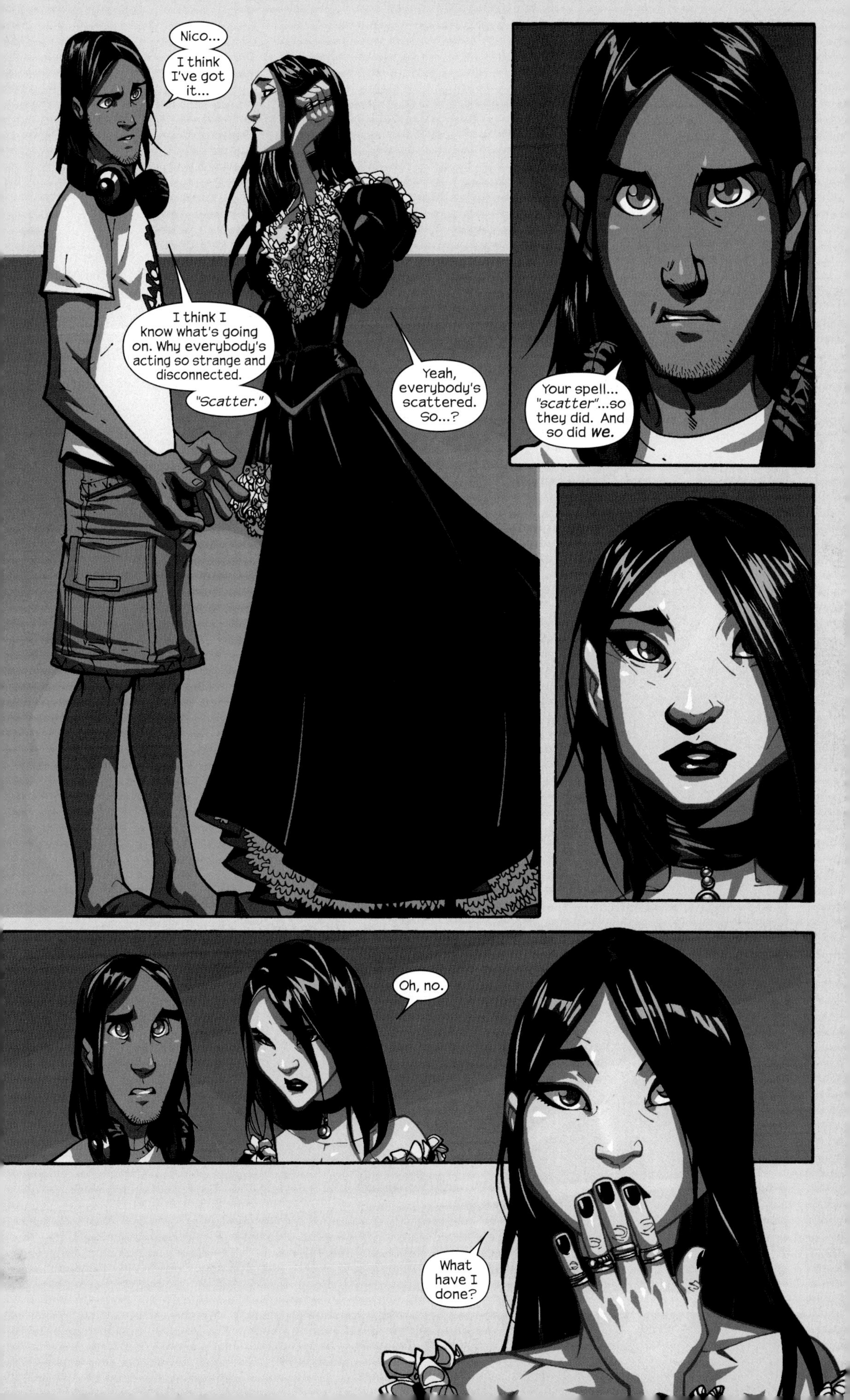
Nico...
I think I've got it...
I think I know what's going on. Why everybody's acting so strange and disconnected.
"Scatter."
Yeah, everybody's scattered. So...?
Your spell... "scatter"...so they did. And so did **we.**
Oh, no.
What have I done?

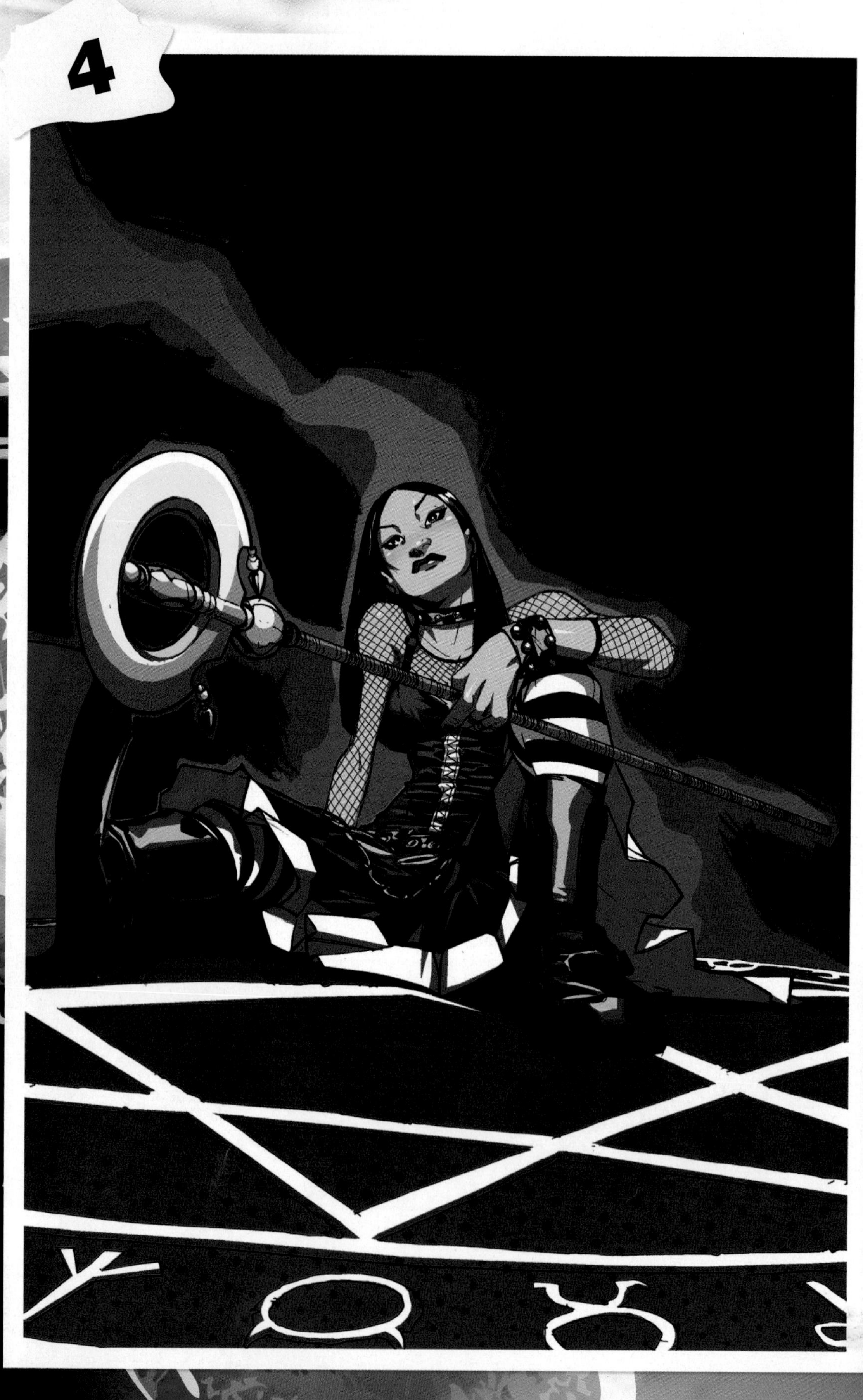
4

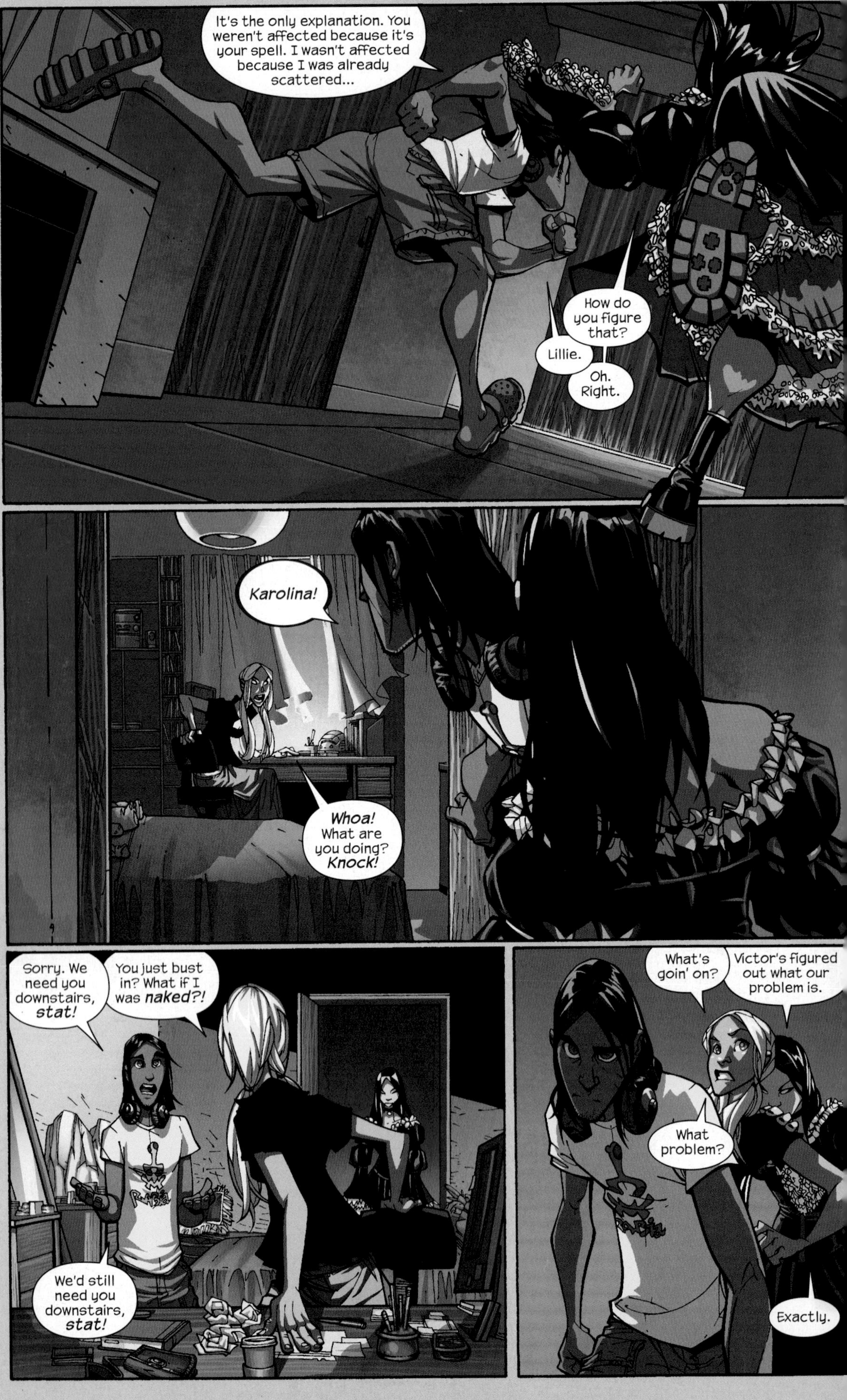
It's the only explanation. You weren't affected because it's your spell. I wasn't affected because I was already scattered...
How do you figure that?
Lillie.
Oh. Right.
Karolina!
Whoa! What are you doing? Knock!
Sorry. We need you downstairs, stat!
You just bust in? What if I was naked?!
We'd still need you downstairs, stat!
What's goin' on?
Victor's figured out what our problem is.
What problem?
Exactly.

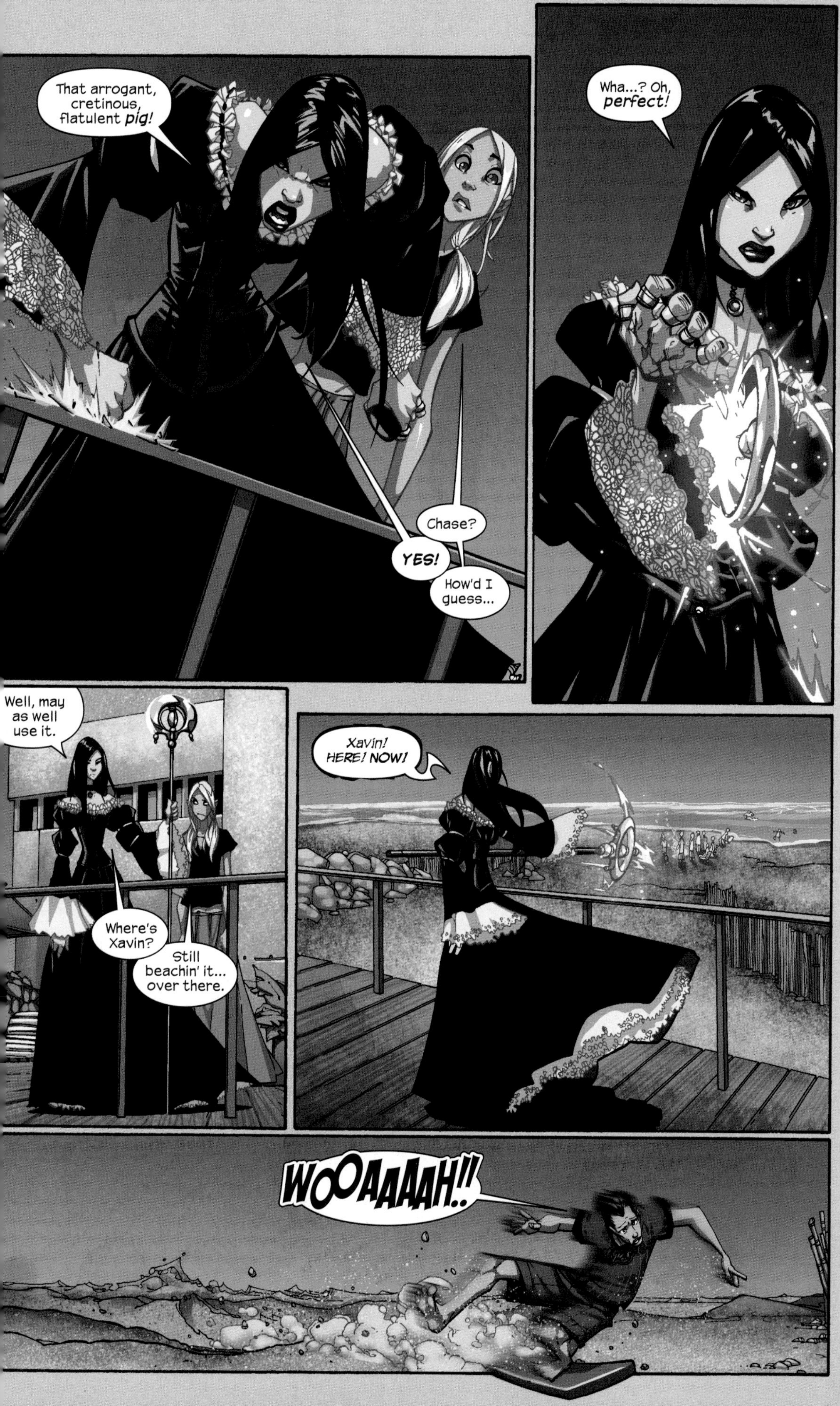
That arrogant, cretinous, flatulent pig!
Chase?
YES!
How'd I guess...
Wha...? Oh, perfect!
Well, may as well use it.
Where's Xavin?
Still beachin' it... over there.
Xavin! HERE! NOW!
WOOAAAAH!!..

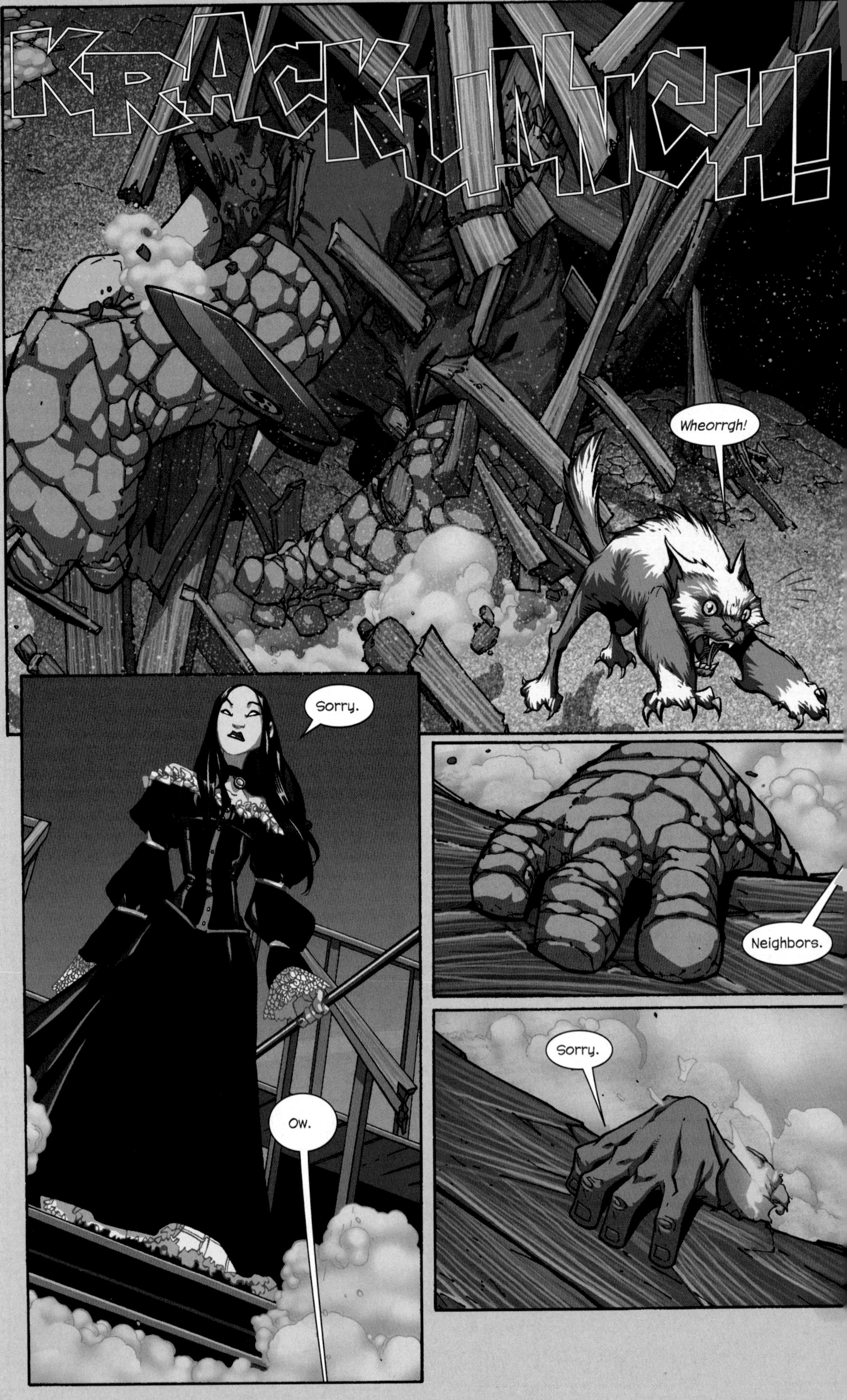
KRACKUMMCH!
Wheorrgh!
Sorry.
Neighbors.
Sorry.
Ow.

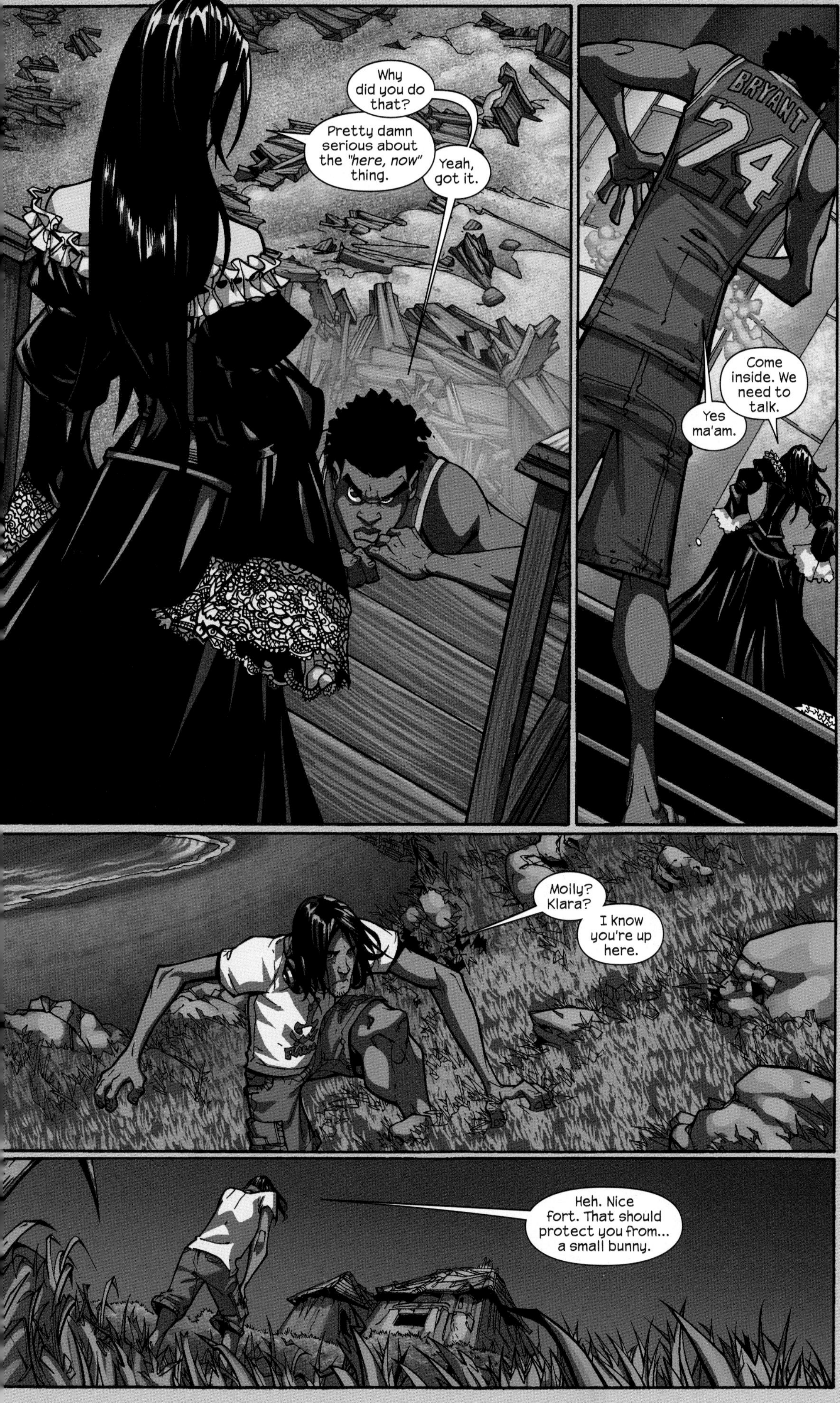
Why did you do that?
Pretty damn serious about the *"here, now"* thing.
Yeah, got it.
BRYANT 24
Come inside. We need to talk.
Yes ma'am.
Molly? Klara?
I know you're up here.
Heh. Nice fort. That should protect you from... a small bunny.

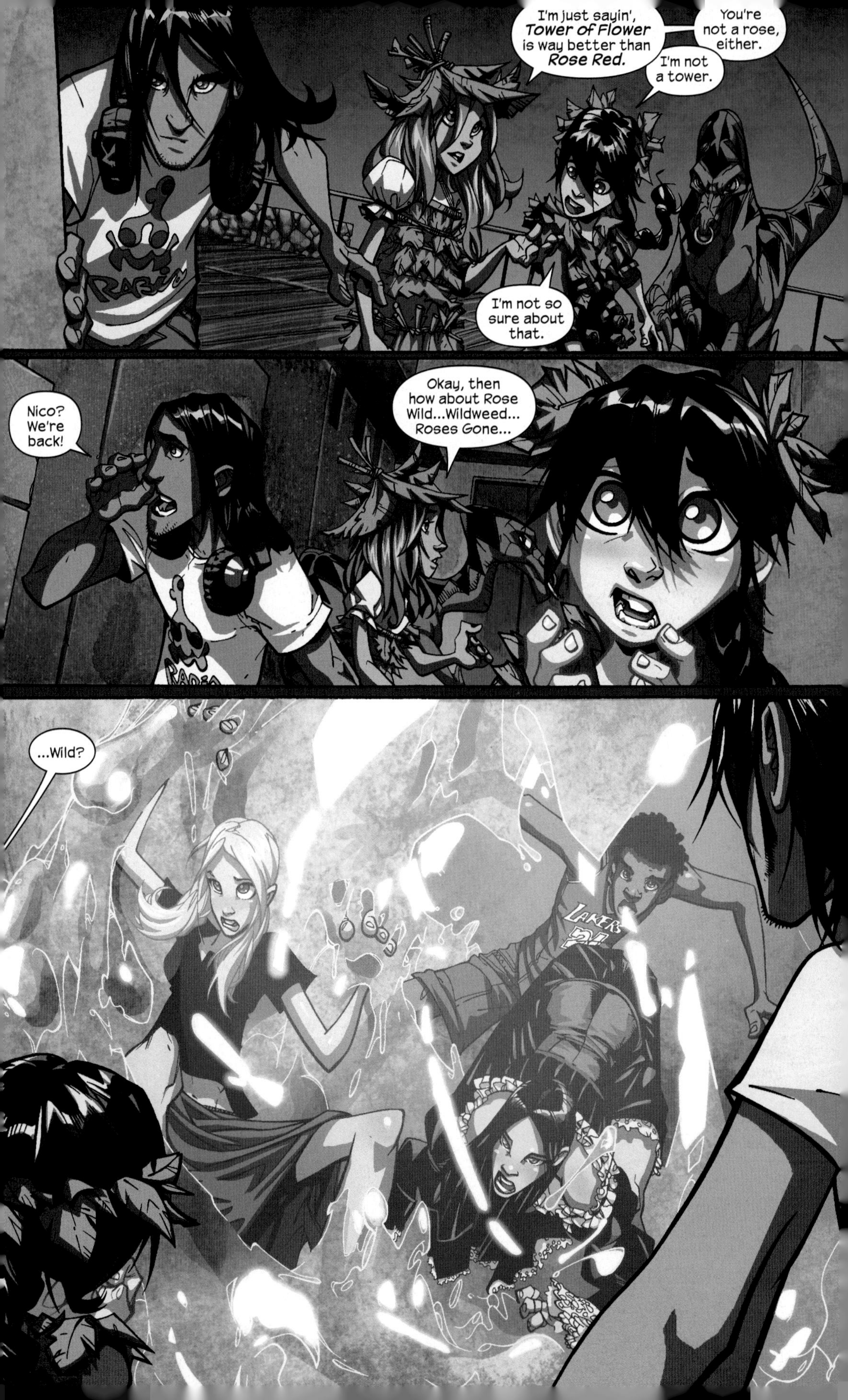
I'm just sayin', *Tower of Flower* is way better than *Rose Red.*
You're not a rose, either.
I'm not a tower.
I'm not so sure about that.
Nico? We're back!
Okay, then how about Rose Wild...Wildweed... Roses Gone...
...Wild?
LAKERS

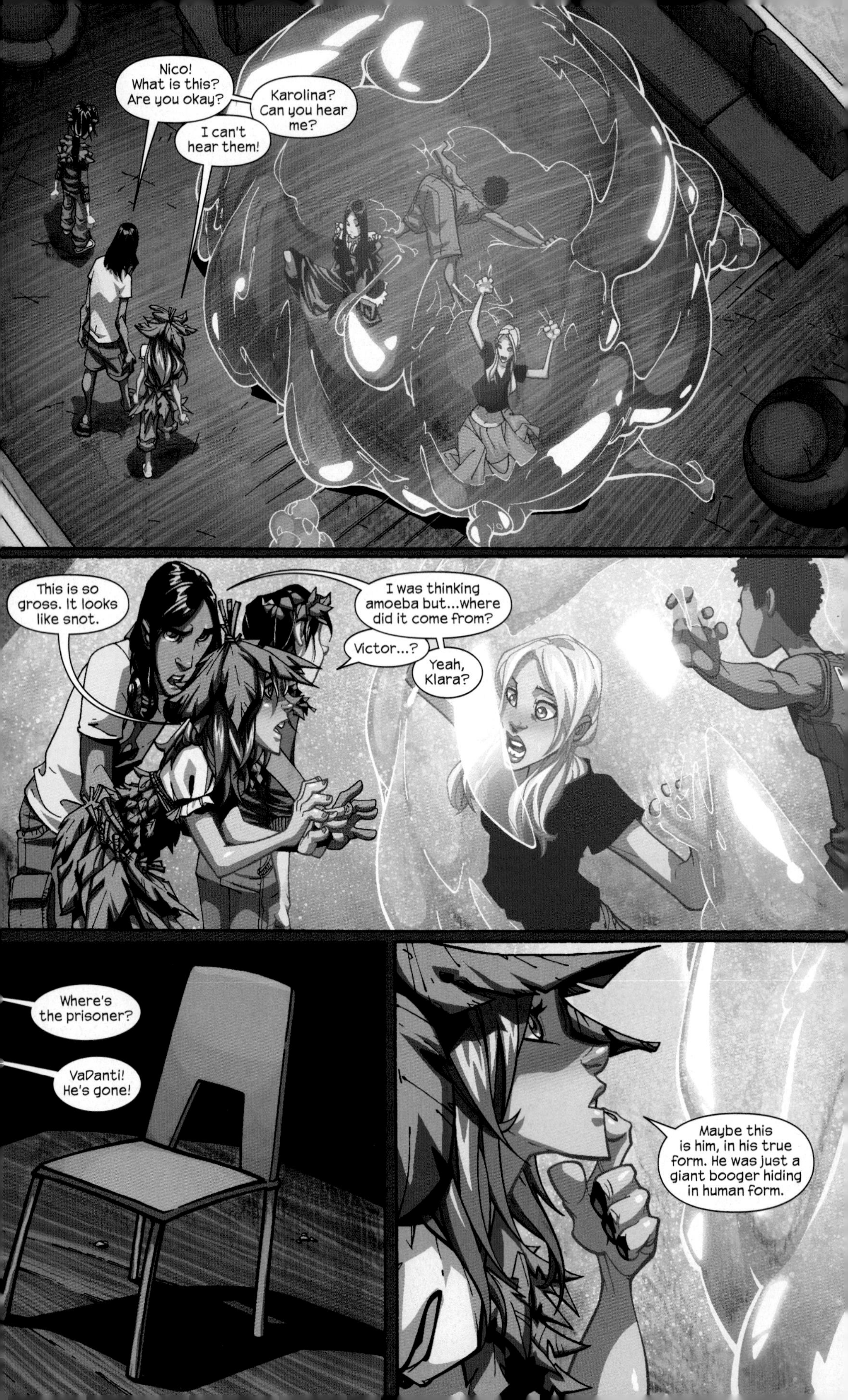
Nico! What is this? Are you okay?
Karolina? Can you hear me?
I can't hear them!
This is so gross. It looks like snot.
I was thinking amoeba but...where did it come from?
Victor...?
Yeah, Klara?
Where's the prisoner?
VaDanti! He's gone!
Maybe this is him, in his true form. He was just a giant booger hiding in human form.

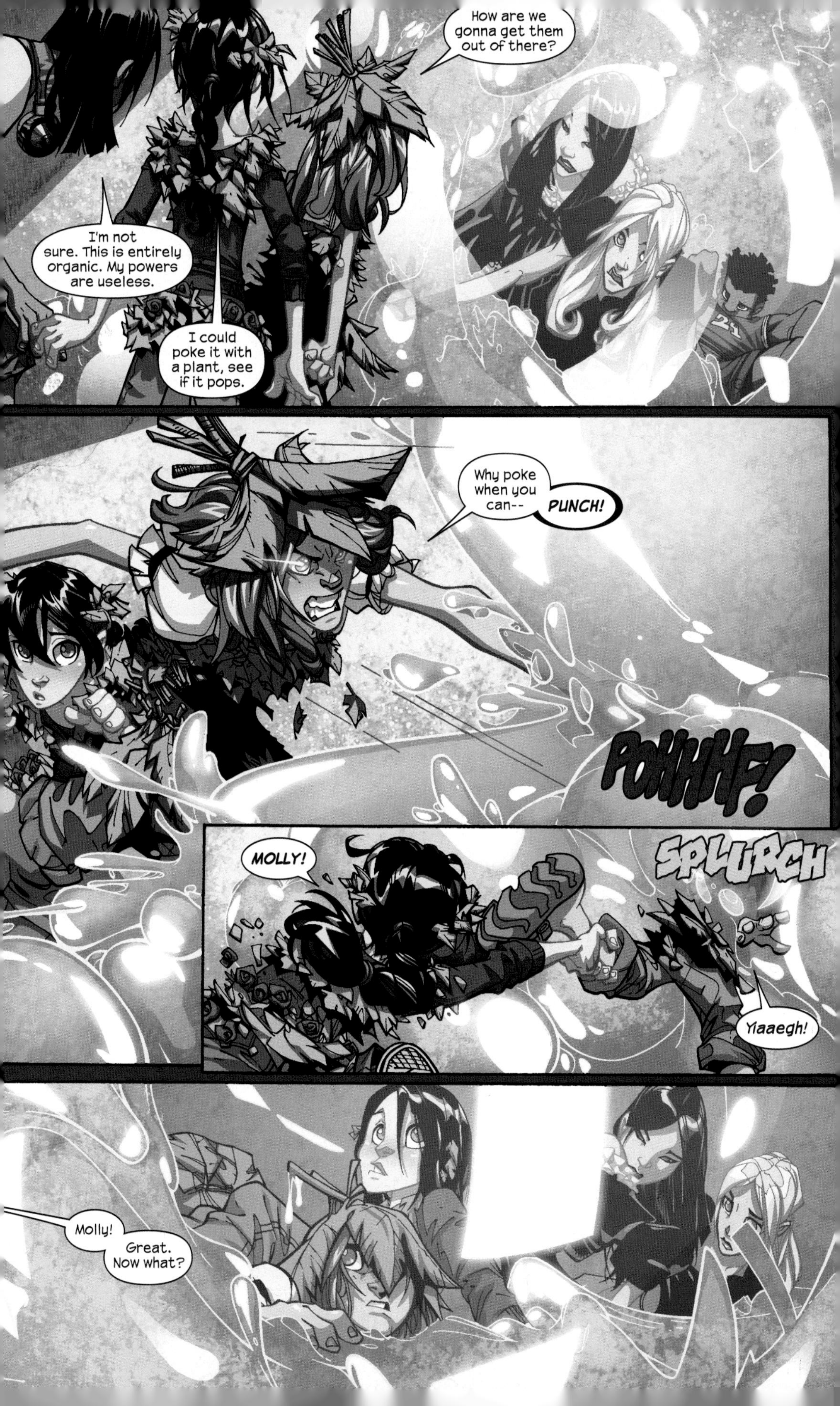
How are we gonna get them out of there?
I'm not sure. This is entirely organic. My powers are useless.
I could poke it with a plant, see if it pops.
Why poke when you can--
PUNCH!
POHHHF!
MOLLY!
SPLURCH
Yiaaegh!
Molly!
Great. Now what?

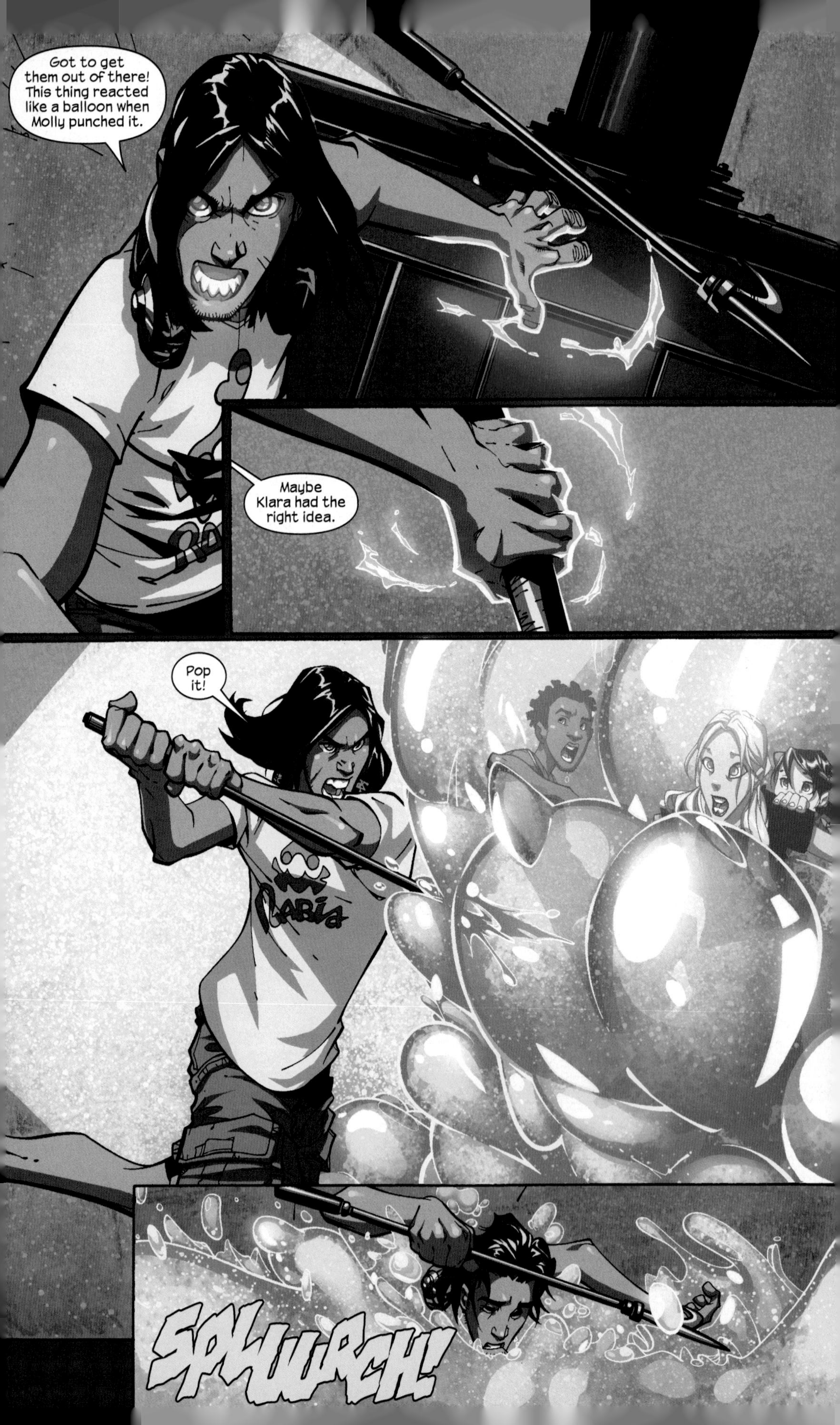
Got to get them out of there! This thing reacted like a balloon when Molly punched it.
Maybe Klara had the right idea.
Pop it!
SPLUURCH!

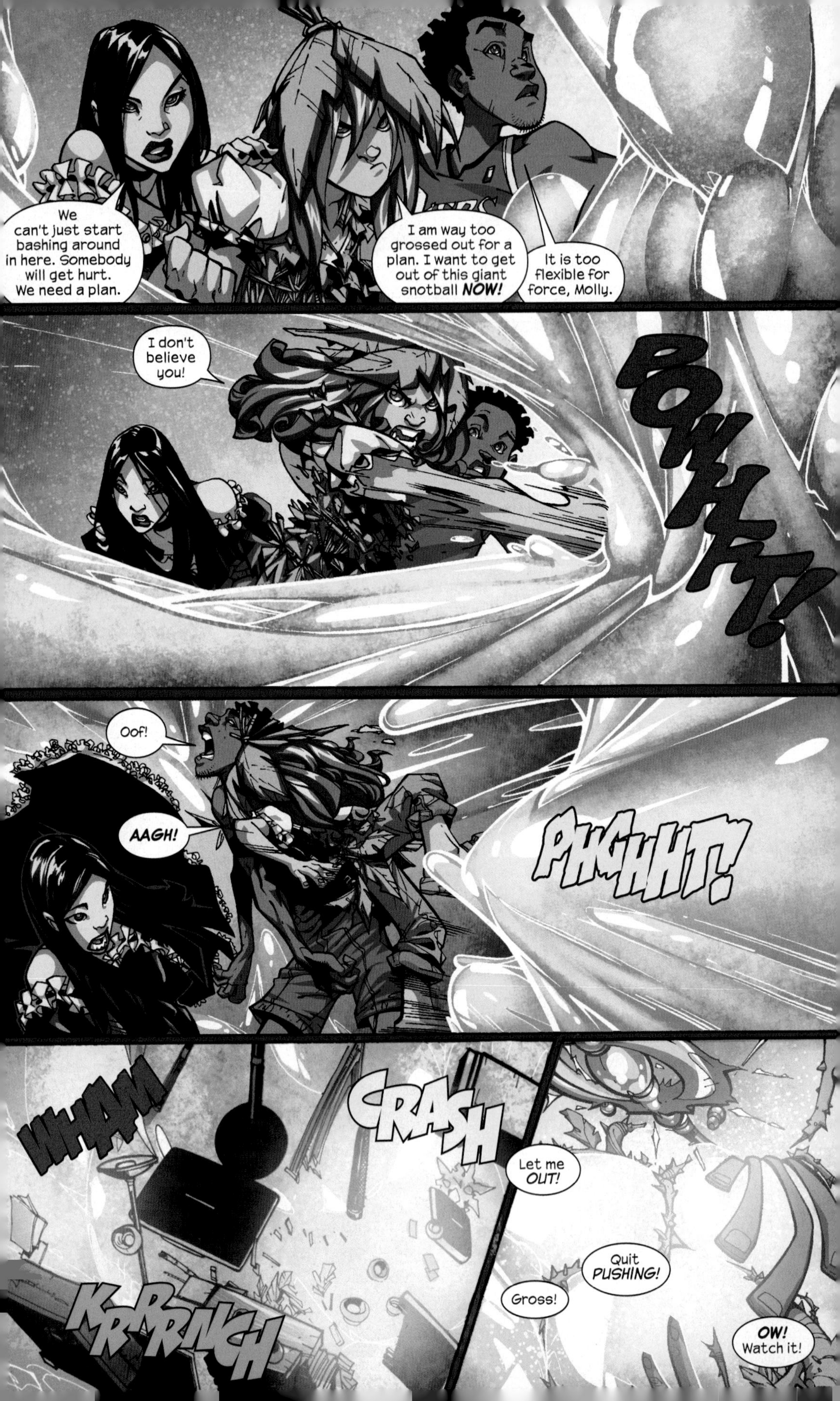

We can't just start bashing around in here. Somebody will get hurt. We need a plan.
I am way too grossed out for a plan. I want to get out of this giant snotball NOW!
It is too flexible for force, Molly.
I don't believe you!
BOWHFT!
Oof!
AAGH!
PHGHHT!
WHAM
CRASH
KRRRNCH
Let me OUT!
Quit PUSHING!
Gross!
OW! Watch it!

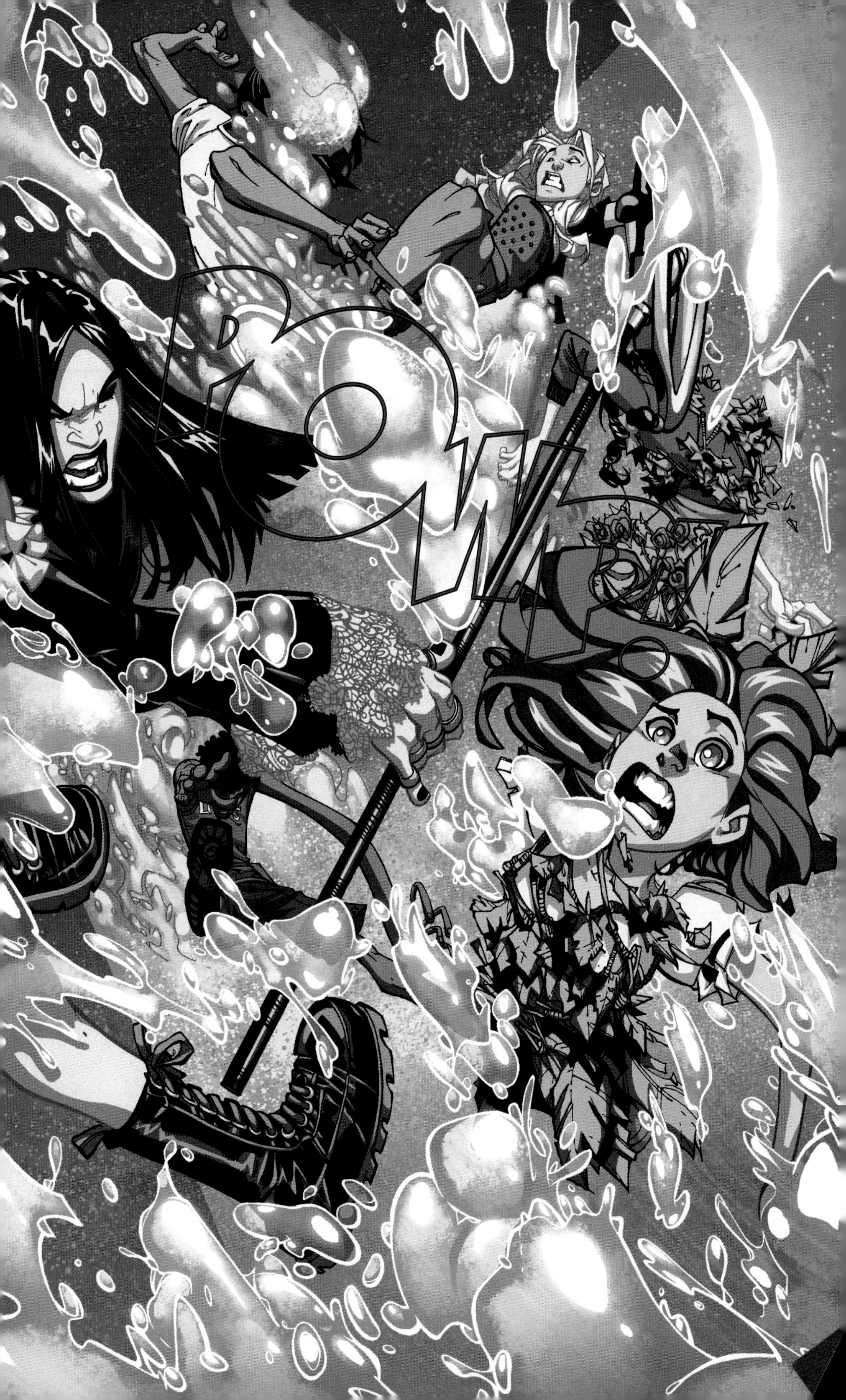

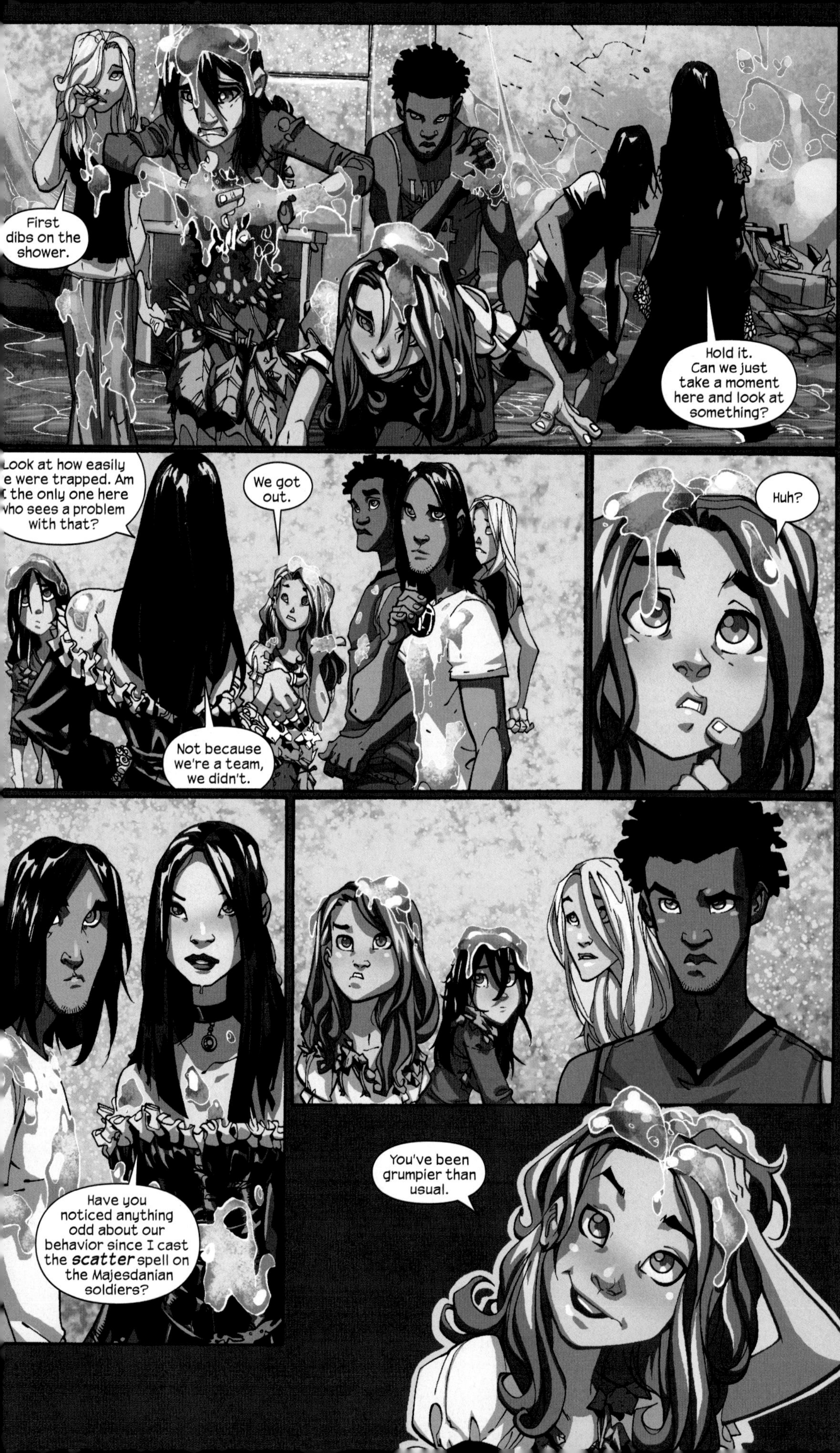
First dibs on the shower.
Hold it. Can we just take a moment here and look at something?
Look at how easily e were trapped. Am I the only one here who sees a problem with that?
We got out.
Not because we're a team, we didn't.
Huh?
Have you noticed anything odd about our behavior since I cast the *scatter* spell on the Majesdanian soldiers?
You've been grumpier than usual.

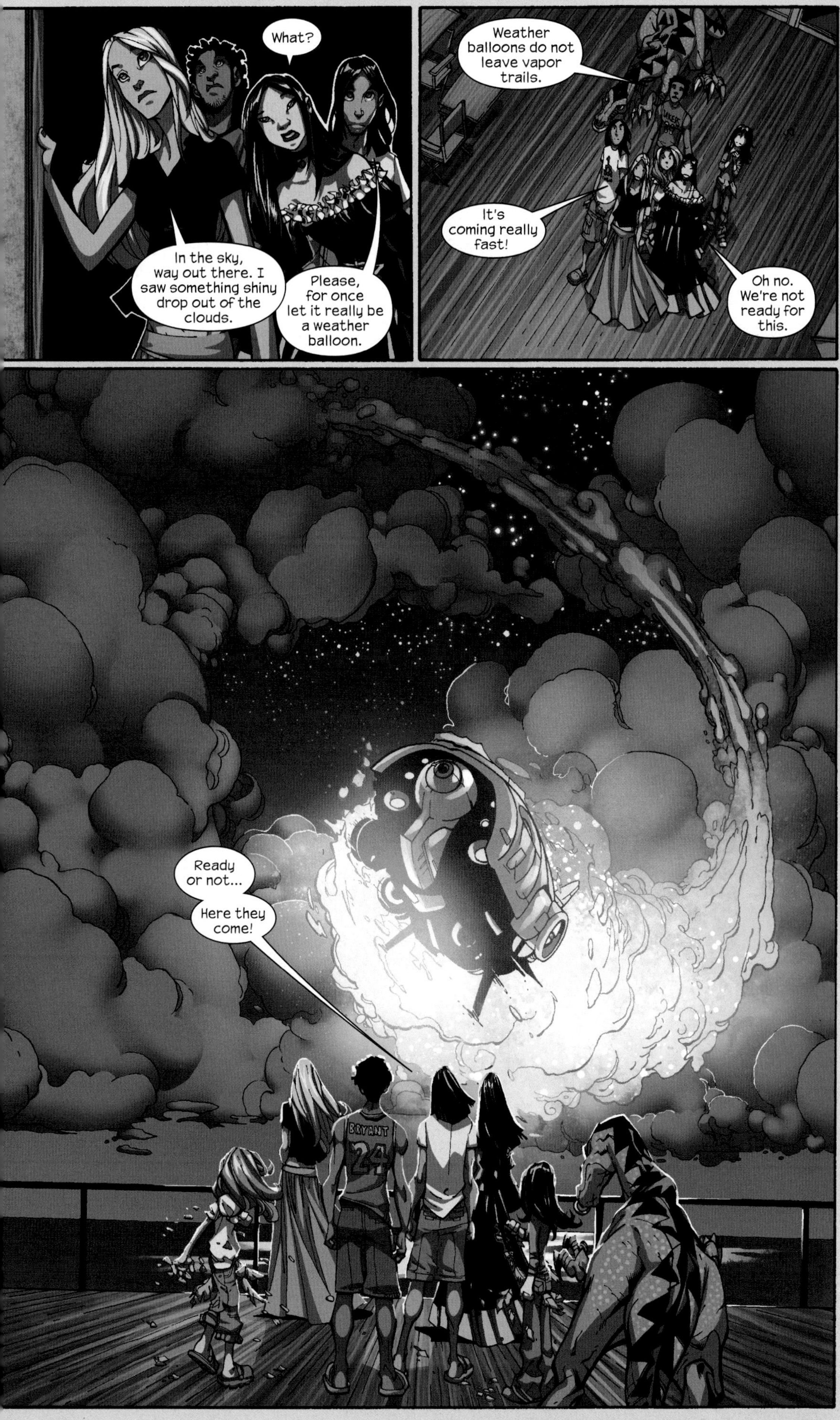
What?
In the sky, way out there. I saw something shiny drop out of the clouds.
Please, for once let it really be a weather balloon.
Weather balloons do not leave vapor trails.
It's coming really fast!
Oh no. We're not ready for this.
Ready or not...
Here they come!
BRYANT 24

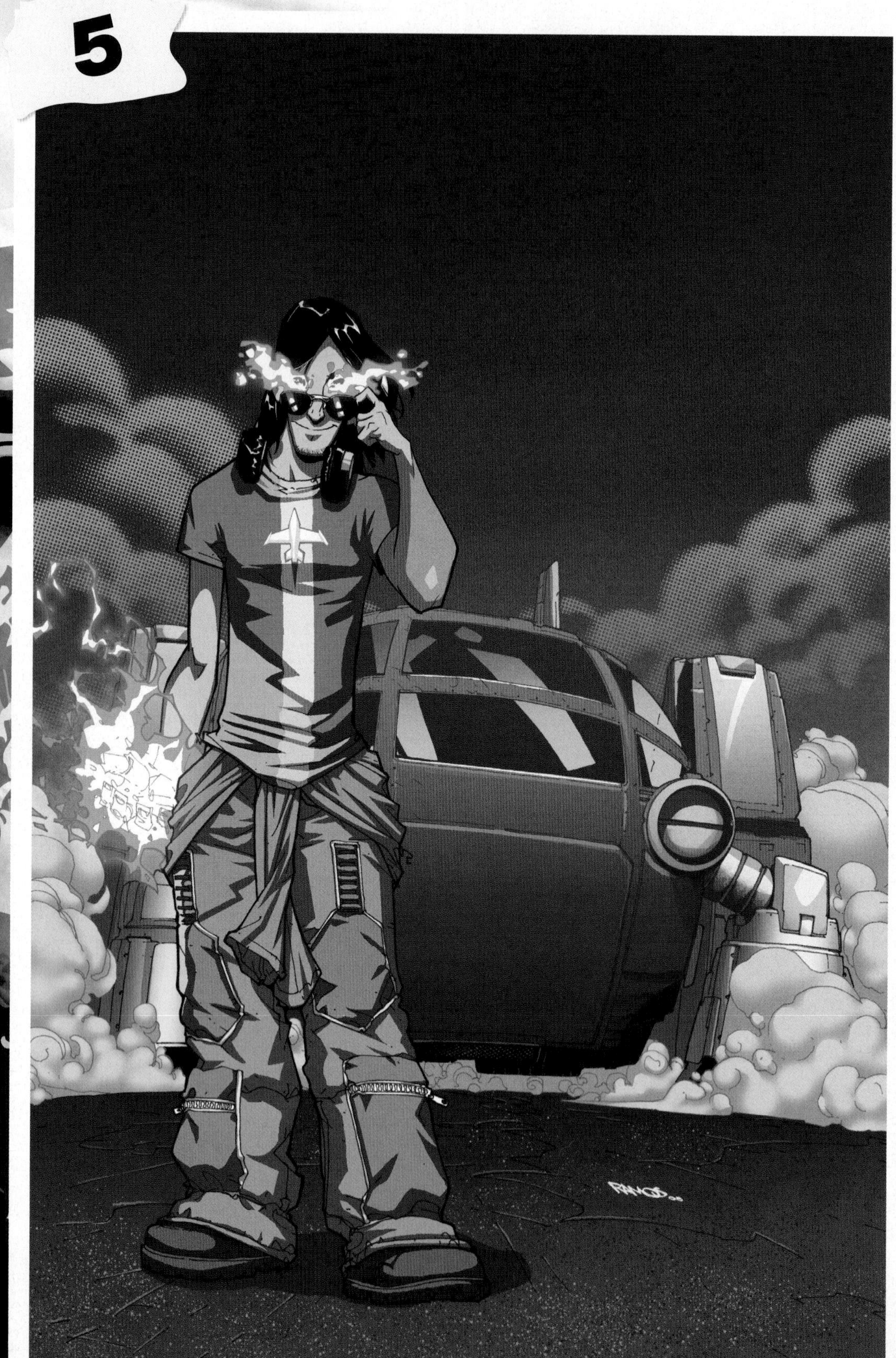
5

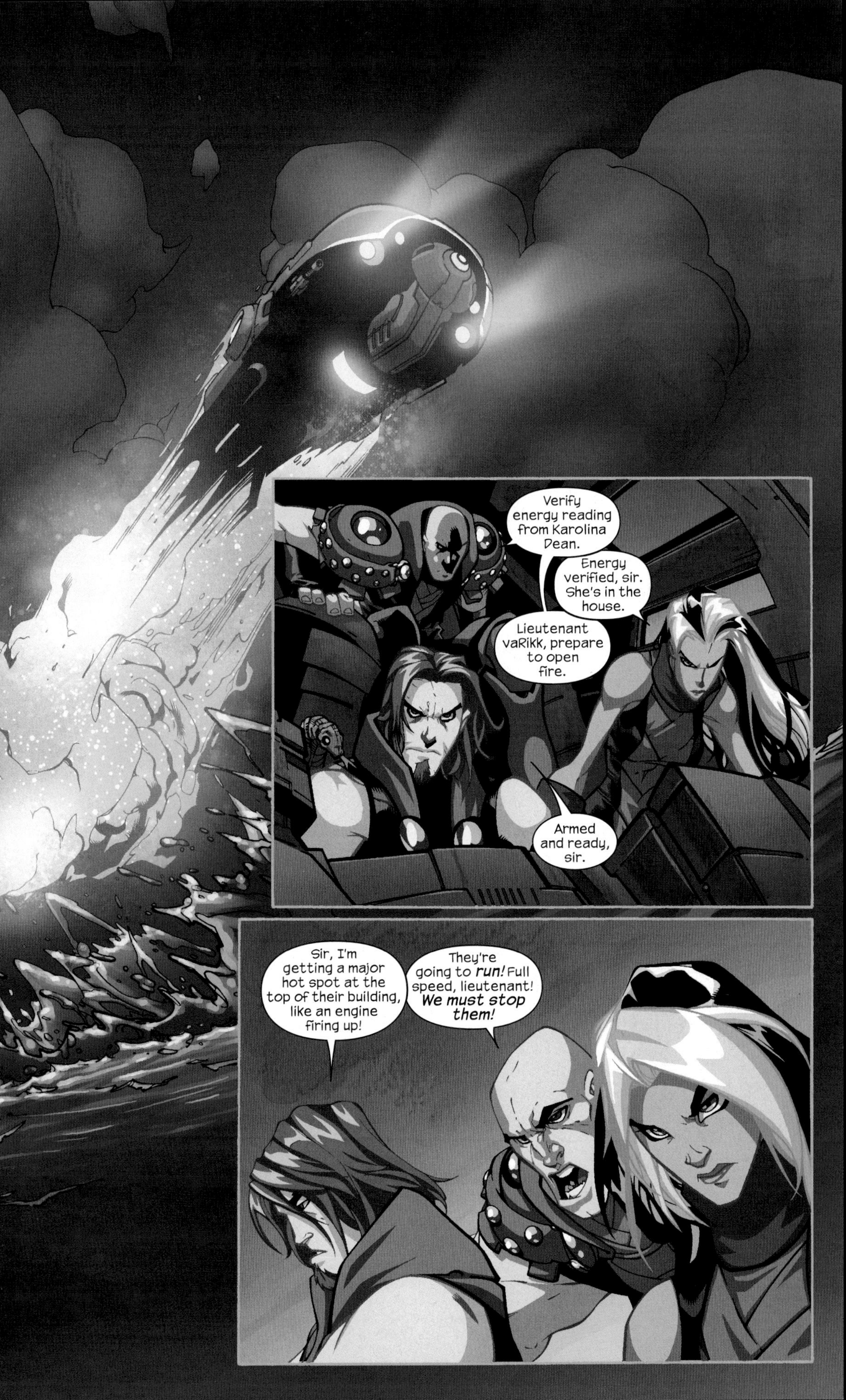
Verify energy reading from Karolina Dean.
Energy verified, sir. She's in the house.
Lieutenant vaRikk, prepare to open fire.
Armed and ready, sir.
Sir, I'm getting a major hot spot at the top of their building, like an engine firing up!
They're going to *run!* Full speed, lieutenant! ***We must stop them!***

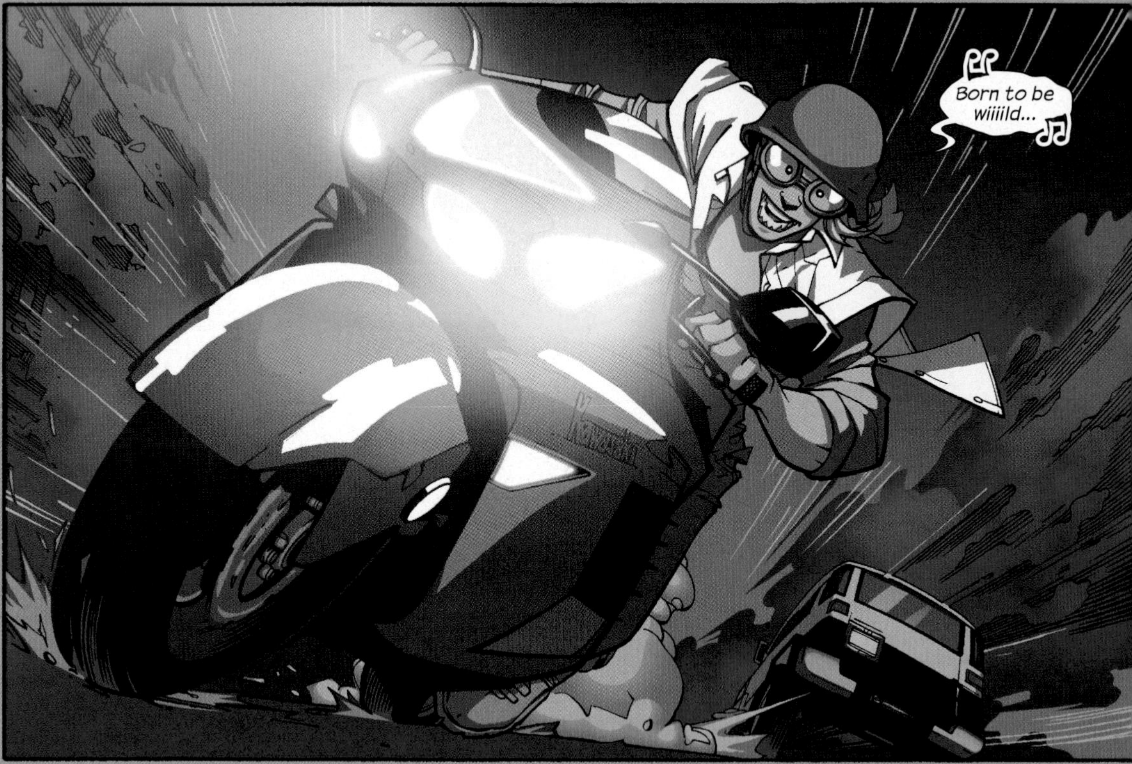
Born to be wiiiild...

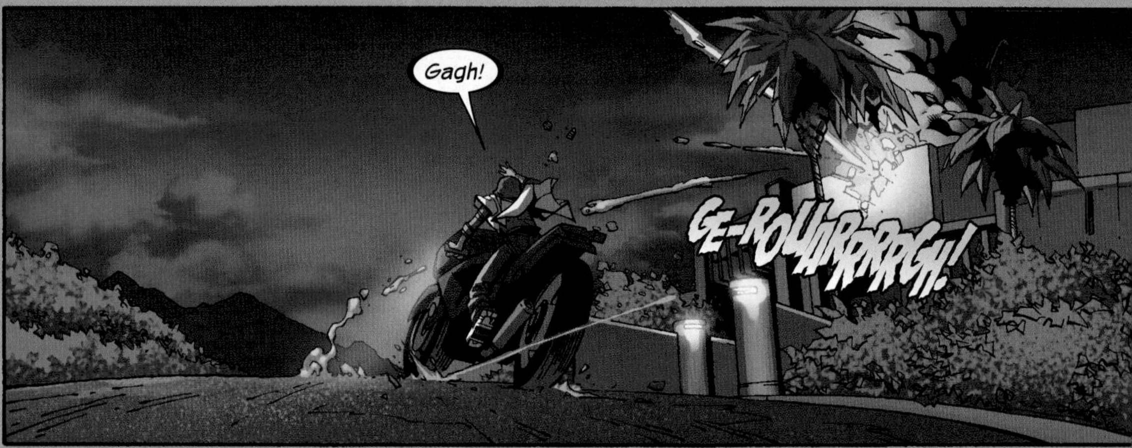
Gagh!
GE-ROUARRRRGH!

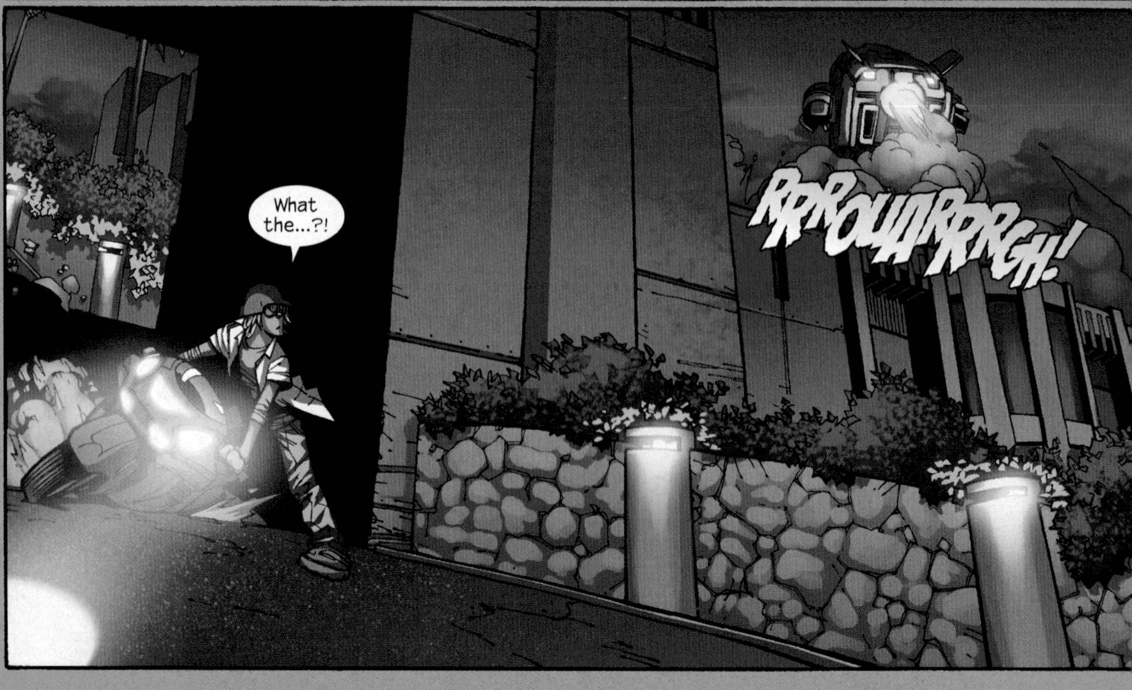
What the...?!
RRROUARRRGH!

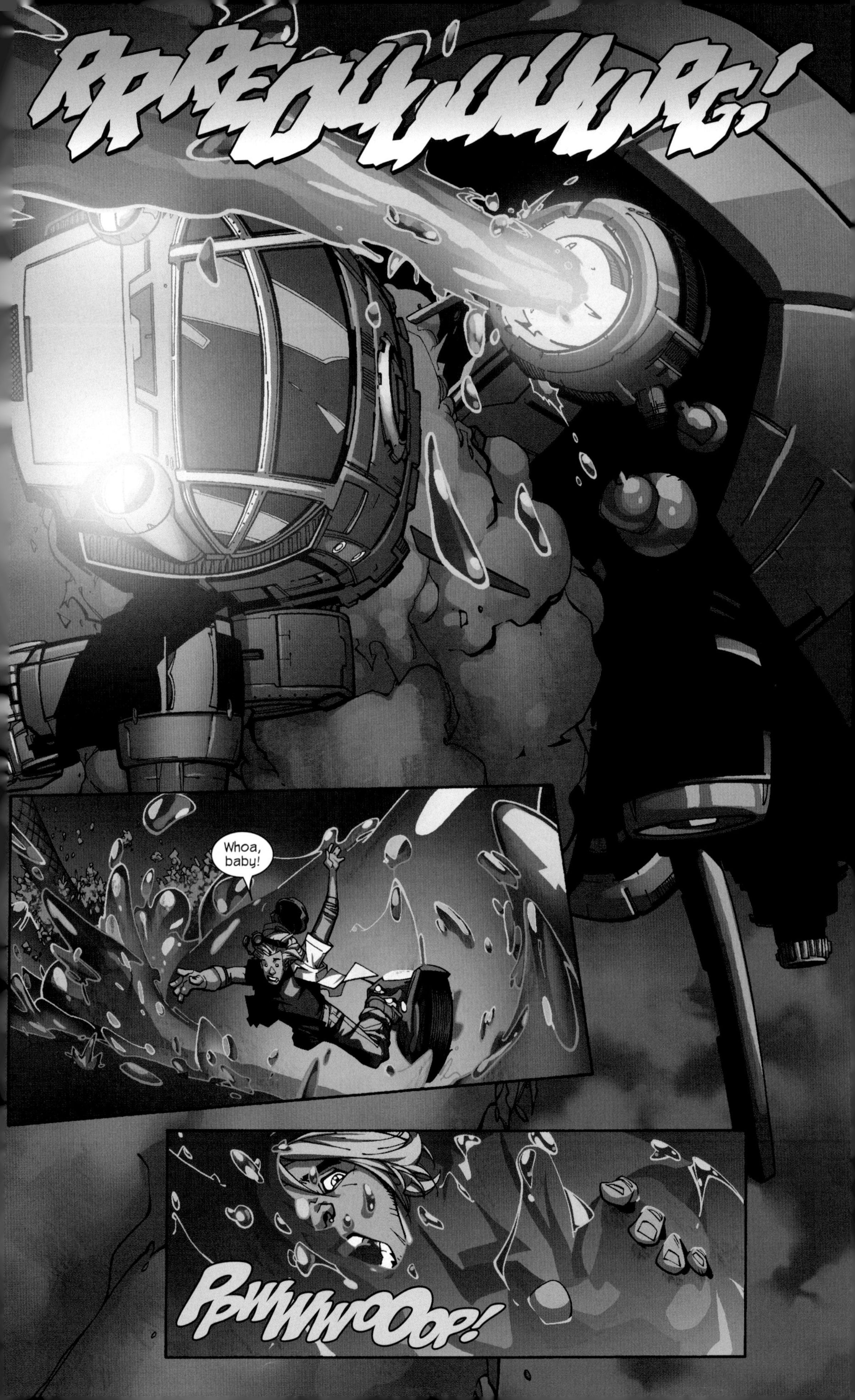
RRREOWWWWRG!
Whoa, baby!
PSHWWWOOOP!

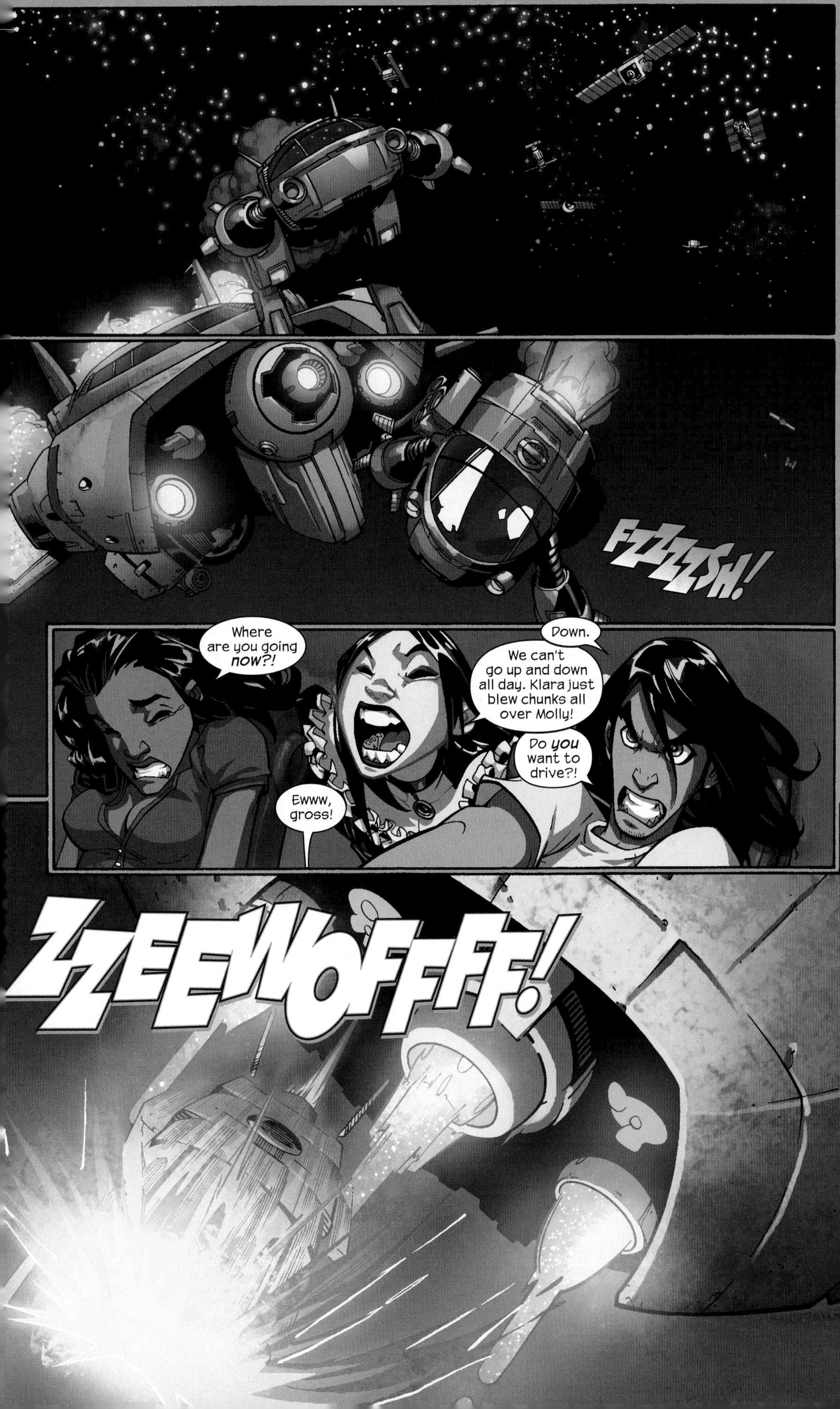
FZZZZSH!
Where are you going now?!
Down.
We can't go up and down all day. Klara just blew chunks all over Molly!
Do you want to drive?!
Ewww, gross!
ZZEEWOFFFF!

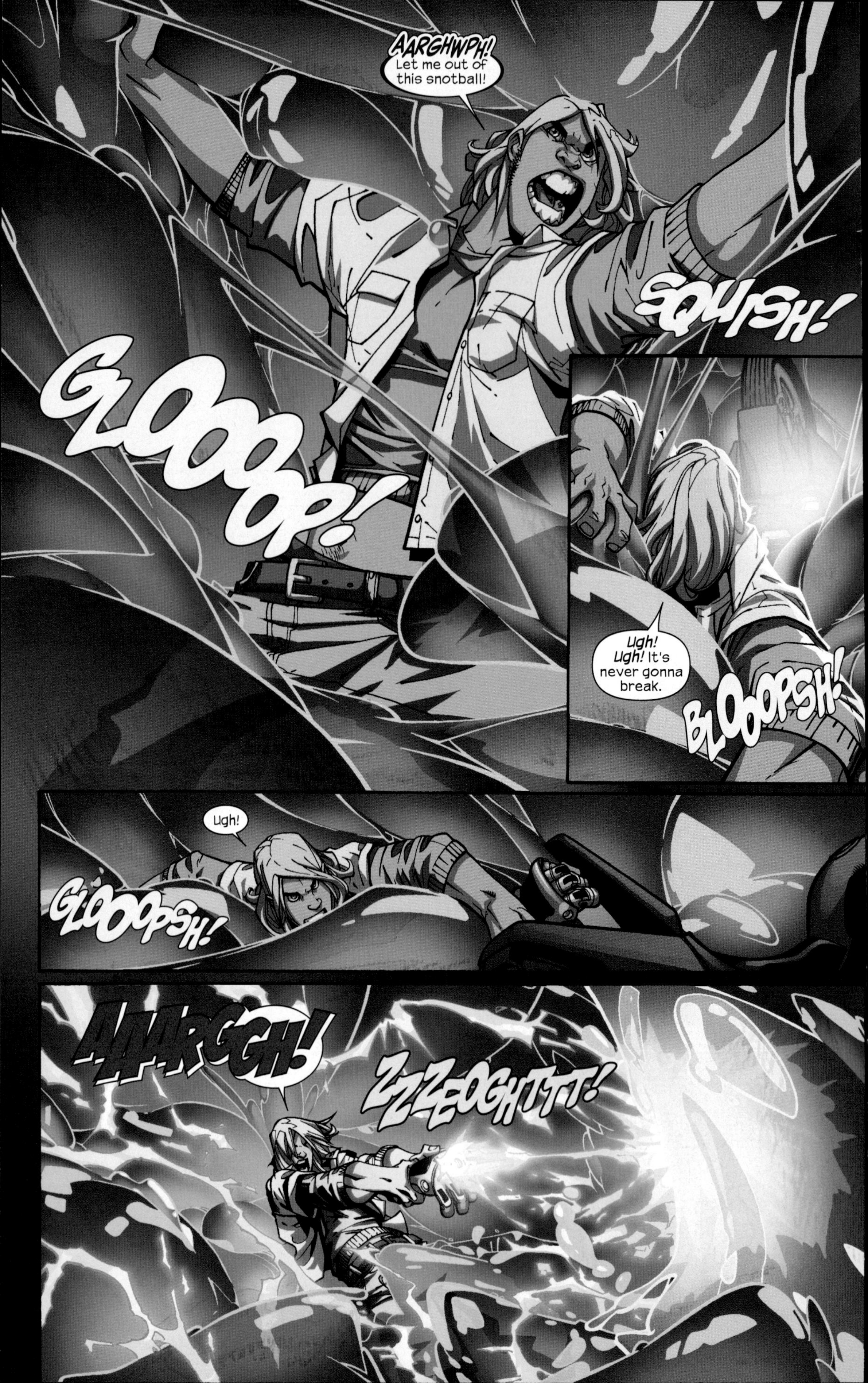
AARGHWPH! Let me out of this snotball!
SQUISH!
GLOOOOOP!
Ugh! Ugh! It's never gonna break.
BLOOOPSH!
Ugh!
GLOOOPSH!
AAARGGH!
ZZZEOGHTTT!

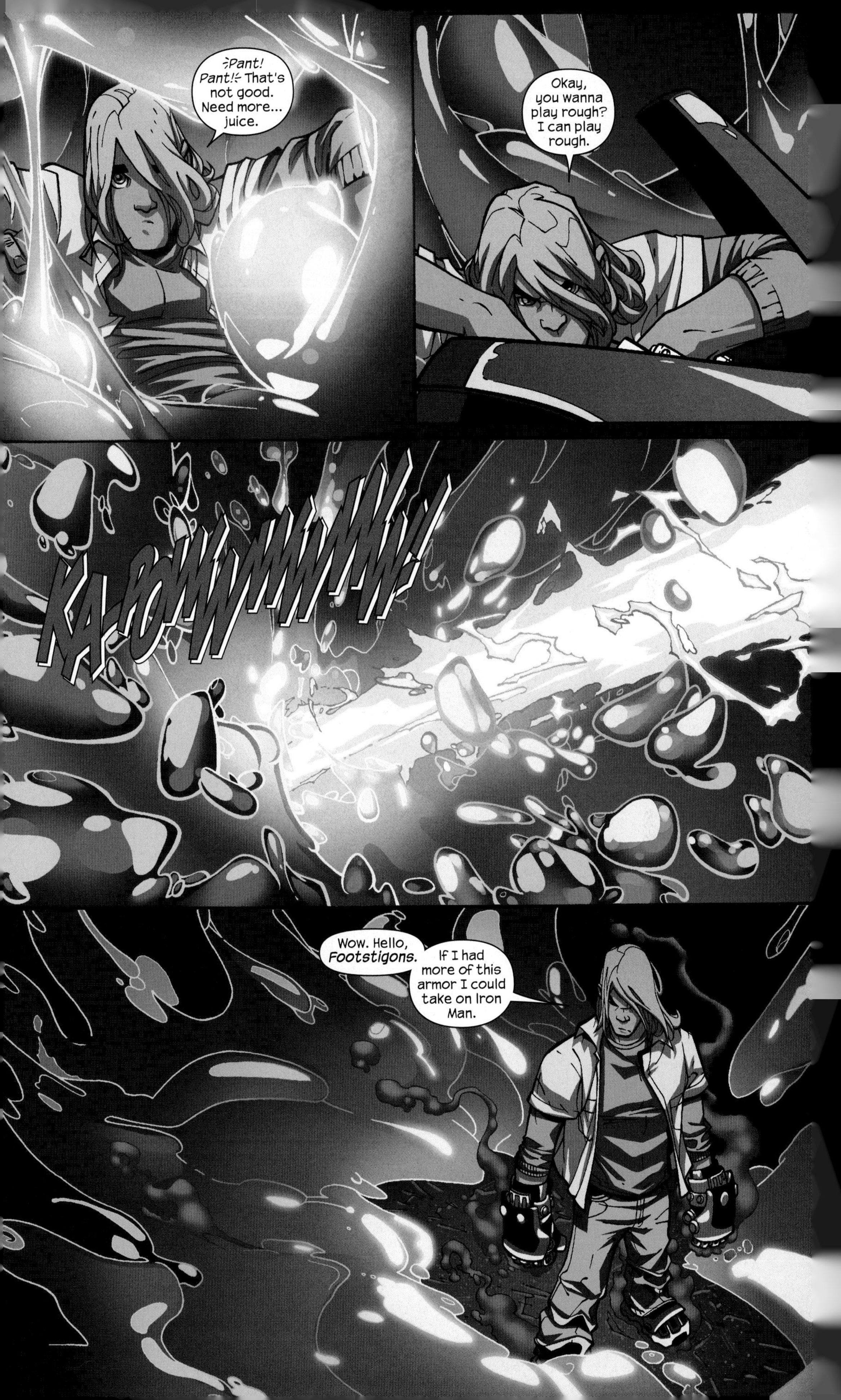

Pant! Pant! That's not good. Need more... juice.
Okay, you wanna play rough? I can play rough.
KA-POWWWWW!
Wow. Hello, Footstigons.
If I had more of this armor I could take on Iron Man.

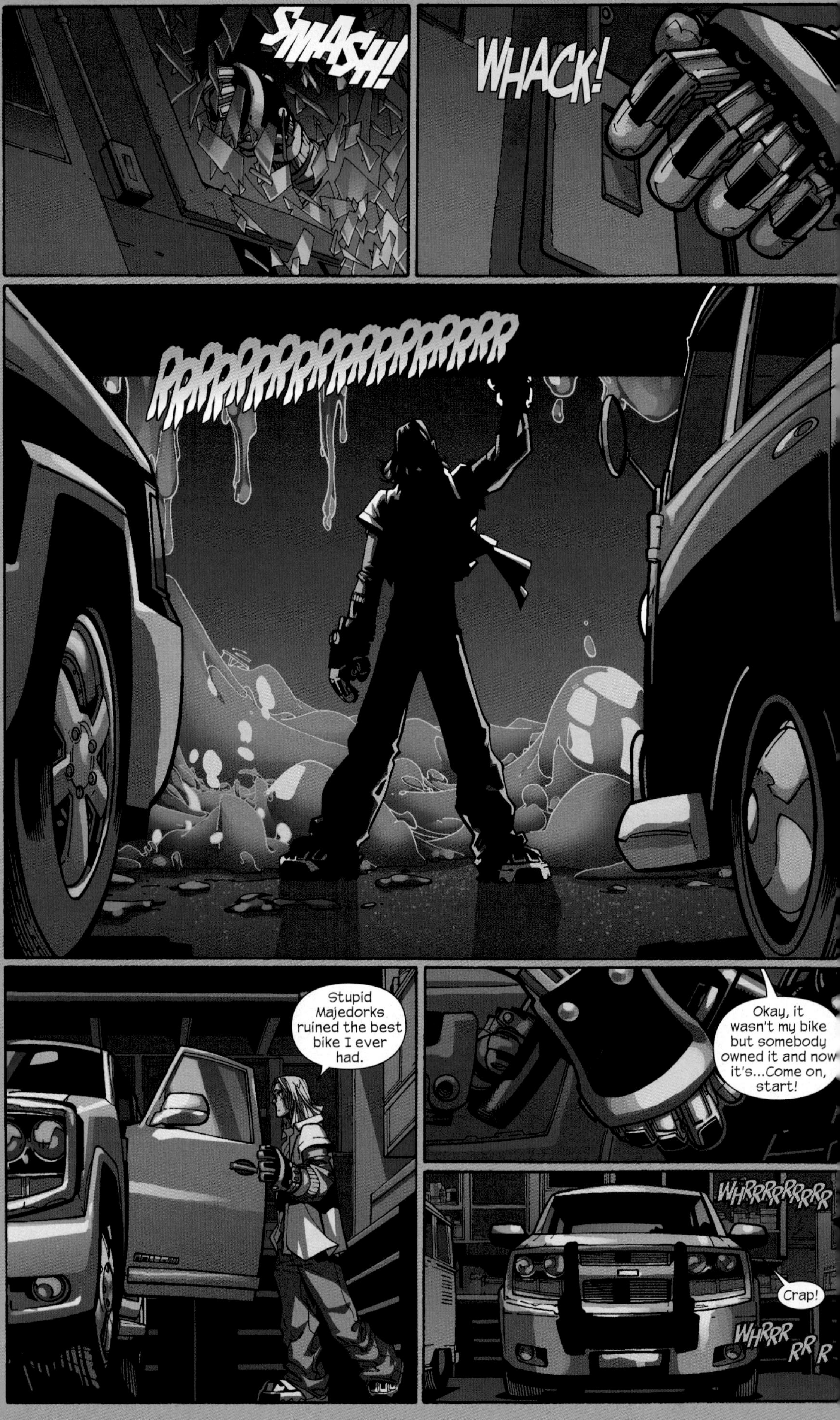
SMASH!
WHACK!
RRRRRRRRRRRRRRRRRRRRRRR
Stupid Majedorks ruined the best bike I ever had.
Okay, it wasn't my bike but somebody owned it and now it's...Come on, start!
WHRRRRRRRRR
Crap!
WHRRR RRR

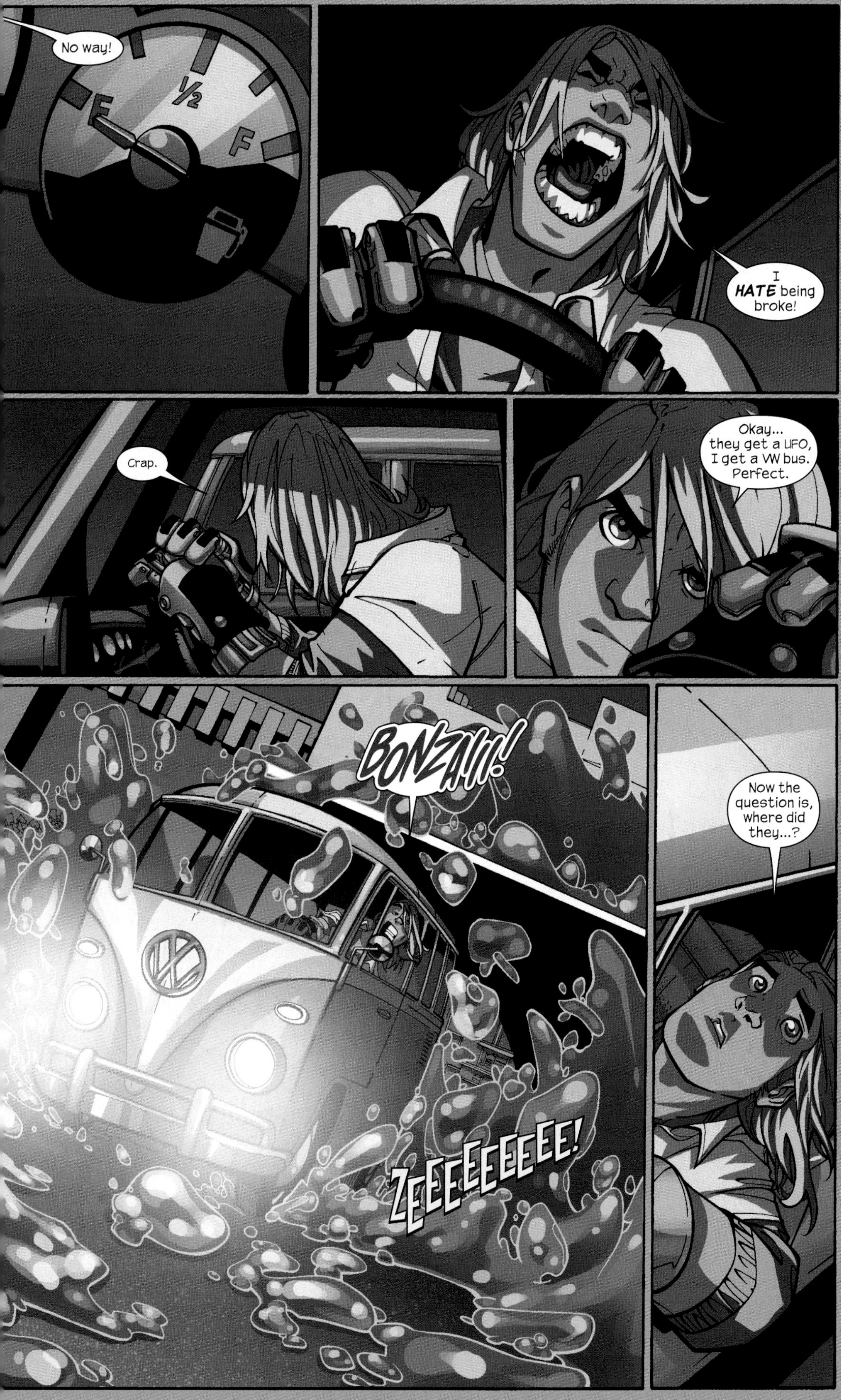
No way!
I HATE being broke!
Crap.
Okay... they get a UFO, I get a VW bus. Perfect.
BONZAIII!
ZEEEEEEEEE!
Now the question is, where did they...?

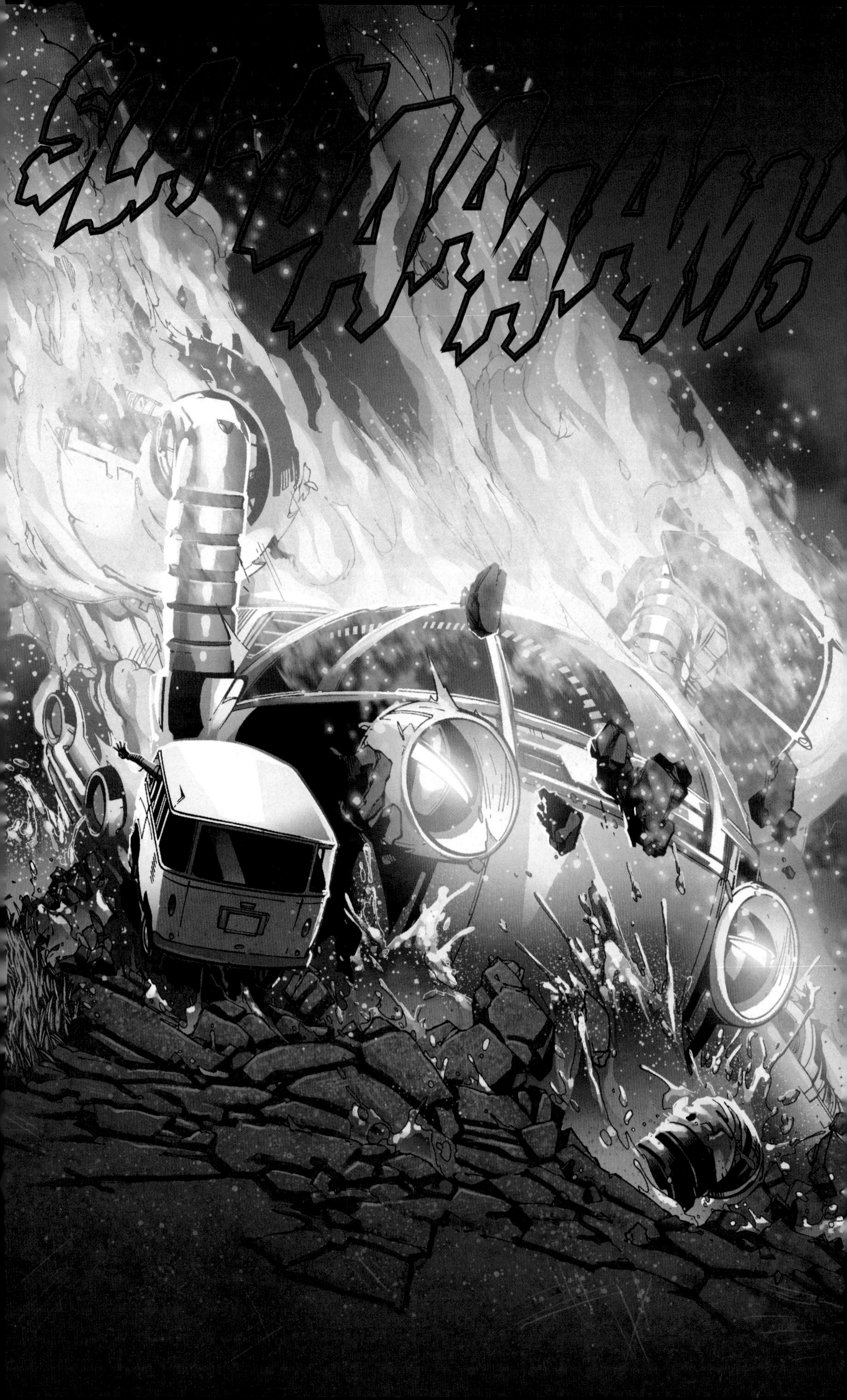

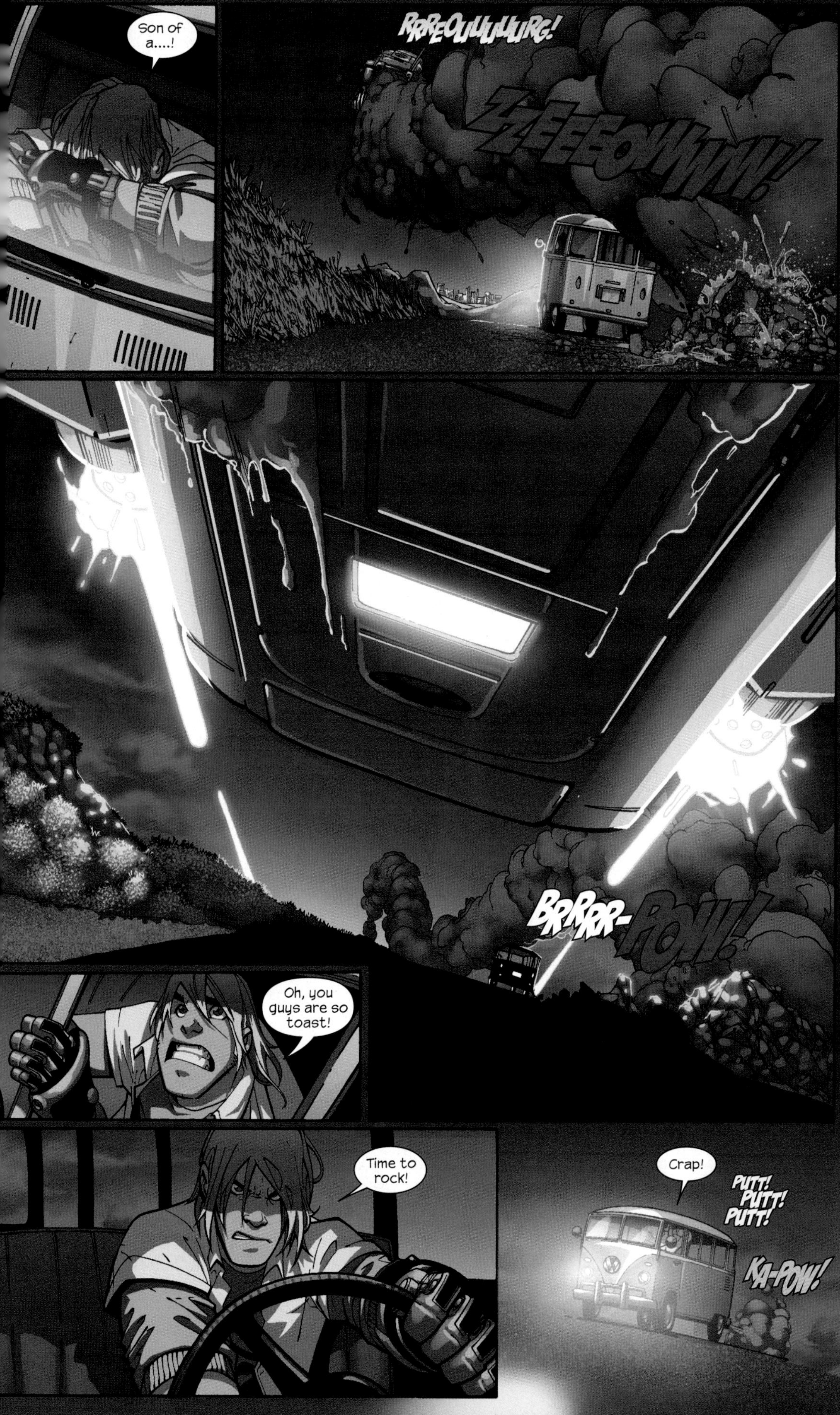
Son of a....!
RRREOUUUUURG!
ZZEEE-OWWW!
BRRRR-POW!
Oh, you guys are so toast!
Time to rock!
Crap!
PUTT! PUTT! PUTT!
KA-POW!

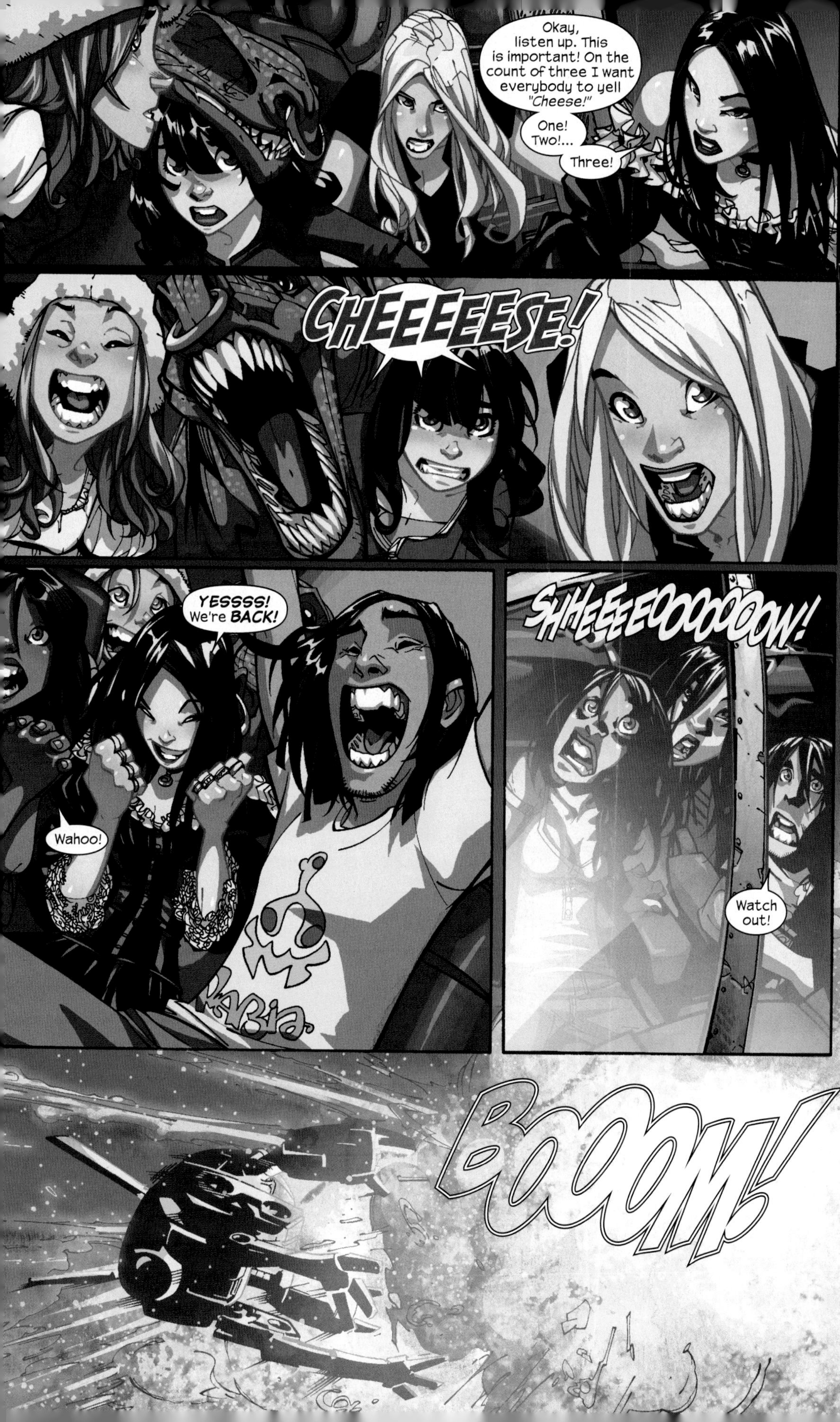

Okay, listen up. This is important! On the count of three I want everybody to yell "Cheese!"
One! Two!...
Three!
CHEEEEESE!
YESSSS! We're BACK!
Wahoo!
SHHEEEEOOOOOOW!
Watch out!
BOOOM!

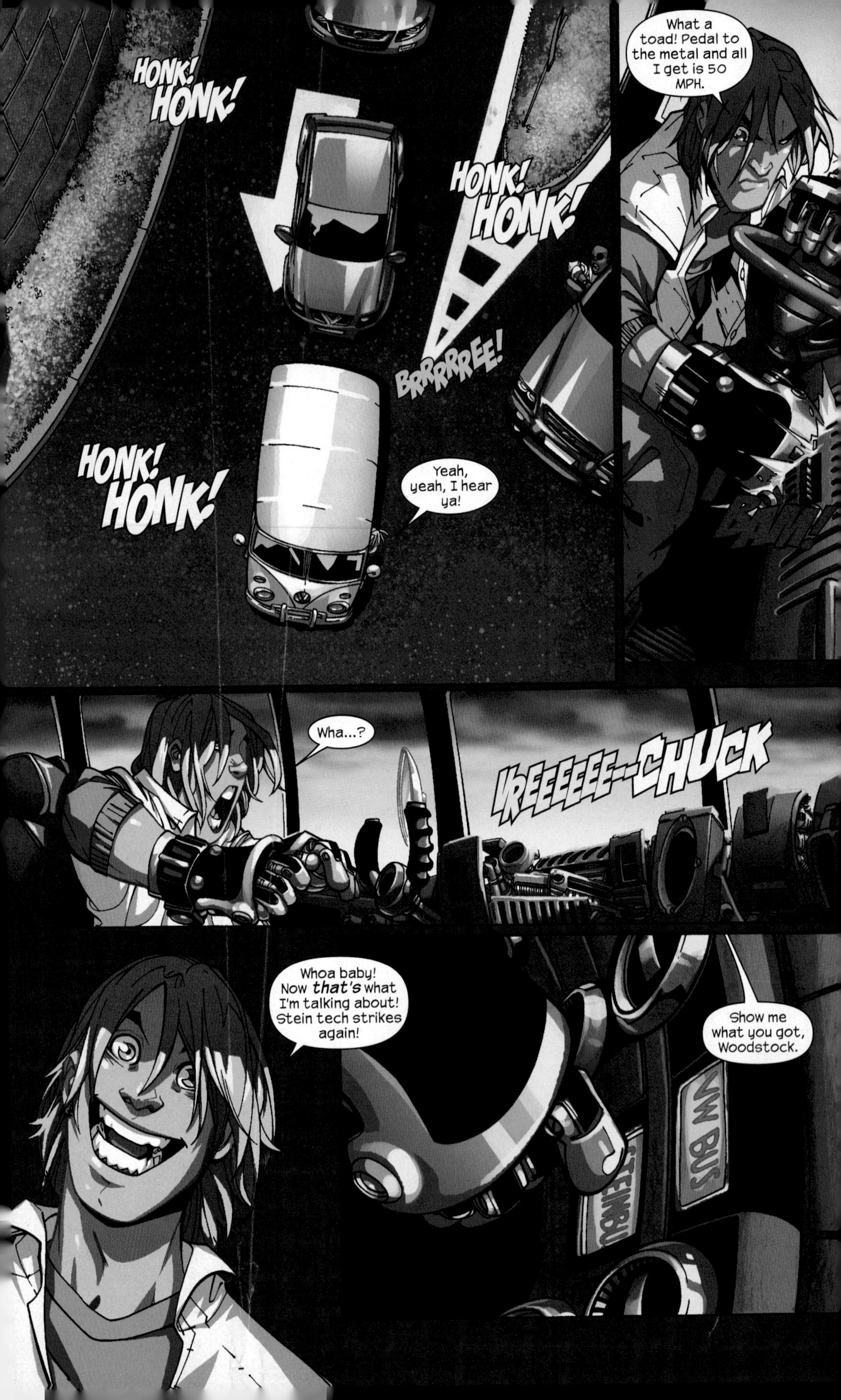
HONK! HONK!
HONK! HONK!
BRRRRREE!
HONK! HONK!
Yeah, yeah, I hear ya!
What a toad! Pedal to the metal and all I get is 50 MPH.
Wha...?
VREEEEEE-CHUCK
Whoa baby! Now that's what I'm talking about! Stein tech strikes again!
Show me what you got, Woodstock.
VW BUS

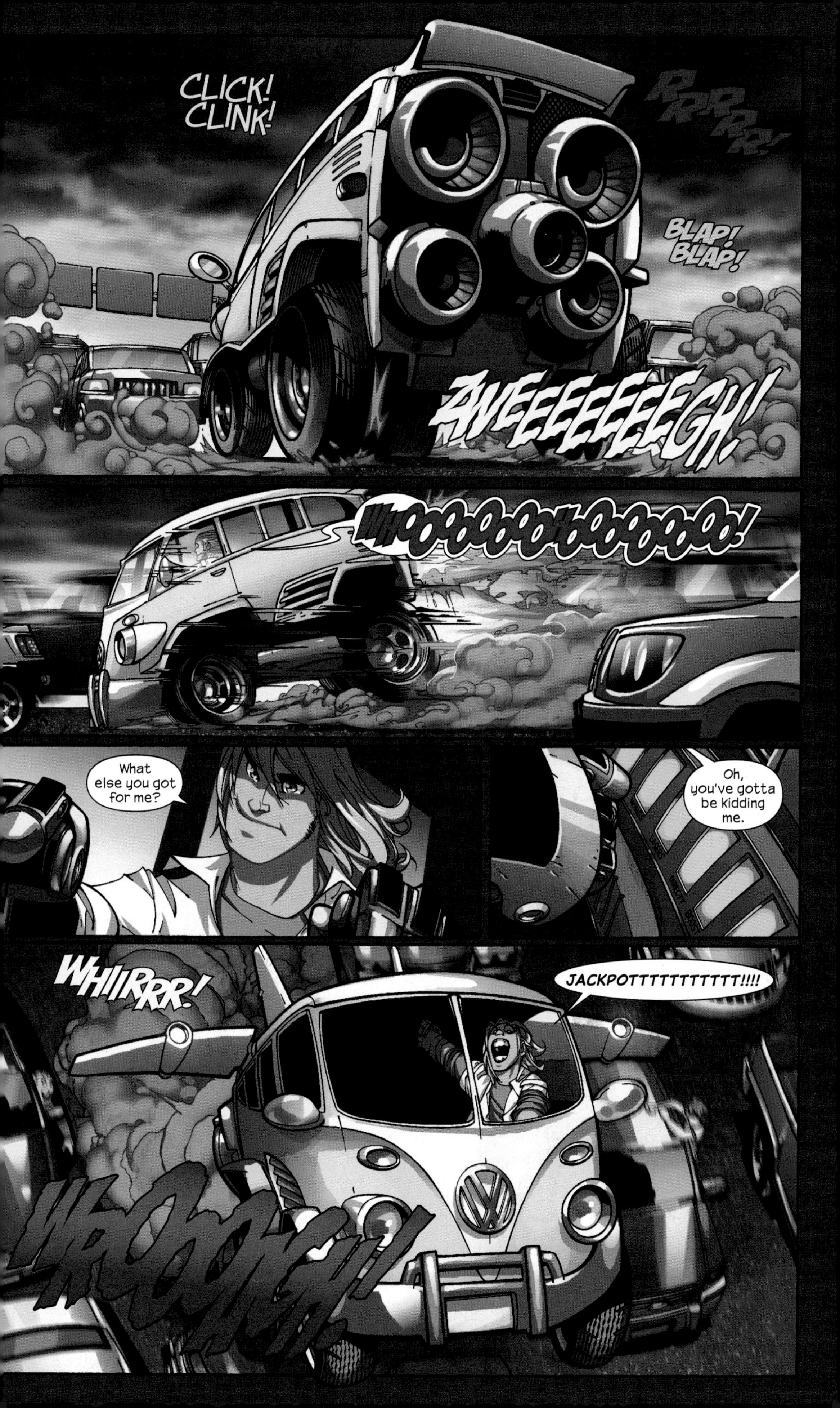
CLICK! CLINK!
RRRRR!
BLAP! BLAP!
ZWEEEEEEEEGH!
WHOOOOOOOOOOOOOOO!
What else you got for me?
Oh, you've gotta be kidding me.
WHIIRRR!
JACKPOTTTTTTTTTTT!!!!

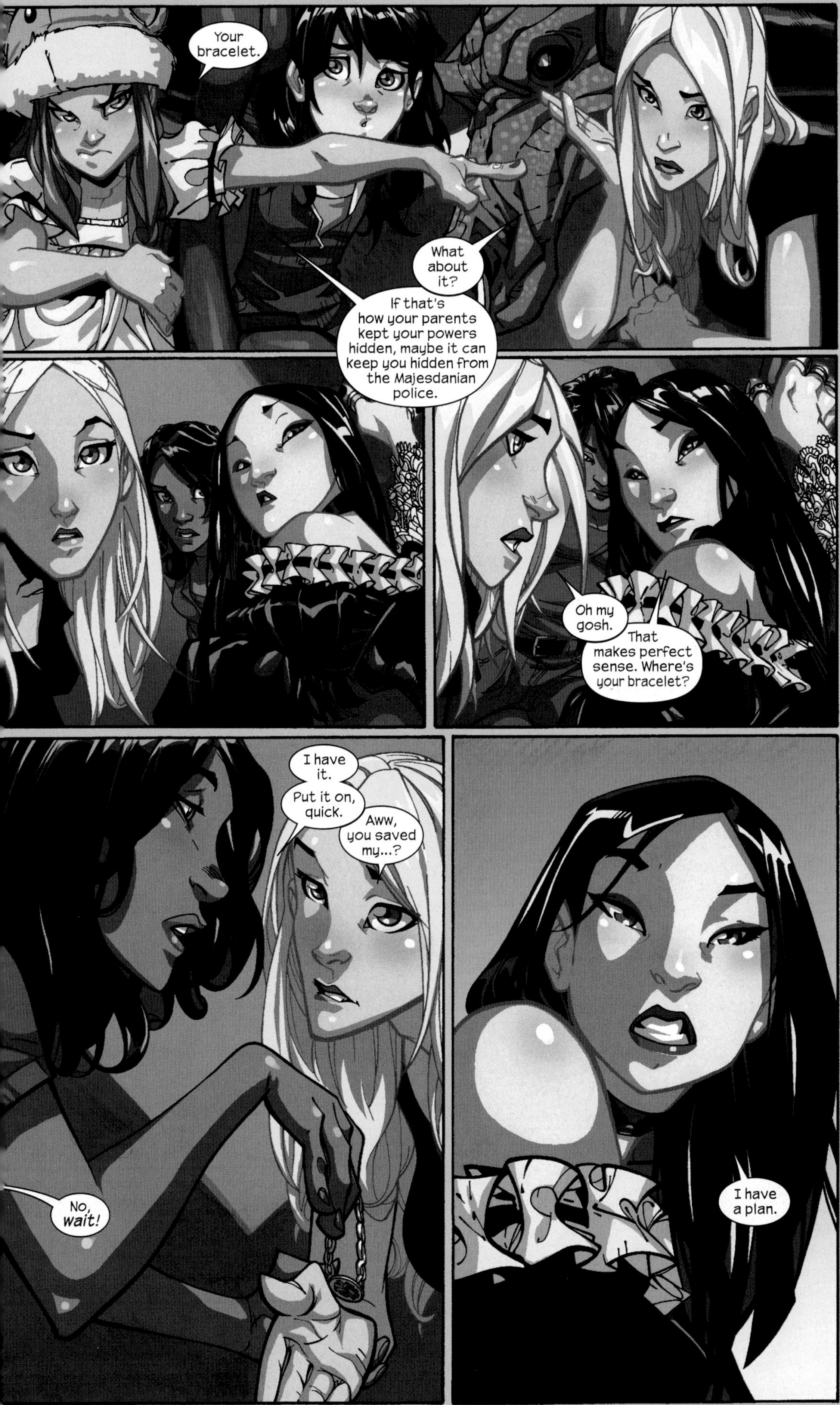
Your bracelet.
What about it?
If that's how your parents kept your powers hidden, maybe it can keep you hidden from the Majesdanian police.
Oh my gosh.
That makes perfect sense. Where's your bracelet?
I have it.
Put it on, quick.
Aww, you saved my...?
No, wait!
I have a plan.

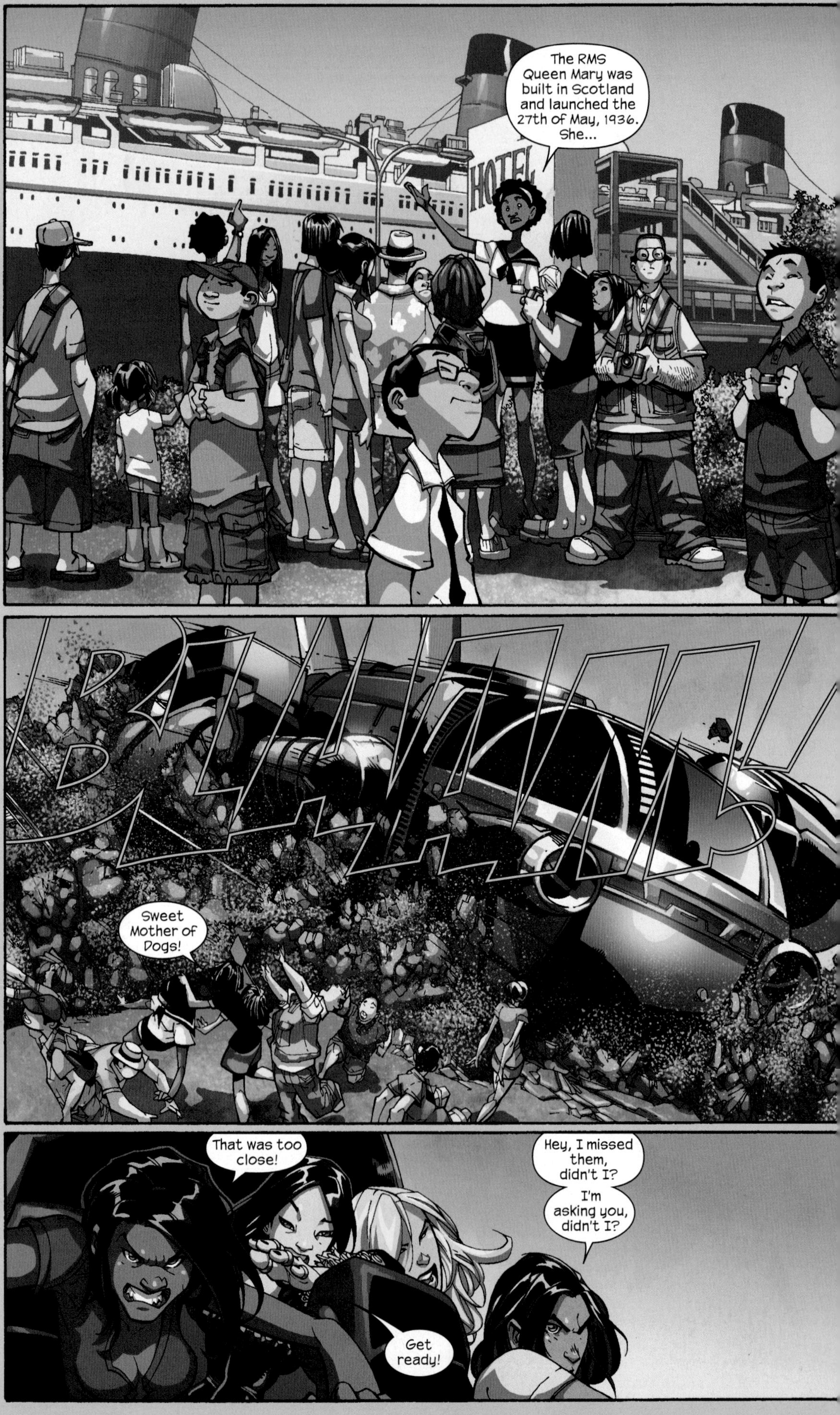
The RMS Queen Mary was built in Scotland and launched the 27th of May, 1936. She...
HOTEL
BLAMMM
Sweet Mother of Dogs!
That was too close!
Hey, I missed them, didn't I?
I'm asking you, didn't I?
Get ready!

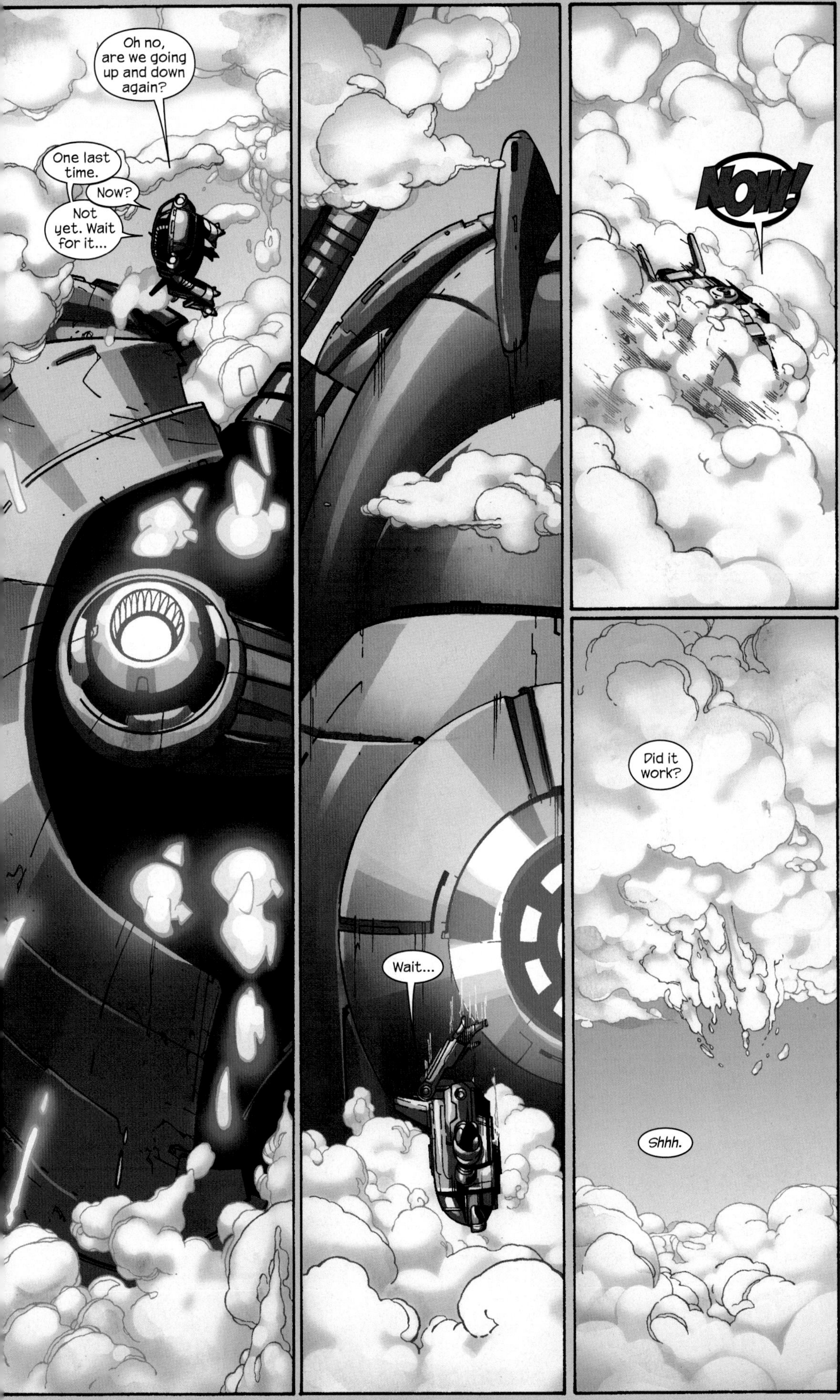

Oh no, are we going up and down again?
One last time.
Now?
Not yet. Wait for it...
Wait...
NOW!
Did it work?
Shhh.

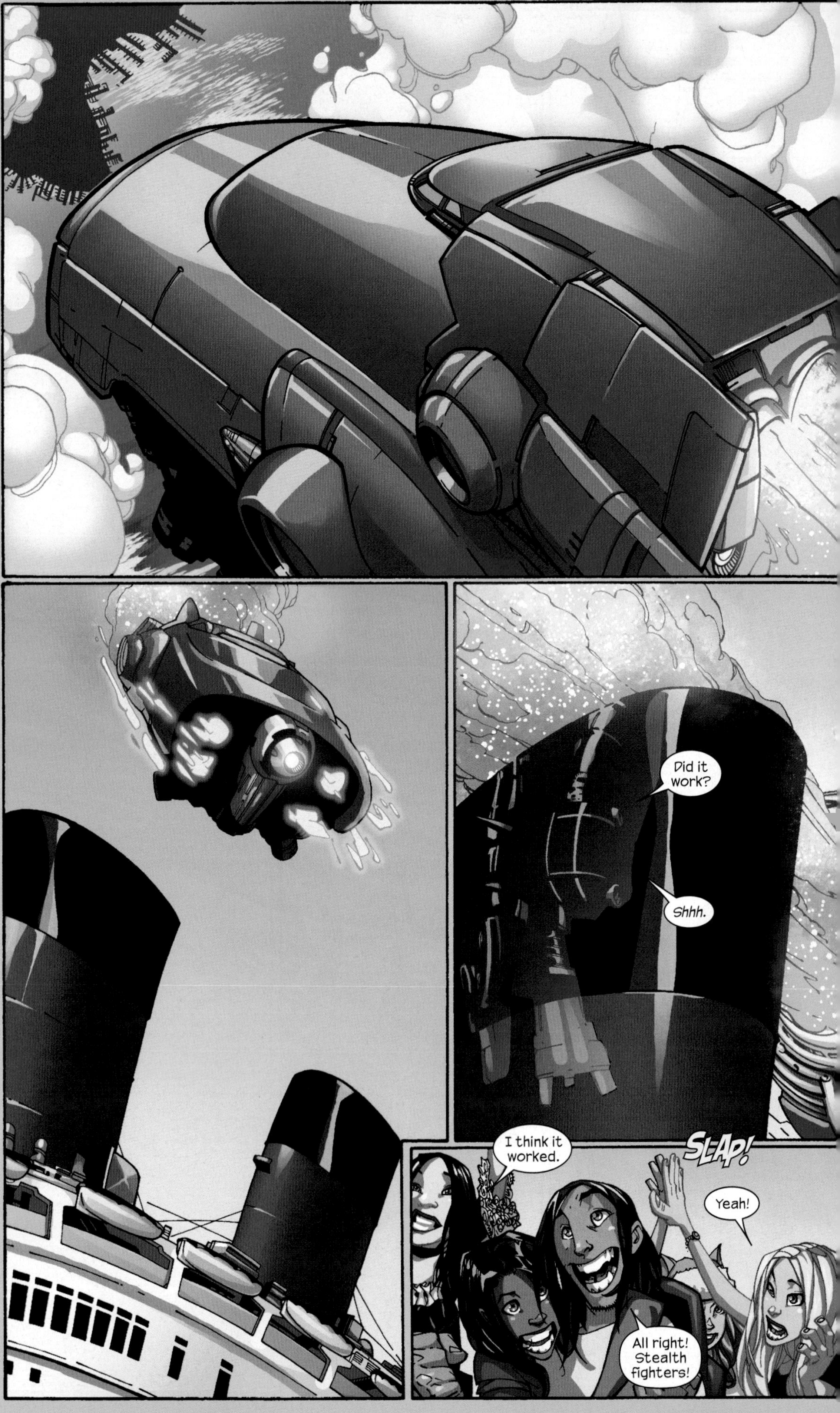
Did it work?
Shhh.
I think it worked.
SLAP!
Yeah!
All right! Stealth fighters!

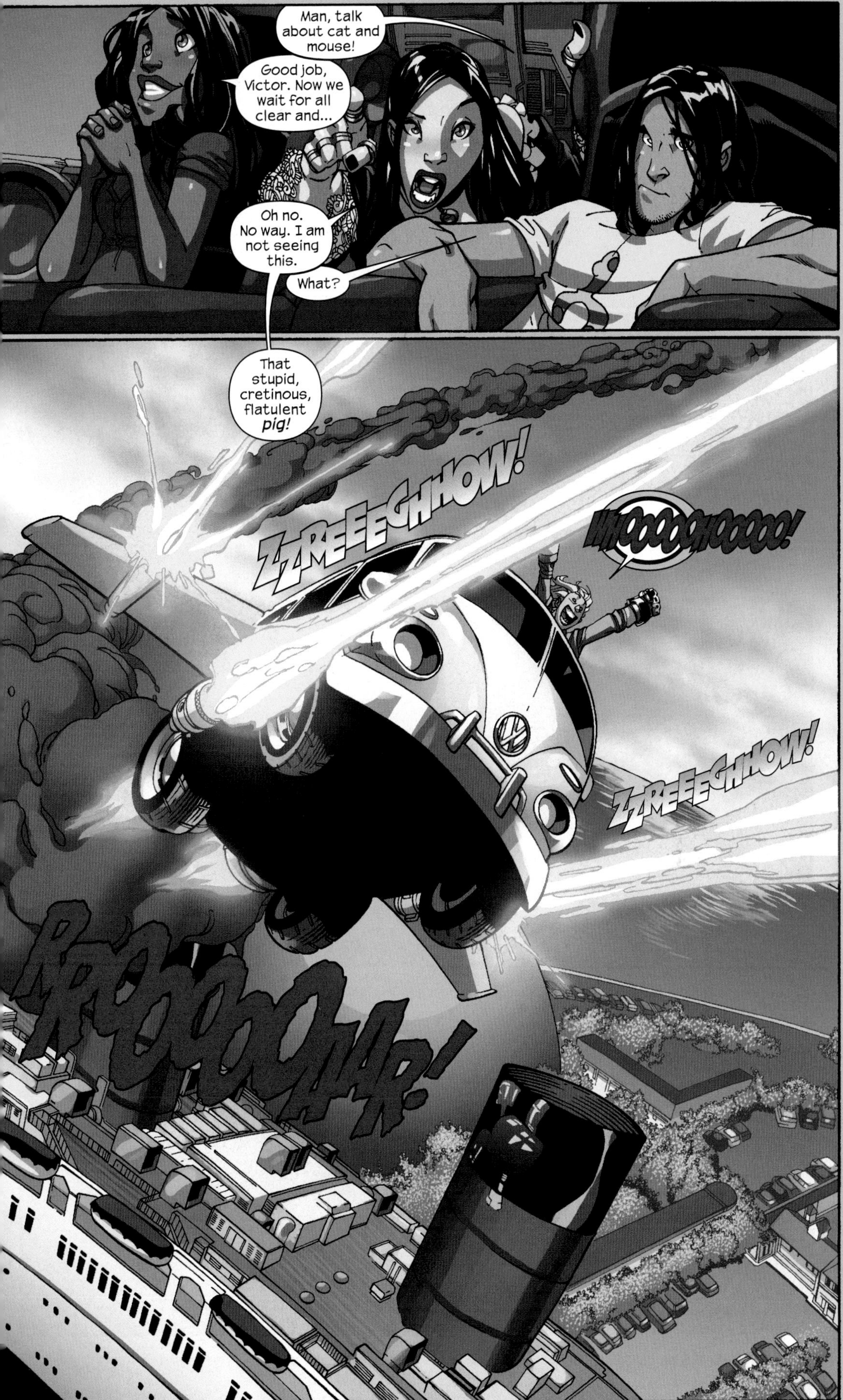

Man, talk about cat and mouse!
Good job, Victor. Now we wait for all clear and...
Oh no. No way. I am not seeing this.
What?
That stupid, cretinous, flatulent *pig!*
ZZREEEGHHOW!
WHOOOOGHOOOOO!
ZZREEEGHHOW!
RROOOOOAR!

6

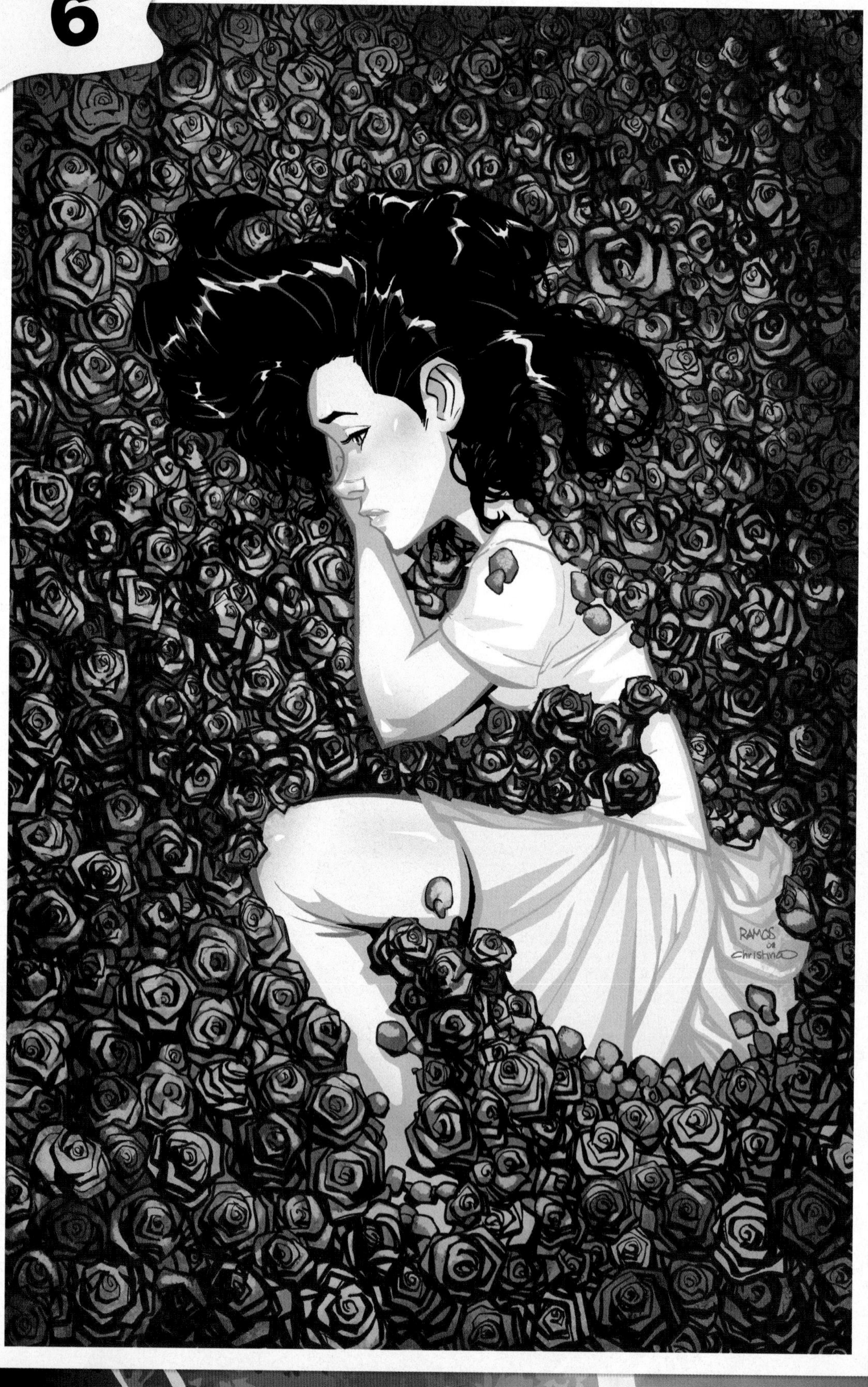
RAMOS
08
Christina

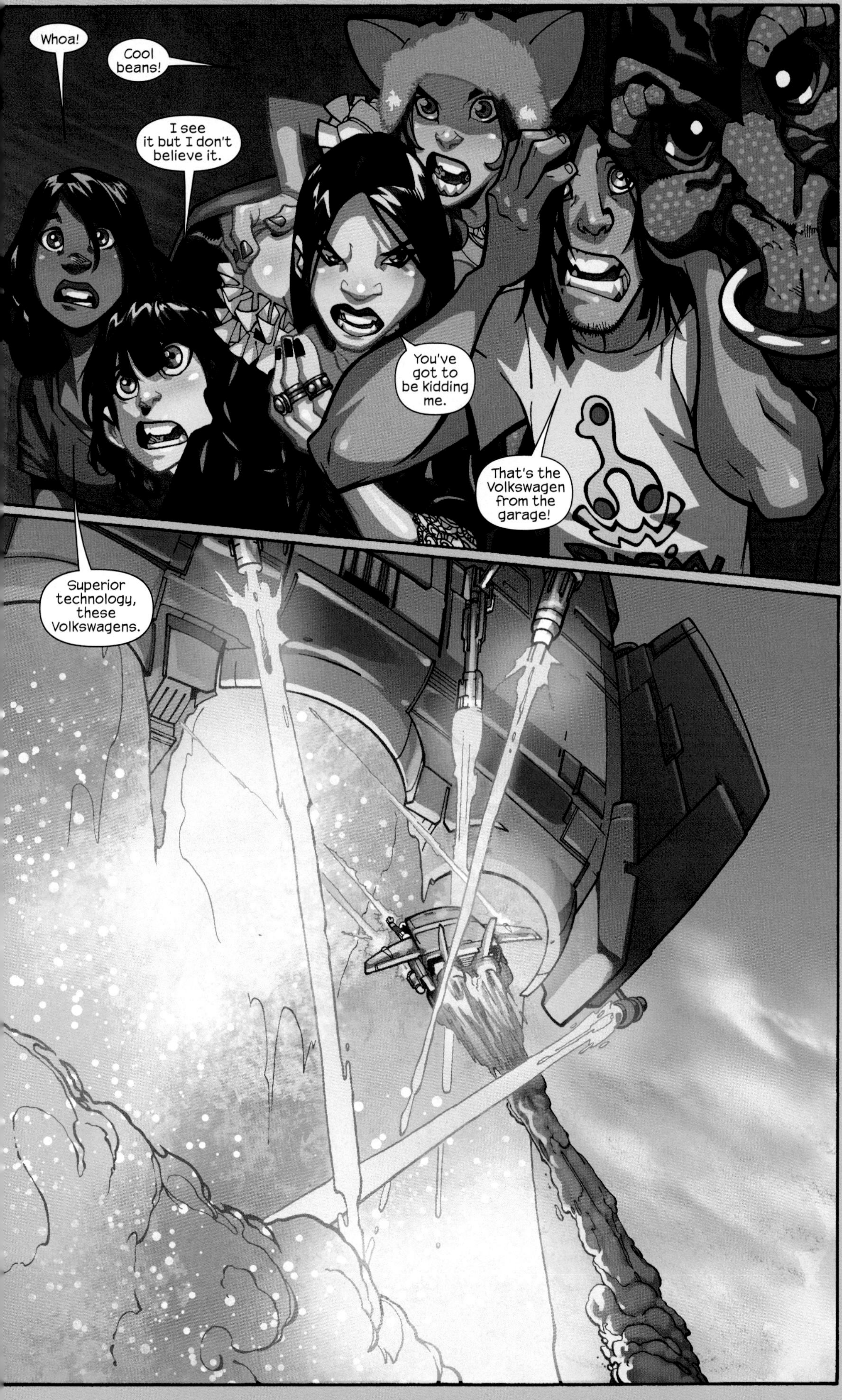
Whoa!
Cool beans!
I see it but I don't believe it.
You've got to be kidding me.
That's the Volkswagen from the garage!
Superior technology, these Volkswagens.

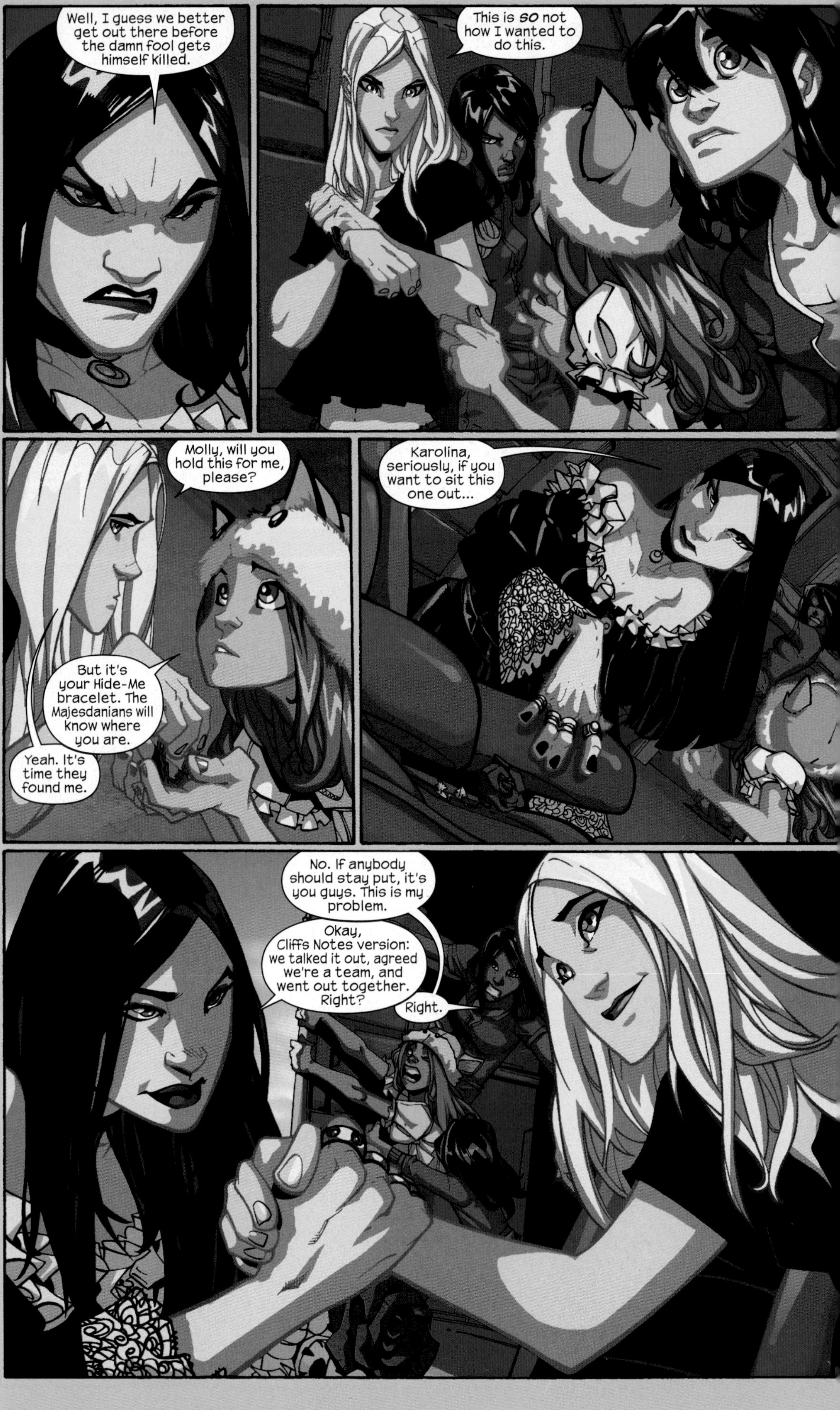
Well, I guess we better get out there before the damn fool gets himself killed.
This is SO not how I wanted to do this.
Molly, will you hold this for me, please?
But it's your Hide-Me bracelet. The Majesdanians will know where you are.
Yeah. It's time they found me.
Karolina, seriously, if you want to sit this one out...
No. If anybody should stay put, it's you guys. This is my problem.
Okay, Cliffs Notes version: we talked it out, agreed we're a team, and went out together. Right?
Right.

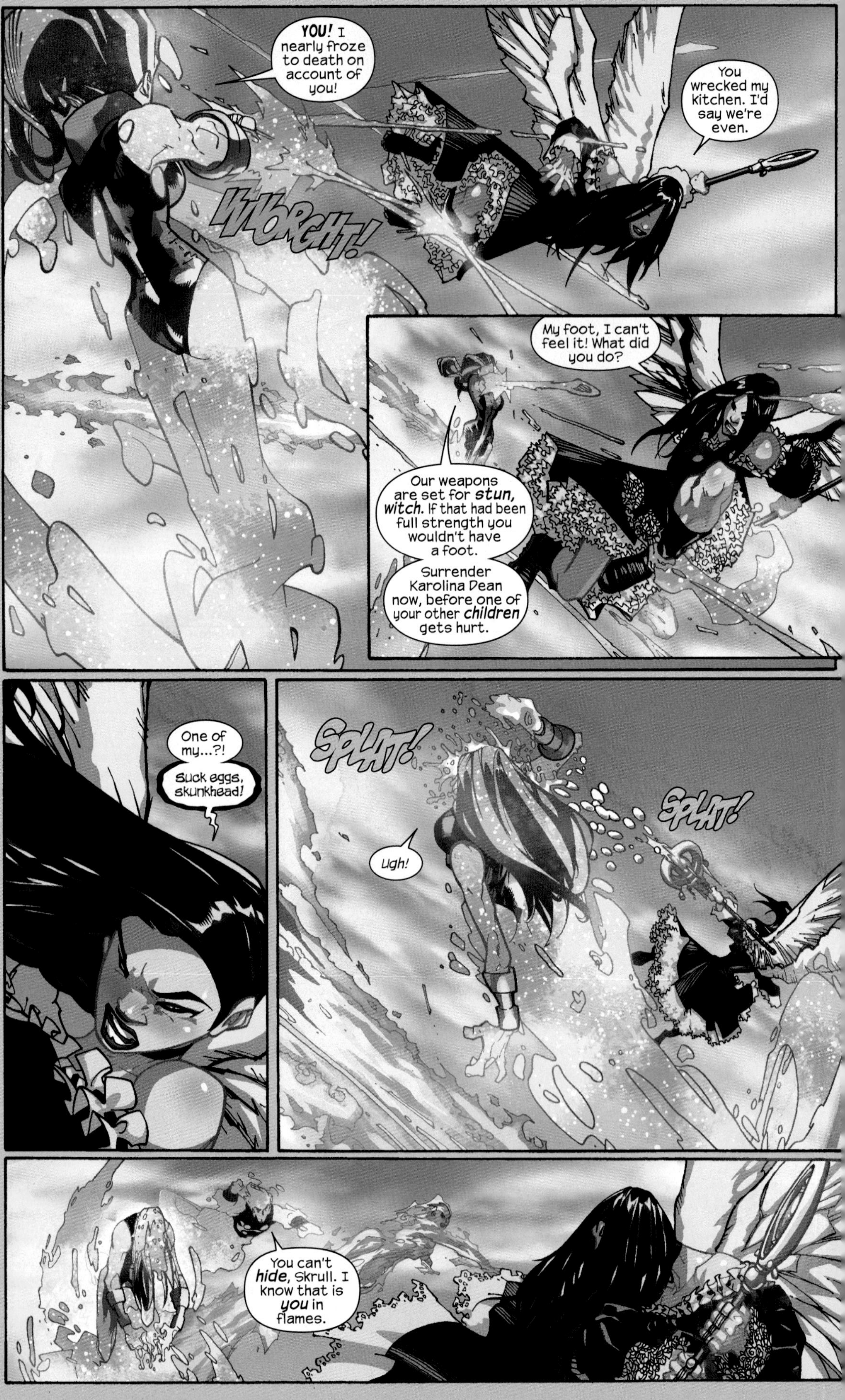
YOU! I nearly froze to death on account of you!
You wrecked my kitchen. I'd say we're even.
WHORGHT!
My foot, I can't feel it! What did you do?
Our weapons are set for stun, witch. If that had been full strength you wouldn't have a foot.
Surrender Karolina Dean now, before one of your other children gets hurt.
One of my...?!
Suck eggs, skunkhead!
SPLAT!
SPLAT!
Ugh!
You can't hide, Skrull. I know that is you in flames.

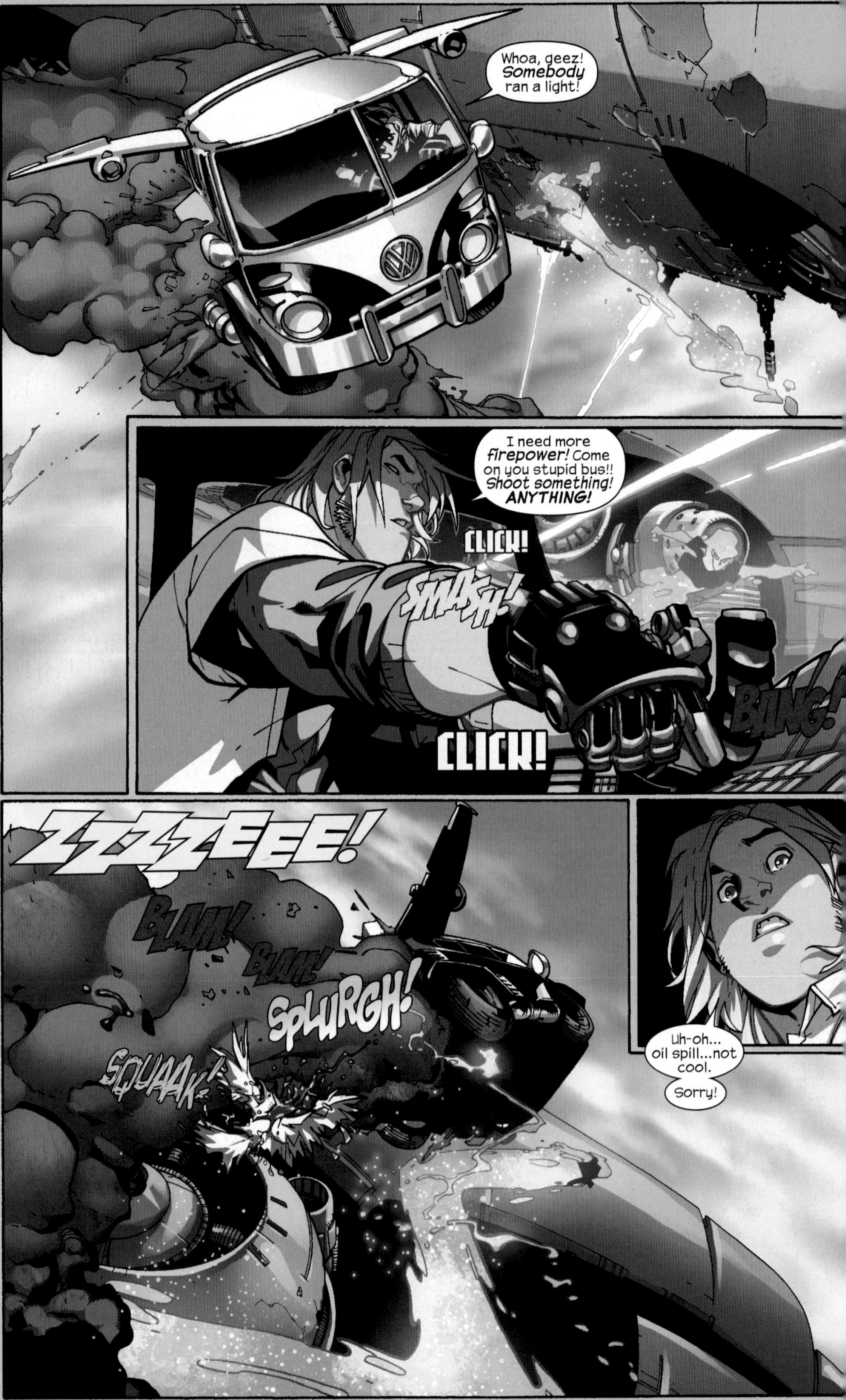

Whoa, geez! Somebody ran a light!
I need more firepower! Come on you stupid bus!! Shoot something! ANYTHING!
CLICK!
SMASH!
CLICK!
BANG!
ZZZZEEE!
BLAM!
BLAM!
SPLURGH!
SQUAAK!
Uh-oh... oil spill...not cool.
Sorry!

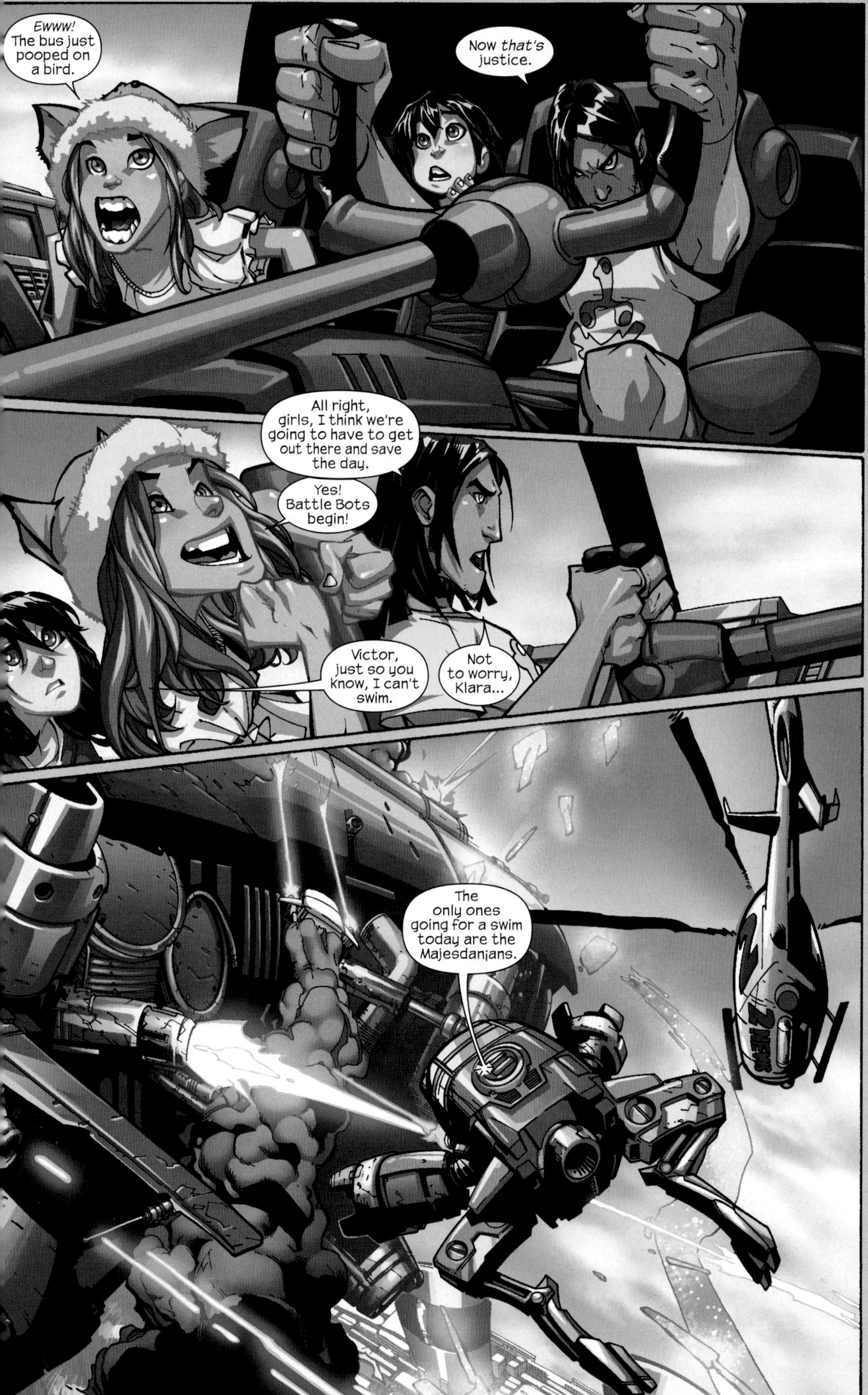

Ewww! The bus just pooped on a bird.
Now *that's* justice.
All right, girls, I think we're going to have to get out there and save the day.
Yes! Battle Bots begin!
Victor, just so you know, I can't swim.
Not to worry, Klara...
The only ones going for a swim today are the Majesdanians.
2 NEWS

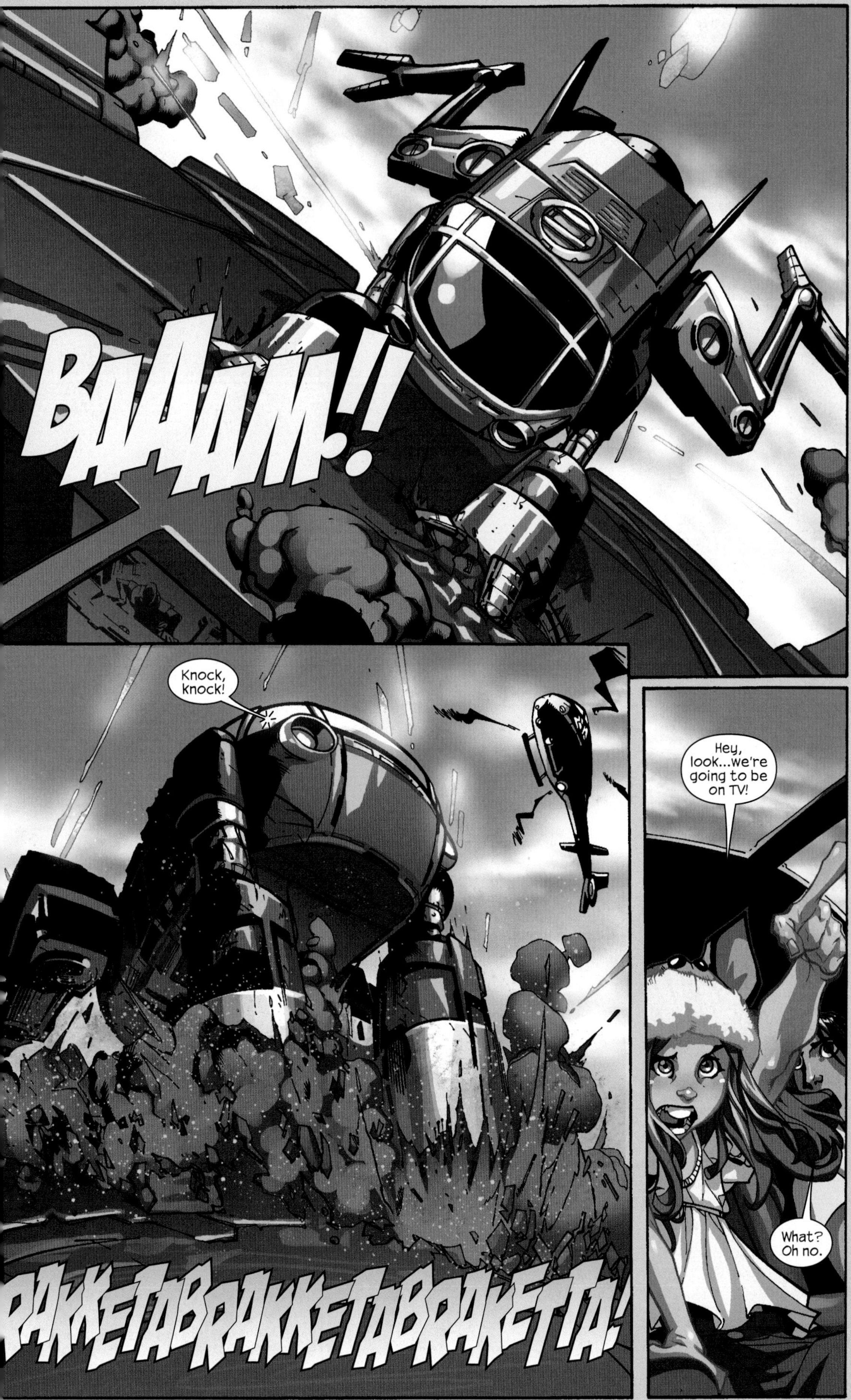
BAAAM!!
Knock, knock!
Hey, look...we're going to be on TV!
What? Oh no.
RAKKETABRAKKETABRAKETTA!

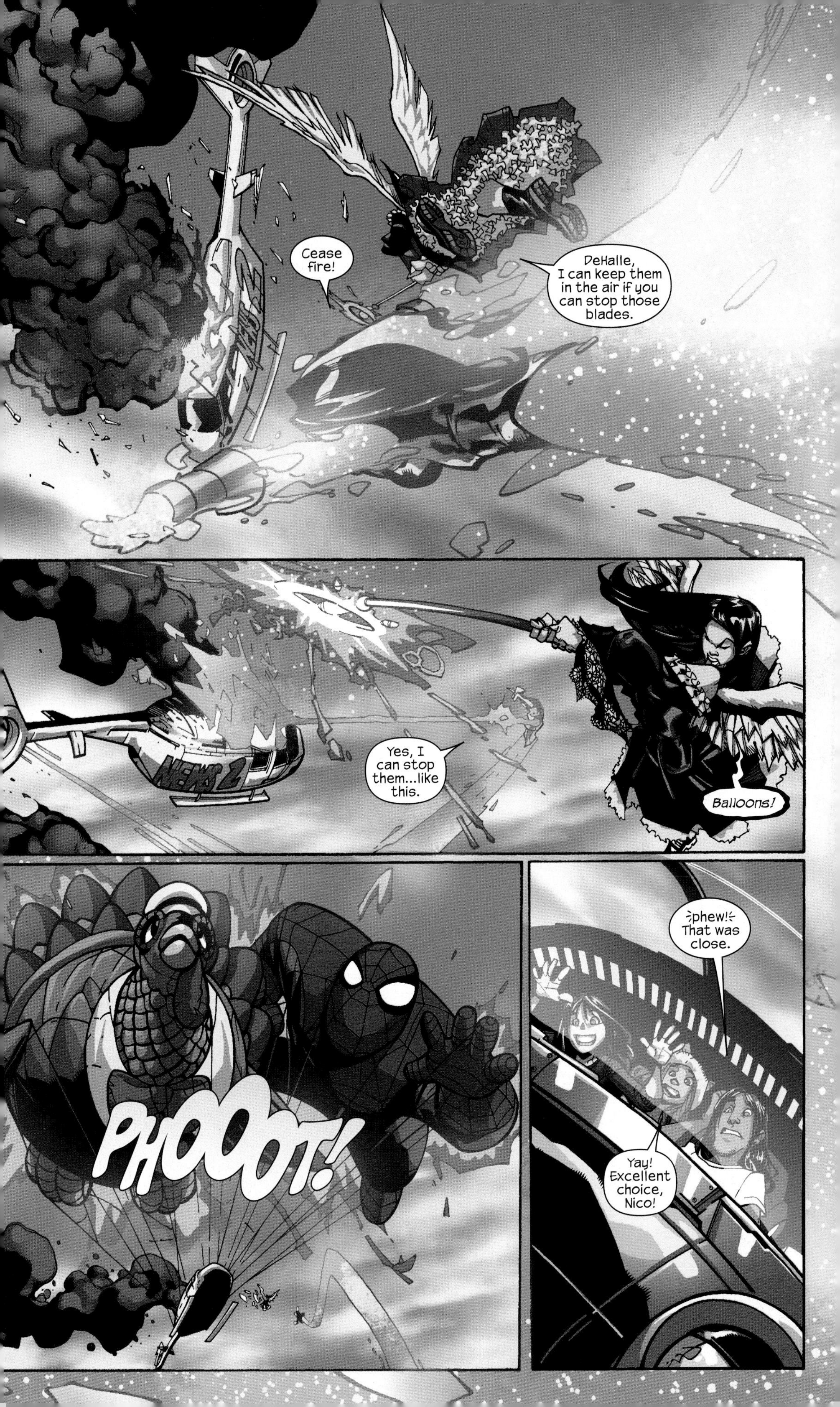
Cease fire!
DeHalle, I can keep them in the air if you can stop those blades.
NEWS 2
Yes, I can stop them...like this.
Balloons!
PHOOOT!
phew! That was close.
Yay! Excellent choice, Nico!

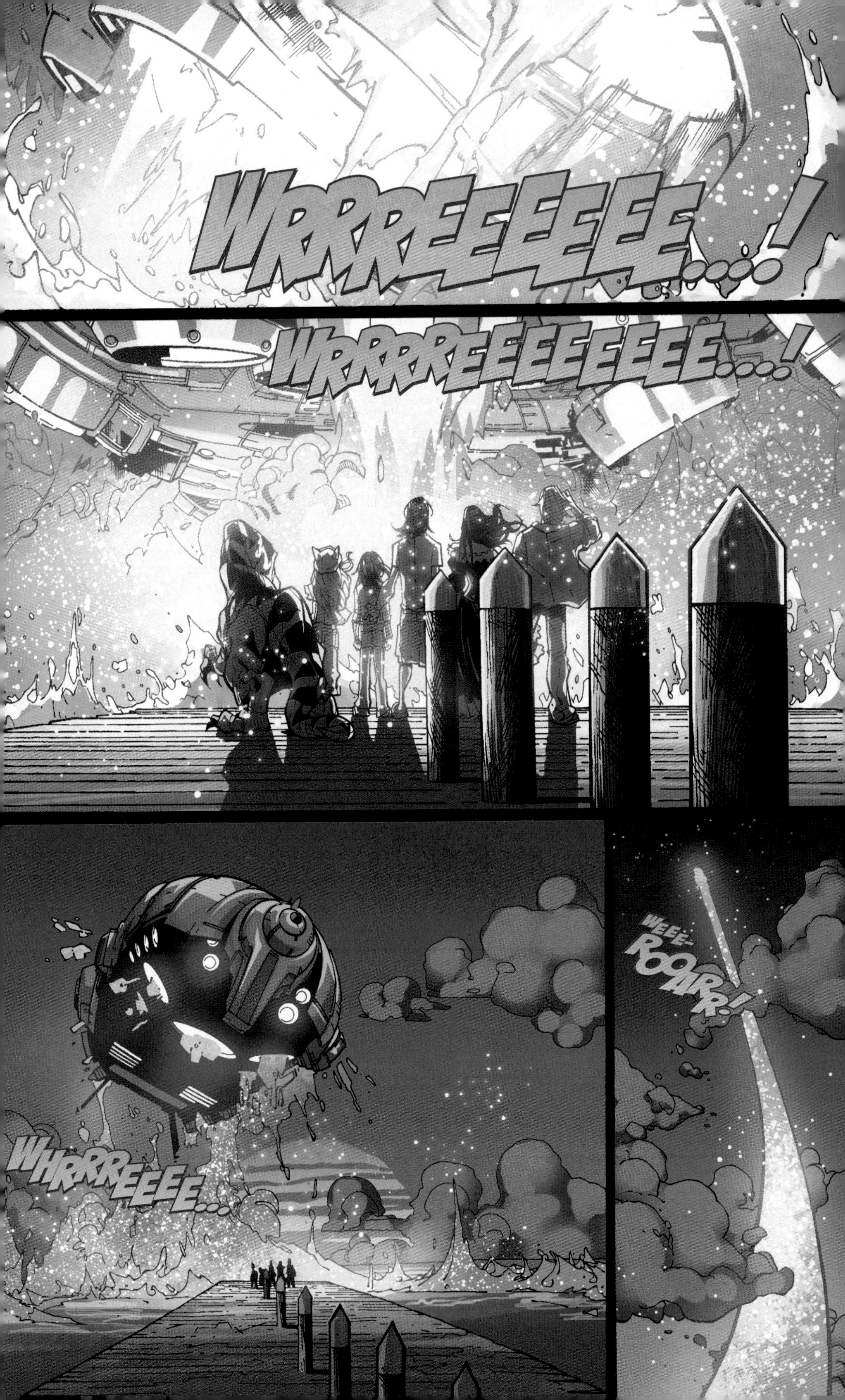
WRRREEEEEE...!
WRRRRREEEEEEEE...!
WHRRRREEEE...
WEEE-ROOARR!

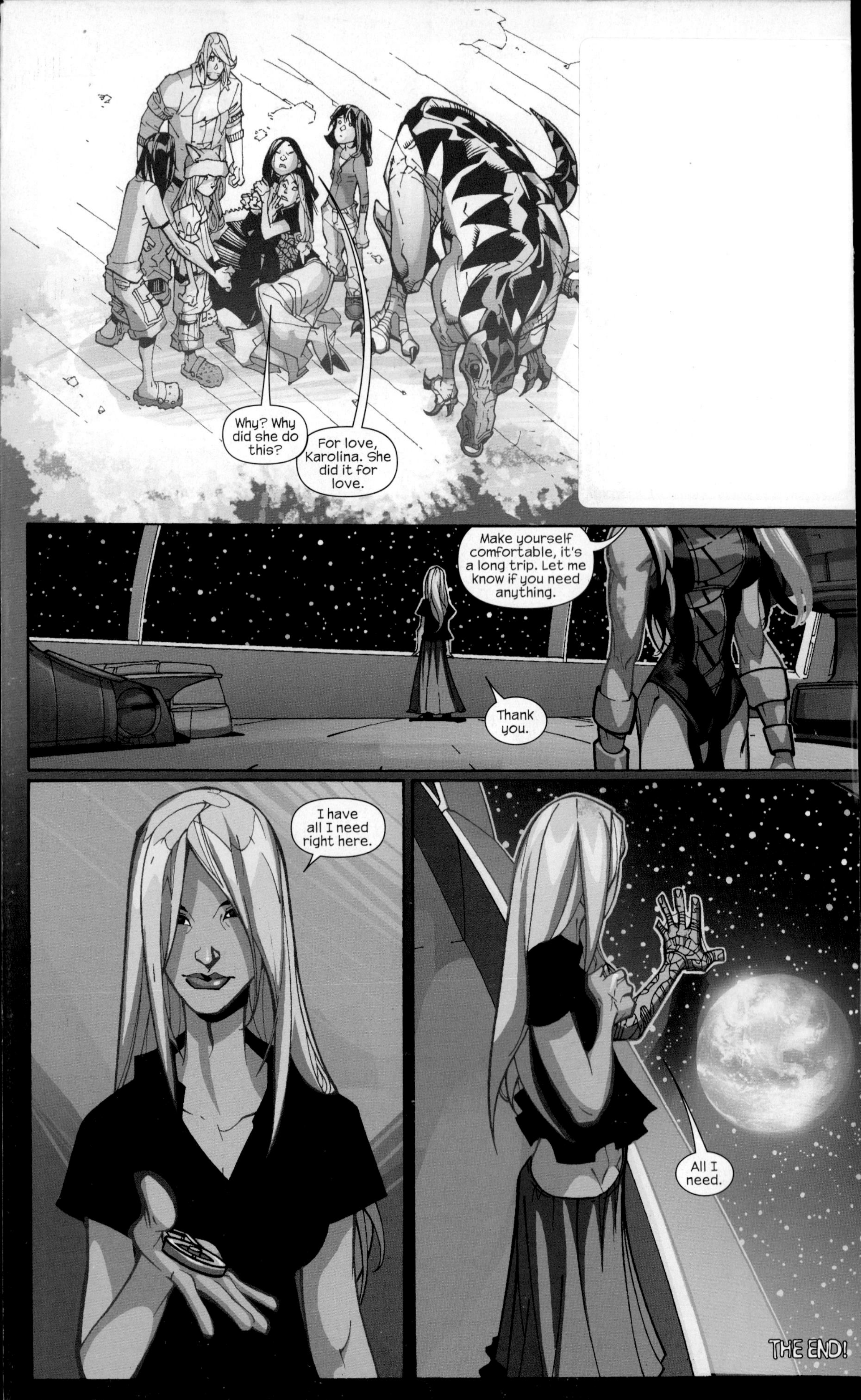
Why? Why did she do this?
For love, Karolina. She did it for love.
Make yourself comfortable, it's a long trip. Let me know if you need anything.
Thank you.
I have all I need right here.
All I need.
THE END!